Frommer's®

Barcelona
day BY day™

2nd Edition

by Neil Edward Schlecht

WILEY
Wiley Publishing, Inc.

Contents

Published by:

Wiley Publishing, Inc.

111 River St.
Hoboken, NJ 07030-5774

ISBN 978-0-470-62780-8 (paper); ISBN 978-0-470-91249-2 (ebk)

Editor: Jennifer Reilly
Production Editor: Michael Brumitt
Photo Editor: Richard Fox
Cartographer: Andrew Murphy
Production by Wiley Indianapolis Composition Services

For information on our other products and services or to obtain technical support, please contact our Customer Care Department within the U.S. at 877/762-2974, outside the U.S. at 317/572-3993 or fax 317/572-4002.

Wiley also publishes its books in a variety of electronic formats. Some content that appears in print may not be available in electronic formats.

Manufactured in China

5   4   3   2   1

A Note from the Editorial Director

Organizing your time. That's what this guide is all about.

Other guides give you long lists of things to see and do and then expect you to fit the pieces together. The Day by Day guides are different. These guides tell you the best of everything, and then they show you how to see it *in the smartest, most time-efficient way*. Our authors have designed detailed itineraries organized by time, neighborhood, or special interest. And each tour comes with a bulleted map that takes you from stop to stop.

Hoping to tour the best in *modernista* architecture, stroll down La Rambla, or taste your way through gourmet Barcelona? Planning a walk through La Ribera, or plotting a day of fun-filled activities with the kids? Whatever your interest or schedule, the Day by Days give you the smartest routes to follow. Not only do we take you to the top attractions, hotels, and restaurants, but we also help you access those special moments that locals get to experience—those "finds" that turn tourists into travelers.

The Day by Days are also your top choice if you're looking for one complete guide for all your travel needs. The best hotels and restaurants for every budget, the greatest shopping values, the wildest nightlife—it's all here.

Why should you trust our judgment? Because our authors personally visit each place they write about. They're an independent lot who say what they think and would never include places they wouldn't recommend to their best friends. They're also open to suggestions from readers. If you'd like to contact them, please send your comments our way at feedback@frommers.com, and we'll pass them on.

Enjoy your Day by Day guide—the most helpful travel companion you can buy. And have the trip of a lifetime.

Warm regards,

Kelly Regan

Kelly Regan, Editorial Director
Frommer's Travel Guides

About the Author

Neil Edward Schlecht is a freelance writer based in northwestern Connecticut. His first exposure to Spain was teaching English for a summer at Col.legi Sant Ignasi in Barcelona. He returned to the Catalan capital just before the 1992 Olympics and spent most of the decade there, working on social and economic development projects for the European Union and later as a contributing writer for a Spanish art and antiques magazine. He is the author of more than a dozen travel guides to spots around the world, including *Mallorca & Menorca Day by Day*, *Frommer's Peru*, and *Buenos Aires Day by Day*. But little motivates him like the chance to discover new restaurants, wines, and cycling routes in Spain.

Acknowledgments

Many thanks to Jennifer Reilly, my very patient and thorough editor, and María Lluisa Albacar of Barcelona Turisme, for her greatly appreciated assistance in one of my favorite cities in the world.

An Additional Note

Please be advised that travel information is subject to change at any time—and this is especially true of prices. We therefore suggest that you write or call ahead for confirmation when making your travel plans. The authors, editors, and publisher cannot be held responsible for the experiences of readers while traveling. Your safety is important to us, however, so we encourage you to stay alert and be aware of your surroundings.

Star Ratings, Icons & Abbreviations

Every hotel, restaurant, and attraction listing in this guide has been ranked for quality, value, service, amenities, and special features using a **star-rating system.** Hotels, restaurants, attractions, shopping, and nightlife are rated on a scale of zero stars (recommended) to three stars (exceptional). In addition to the star-rating system, we also use a **kids icon** to point out the best bets for families. Within each tour, we recommend cafes, bars, or restaurants where you can take a break. Each of these stops appears in a shaded box marked with a coffee-cup-shaped bullet ☕.

The following **abbreviations** are used for credit cards:

AE	American Express	DISC	Discover	V	Visa
DC	Diners Club	MC	MasterCard		

Travel Resources at Frommers.com

Frommer's travel resources don't end with this guide. Frommer's website, **www.frommers.com**, has travel information on more than 4,000 destinations. We update features regularly, giving you access to the most current trip-planning information and the best airfare, lodging, and car-rental bargains. You can also listen to podcasts, connect with other Frommers.com members through our active-reader forums, share your travel photos, read blogs from guidebook editors and fellow travelers, and much more.

A Note on Prices

In the "Take a Break" and "Best Bets" sections of this book, we have used a system of dollar signs to show a range of costs for 1 night in a hotel (the price of a double-occupancy room) or the cost of an entree at a restaurant. Use the following table to decipher the dollar signs:

Cost	Hotels	Restaurants
$	under $100	under $10
$$	$100–$200	$10–$20
$$$	$200–$300	$20–$30
$$$$	$300–$400	$30–$40
$$$$$	over $400	over $40

How to Contact Us

In researching this book, we discovered many wonderful places—hotels, restaurants, shops, and more. We're sure you'll find others. Please tell us about them, so we can share the information with your fellow travelers in upcoming editions. If you were disappointed with a recommendation, we'd love to know that, too. Please write to:

Frommer's Barcelona Day by Day, 2nd Edition
Wiley Publishing, Inc. • 111 River St. • Hoboken, NJ 07030-5774
frommersfeedback@wiley.com

15 Favorite
Moments

15 Favorite **Moments**

1. La Rambla
2. Modernista masterpieces
3. Barri Gòtic
4. Mercat de la Boqueria
5. Palau de la Música
6. Catalan cuisine*
7. Old-school Barcelona*
8. Biking along the beach
9. Cava crawl*
10. La Ribera fashion
11. Classic Catalan culture*
12. Santa María del Mar
13. La Pedrera
14. Blue Tram to Tibidabo
15. Catalunya*

categories not mapped

Previous page: The rooftop chimneys of La Pedrera.

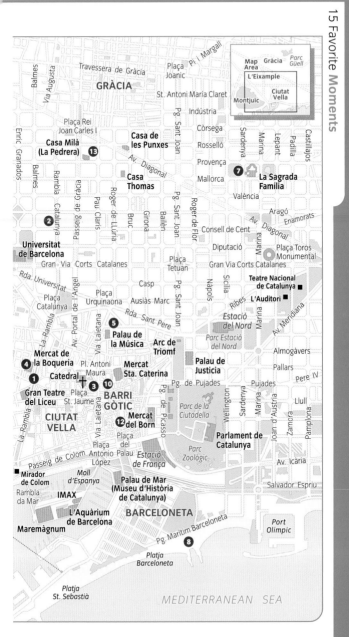

It's not really a shock that Barcelona has become such a hot destination. What is surprising is how long it took most of the world to discover Barcelona's diverse charms, which draw architecture and design fanatics, foodies, culture hounds, history buffs, and those merely in search of an all-night party. These are some of my favorite things to do in the thriving Catalan capital.

1 Joining the throngs on La Rambla. Barcelona's pedestrian-only boulevard is anything but commonplace; it's the epicenter of life in the capital, and joining the vibrant street parade is the best way to immerse yourself in the city. Pick up fresh flowers, kick back at a sidewalk cafe, and come face-to-face with outrageous human statues (but keep an eye on your belongings!). *See p 57.*

2 Marveling at *Modernista* Masterpieces. Beyond the Gaudí must-sees La Pedrera and La Sagrada Família, the L'Eixample grid teems with stunning *modernista* buildings by dozens of architects famous and not. Start on Passeig de Gràcia's stunning Manzana de la Discórdia; then fan out to see innumerable examples of the *modernista* craze

See some outrageous performers on La Rambla.

The modernista *apartment building Casa Batlló.*

that took over Barcelona in the late 19th and early 20th centuries. And don't miss an afternoon relaxing on the serpentine, broken-ceramic benches high above the city at Gaudí's Parc Güell. *See p 24.*

3 Wandering the Barri Gòtic. Barcelona's Gothic Quarter is a mesmerizing labyrinth of medieval buildings and narrow streets; it's a joy to take a stroll and discover a quiet square or picturesque patio. Meander down Sant Sever and slip into Plaça Sant Felip Neri, or along Carrer Banys Nous, lined with antiques shops. *See p 60.*

4 Breathing in La Boqueria. Barcelona's wonderfully redolent food market is a feast for the senses,

La Boqueria is a food-lover's paradise.

with hundreds of colorful stalls overflowing with fresh seafood, wild mushrooms, meats, and vegetables. For a special treat, join locals and sample the goods at a kiosk such as Bar Pintxo or El Quim for breakfast or lunch at the counter. *See p 58.*

⑤ **Tuning into El Palau de la Música.** This mind-blowing 1908 *modernista* concert hall draws hordes for its architectural tours. But there's nothing quite like experiencing a performance here; the spine-tingling monument to Art Nouveau excess takes a backseat to no musician, whether a chamber quartet or Lou Reed. *See p 124.*

⑥ **Sampling cutting-edge Catalan cuisine.** Led by the likes of Ferrán Adriá of El Bulli fame, Catalan cooking has exploded, transforming Barcelona into the hottest dining scene in Europe. From chic tapas bars to minimalist haunts known for their celebrity chefs, Barcelona has become a destination for gastronomic pilgrims. *See p 93.*

⑦ **Dipping into old-school Barcelona.** Unfazed by today's fashions and fast pace are authentic, time-stopping treasures in the old city, portals to an earlier era: a 1920s *modernista* chocolate shop; a *granja*, or "milk bar," serving thick chocolate drinks as it has for 125 years; and a gourmet food and wine

shop in the same family for four generations. All are portals to an earlier era. *See p 46.*

⑧ **Biking along the beach.** Just 2 decades ago, Barcelona turned its back on the Mediterranean and its polluted port; today the revitalized waterfront is lined with leisurely bike paths and immaculate urban beaches. Take a pit stop at one of the city's most traditional seafood haunts in working-class Barceloneta. *See p 90.*

⑨ **Traipsing along on a cava crawl.** You can do a tapas crawl anywhere in Spain, but in Barcelona pre-meal snacks are washed down by glasses of *cava,* Catalan sparkling wine. *Xampanyerías* are friendly spots where good cheer bubbles over. *See p 117.*

Be sure to try the cava (Catalan sparkling wine) while you're visiting the region.

⑩ Discovering cutting-edge fashion on medieval streets. Against a backdrop of Gothic palaces, churches, and centuries-old shops, the tangle of dark but suddenly chic alleyways of the La Ribera/Born district now are also home to dozens of edgy fashion and home-design shops, a delight to discover. *See p 64.*

⑪ Experiencing classic Catalan culture. La Mercé, Barcelona's signature folklore festival, has something for everyone: *castellers* (human towers rising eight levels); *gigants* and *cap grosses* (massive costumed royal figures parading the streets); and devils running, chasing each other down with fireworks in *correfocs*. It's a blast and a quintessential expression of Catalan pride. *See p 161.*

⑫ Reveling in Santa Maria del Mar. This Gothic church, in the heart of bustling La Ribera, is architectural perfection, a model of graceful, soaring dimensions. A rare concert can be thrilling, but it's also a sublime sanctuary on a quiet afternoon. You might catch a society wedding spilling out onto the steps—which you can watch from a wine bar just across the plaza. *See p 65.*

⑬ Dining on the Roof at La Pedrera. The dreamlike rooftop of Antoni Gaudí's finest private building is topped by surreal-looking chimneys, but it really comes to life during "Nits de Cuina," a summer eve's program of gourmet Catalan dinners served by elite, Michelin-starred Barcelona chefs (the jazz concerts formerly held on the terrace have been moved to a concert hall within). With a view of the city and the lights of elegant Passeig de Gràcia below, it's got to be the city's most enviable dining space. *See p 9,* ❷.

⑭ Hopping the Blue Tram to Tibidabo. Appreciate how Barcelona gracefully stretches from the surrounding hills out to the sea on the old trolley *(Tramvia Blau)* up to Tibidabo, the hilltop overlooking the city. On a clear day, you can survey the perfect grid system of L'Eixample and maybe even pick out Mallorca in the distant Mediterranean. *See p 22.*

⑮ Getting a taste of Catalunya. Sample even more Catalan flavor just a couple of hours outside the capital: Ride an aerial cable car to Montserrat, a monastery cleaved into a mountain; discover the idiosyncratic spots where Salvador Dalí's mad genius erupted; or lose yourself in the pristine, ancient Jewish quarter of Girona. *See p 146.* ●

Explore Dalí's stomping grounds, including the Teatre Museu Dalí in Figueres.

1 The Best
Full-Day Tours

The Best **in One Day**

1 La Sagrada Família
2 La Pedrera
3 Casa Batlló
4 Casa Amatller
5 Casa Lleó Morera
6 Tapas 24
7 Rambla de Catalunya
8 La Rambla
9 Mercat de la Boqueria
10 Ciutat Vella shopping
11 Bar del Pi
12 Catedral de Barcelona
13 Plaça del Rei

Previous page: La Sagrada Família.

This very full day, a "greatest hits" tour, begins with the best of Barcelona's *modernista* architecture in the morning, is followed by a stroll down the epic Rambla, and ends with the highlights of the *Ciutat Vella*, or Old City. You'll need your walking shoes. The tour is excellent any day of the week, though on Sundays La Boquería, Barcelona's famed food market, is closed. START: **Metro to Sagrada Família.**

1 ★★★ kids **La Sagrada Família.** Antoni Gaudí's unfinished legacy, the soaring "Holy Family" church, is a testament to his singular vision: the art of the impossible. This mind-altering creation—the best-known, if not necessarily the best example, of *modernisme*—has become Barcelona's calling card. Begun in 1882, its eight bejeweled spires drip like melting candlesticks, and virtually every square inch of the surface explodes with intricate spiritual symbols. Gaudí was run over by a tram long before it could be finished, and at present it remains only an otherworldly facade. Though many believe it should be left unfinished, a private foundation works furiously to finish the church—now projected for 2026, the centennial of Gaudí's death. For the foreseeable future, the church will remain under a forest of cranes. ⏲ 1 hr. c/ Mallorca, 401. ☎ 93-207-30-31. www. sagradafamilia.org. Admission 12€ adults; 16€ guided tour. Daily Oct–Mar 9am–6pm; Apr–Sept 9am–8pm. Metro: Sagrada Família.

2 ★★★ kids **La Pedrera.** Thought by many to be the crowning glory of the *modernista* movement, Antoni Gaudí's avant-garde apartment building Casa Milà is better known as La Pedrera, or Stone Quarry, for its wavy mass of limestone. The exterior seems carved out of nature: It undulates like ocean waves along Passeig de Gràcia and around the corner onto Provença Street. The fascinating roof,

Detailed carving work on La Sagrada Família.

what most people come to see, is guarded by a set of warrior-like chimneys that look like the inspiration for Darth Vader. ⏲ 1 hr. Pg. de Gràcia, 92 (at Provença). ☎ 902-40-09-73 or 902-10-12-12 for advance tickets. www.fundaciocaixacatalunya. org. Admission 10€ adults, 6€ students; also part of ArticketBCN joint admission. Audioguide 3€. Nov–Feb daily 9am–6pm; Mar–Oct daily 10am–8pm. Closed Dec 25–26 and Jan 1–6. Metro: Diagonal or Provença.

3 ★★★ **Casa Batlló.** The centerpiece of the so-called "Block of Discord," Casa Batlló owes its extraordinary facade to Antoni Gaudí, who completed a remodeling in 1906. Thought to represent the legend of Saint George (patron saint

Top Attractions: Practical Matters

ArticketBCN Discounts: With a single ticket (www.articketbcn. org) you can visit seven top art museums, including La Pedrera, Museu Picasso, Museu Nacional d'Art de Catalunya (MNAC), Fundació Joan Miró, Fundació Antoni Tàpies, and Museu d'Art Contemporani de Barcelona (MACBA). Purchase the ticket (22€; good for 6 months) at museum ticket offices, the Plaça de Catalunya Tourist Information Office, the Caixa Catalunya bank, or by phone or online with Tel.Entrada (☎ 902-101-212 or 34-93-326-29-46 from abroad; www.telentrada.com). Another useful, all-purpose pass is the **Barcelona Card** (good for 2–5 consecutive days; 26€–42€ adults, 22€–33€ children), which includes free public transport and discounts at over 80 museums, tourist sights, cultural venues, restaurants, and more, as well as free admission to a handful of activities and museums. The card can be purchased online (10% discount; bcnshop.barcelonaturisme.com) or at the Plaça de Catalunya Tourist Information Office.

of Catalunya) and his dragon, the house glimmers with fragments of colorful ceramics, while the roof curves like the blue-green scales of a dragon's back, and balconies evoke Carnavalesque masks or menacing monster jaws. The sinuous interior, full of custom Gaudí-designed

La Pedrera is considered one of Antoni Gaudí's masterpieces (p 9).

furniture, is similarly stunning (though tours are unexpectedly pricey). Circle around back to see the rear of the building, and glimpse another *modernista* masterpiece across the street on carrer Aragó, the former publishing house by Lluís Domènech i Montaner, now a museum dedicated to the contemporary painter Antoni Tàpies. ⏱ *45 min. Pg. de Gràcia, 43.* ☎ *93-488-06-66. www.casabatllo.es. Admission 18€ adults, 14€ children and students, free for children 4 and under. Daily 9am–8pm. Metro: Pg. de Gràcia.*

❹ ★★ **Casa Amatller.** Puig i Cadafalch, a Gaudí contemporary, created this brilliant house—the first building on the Manzana de la Discòrdia block of Passeig de Gràcia—in 1900. It has a medieval-looking, ceramics-covered facade, topped by a distinctive Flemish-inspired roof and beautiful carved stone and ironwork of themes related to the chocolate business and hobbies of the original owners.

🕐 20 min. Pg. de Gràcia, 41. ☎ 93-487-72-17. www.amatller.org. Ground floor open to public (free admission) Mon–Sat 10am–8pm; Sun 10am–3pm. Metro: Pg. de Gràcia.

❺ ★ Casa Lleó Morera. The final member of the "Block of Discord" triumvirate, this gorgeously ornate corner house, built in 1905 by D i M, who designed El Palau de la Música Catalana, is especially appealing when illuminated at night. The building is now home to the upscale leather-goods purveyor Loewe, which lamentably destroyed a good part of the lower facade and sumptuous interior ground floor. *Pg. de Gràcia, 35. Except for the Loewe store, the house cannot be visited. Metro: Pg. de Gràcia.*

❻ ★★ Tapas 24. The informal tapas bar of acclaimed chef Carles Abellán, who's in the kitchen at Comerç 24, is a good-looking pit stop just off Passeig de Gràcia. Grab a snack or lunch of tantalizing small bites with big flavors, and wine and cava by the glass. *c/ Diputaciò, 269.* ☎ 93-488-09-77. $$.

❼ ★★Rambla de Catalunya. Passeig de Gràcia is home to some of the city's finest *modernista* architecture and a wealth of elegant fashion boutiques and high-end home-design emporiums, making it ideal for window shopping. But an even more leisurely stroll is along Rambla de Catalunya, a delightful, pedestrian-only lane lined with trees, shops, cafes, and classic L'Eixample apartment buildings. Cross over on carrer Consell de Cent, teeming with art galleries, and follow Rambla de Catalunya down to Plaça de Catalunya. 🕐 *30 min. Metro: Pg. de Gràcia.*

❽ ★★★ kids La Rambla. Barcelona's monumental boulevard is the centerpiece of life in the Catalan capital. It throbs with activity, as crowds at all hours of the day file past vendors, food markets, cafes, and historic buildings, including the great Liceu opera house. Subdivided into five separate *ramblas,* each of different character and attractions, are a lively succession of newspaper kiosks, fresh-flower stands, bird sellers, and crowd-friendly human statues (mimes) in elaborately

The "dragon's back" atop Casa Batlló.

Fresh flowers are for sale daily on La Rambla.

conceived costumes and face paint. About halfway down the boulevard, to the left as you face the port, is the Plaça Reial, a grand square with cafes, palm trees, arcades, and lampposts designed by *modernista* master Antoni Gaudí. (At night, the lower sectors of La Rambla can get a little sketchy; keep a close eye on your belongings at all times.) ⏲ *45 min. Begin at Pl. de Catalunya. Metro: Catalunya.*

❾ ★★★ kids Mercat de La Boqueria. Europe's largest and surely most dynamic food market, this Catalan classic is the foundation of Barcelona's fascination with food. Wander among the more than 300 stalls and several small bar/restaurants to take in the sights and smells of an amazingly robust gastronomic scene. Keep an eye out for *bolets* and *ceps* (wild mushrooms), massive prawns, eels, and octopus. The colorful bounty is a testament to the fertile region and Catalans' desire for the freshest and tastiest foodstuffs available. True foodies will want to return one early morning when the market is at its liveliest.

⏲ *30 min. La Rambla, 91–101.* ☎ *93-318-25-84. www.boqueria.info. Mon–Sat 8am–8pm. Metro: Liceu.*

❿ Ciutat Vella shopping. The old-city districts Barri Gòtic (Gothic Quarter) and La Ribera are home to dozens of fashion boutiques, bars, and souvenir shops. Check out bustling, pedestrian-only carrer de Petritxol; carrer Ferran; or dark, atmospheric carrer Banys Nous, site of some of the city's best antiques shops; and carrer de la Palla. Across Vía Laetana in the El Born district are some of the chicest fashion boutiques in old Barcelona. ⏲ *1 hr. Metro: Liceu or Jaume I.*

⓫ ★★ Bar del Pi. One of the prettiest squares in the Old City makes a splendid spot to linger at an outdoor cafe, as Barcelonans do. Of the several cafes clustered around the square, Bar del Pi is the most traditional. People-watching opportunities abound, and on weekends artists and artisans set up booths in the plaça. *Pl. Sant Josep Orio, 1.* ☎ *93-302-21-23. $$.*

⑫ ★★ **Catedral de Barcelona.**
The cathedral, the focal point of the
Old City and a splendid example of
Catalan Gothic architecture, was
begun in 1298 but largely completed in the 14th and 15th centuries. Don't miss the carved choir and
surprisingly lush cloister—a welcome oasis in the midst of the medieval Gothic Quarter, with its pond,
magnolias, orange and palm trees,
and white geese. ⏱ 45 min. Pl. de la
Seu, s/n. ☎ 93-342-82-60. www.
catedralbcn.org. Free admission to
cathedral; museum 1€. Elevator to
roof 10:30am–1:30pm and 5–6pm, 2€.
Global ticket for 1–4:30pm guided visit
to museum, choir, rooftop terraces,
and towers, 4€. Cathedral daily
8am–1pm and 4:30–7:30pm; cloister
museum daily 10am–1pm and 4:30–
6:30pm. Metro: Jaume I.

⑬ ★★ **kids** **Plaça del Rei.** One
of the old quarter's most beautiful
and historic squares, the stately Plaça
del Rei is hemmed in by a remaining
section of the old Roman city walls
and the Palau Reial Major, an 11th-
century royal palace and residence
of the kings of Catalunya and Aragón.
According to legend, the *Reyes*

*Mercat de La Boquería is a Barcelona
institution.*

Católicos, King Ferdinand and Queen
Isabella, received Columbus here after
he returned from the New World.
⏱ 1½ hr. Pl. del Rei, s/n. ☎ 93-256-
21-00. www.museuhistoria.bcn.es.
Admission 6€ adults, 3€ students,
free for children under 16. Apr–Sept
Tues–Sat 10am–8pm; Oct–Mar Tues–
Sat 10am–2pm and 4–7pm; year-round
Sun 10am–8pm. Metro: Jaume I.

A snack at Tapas 24 (p 11).

The Best **in Two Days**

1 El Palau de la
Música Catalana

2 Museu Picasso

3 Carrer de Montcada/
Passeig del Born

4 Santa María del Mar

5 La Vinya del Senyor

6 Moll de la Fusta/
Port Vell

7 Beaches/Port Olímpic

On day two, take in art and architecture highlights of the Old City, followed by leisure time at the revitalized waterfront. Begin the day in the atmospheric La Ribera district before moving on to stroll along the harbor, stop for lunch in the beachside district of Barceloneta, and hit the sands in the afternoon for sunbathing or a sunset cocktail, perhaps topped off by dinner along the waterfront.

START: **Metro to Urquinaona.**

1 ★★★ El Palau de la Música Catalana. Domènech i Montaner's magnificent 1908 music hall is over-the-top ornate but indisputably one of Barcelona's *modernista* masterpieces. The relatively sedate exterior is just a tease of what's inside: a riotous fantasy of ceramics, colored glass, and carved pumice, crowned by an enormous yellow, blue, and green stained-glass dome that looks like a swollen raindrop. It's surely the most exuberant music hall you'll ever see. A daytime guided tour addresses the architecture, but there's nothing like experiencing a concert here. ⏱ *1 hr. C/ Sant Francesc de Paula, 2.* ☎ *902-47-54-85 or 93-295-72-00. www.palaumusica. org. Tour 12€ adults, 10€ students and seniors. Tickets can be bought up to 1 week in advance online, by telephone, or from the gift shop (no same-day tickets by phone). Guided tours daily every half-hour 10am–3:30pm (in English on the hour 10am–3pm). Metro: Urquinaona.*

2 ★★ Museu Picasso. Pablo Picasso was born in southern Spain, but he spent much of his youth and early creative years in Barcelona on his way to becoming the most famous artist of the 20th century. The museum is the largest collection of his works in his native country: 2,500 paintings and sculptures, many of them early works, including several from his blue period. *Las Meninas,* a series of 59 often-whimsical interpretations of Velázquez's masterpiece, is the highlight. The museum occupies several exquisite 15th-century palaces on a pedestrian-only street lined with medieval mansions. ⏱ *90 min. c/ Montcada 15–23.* ☎ *93-319-63-10. www. museupicasso.bcn.es. Admission 9€ adults, 6€ students and those 24 and under, free for children 15 and under. Admission part of ArticketBCN. Free admission 1st Sun (3–8pm) of every month. Tues–Sat 10am–8pm; Sun 10am–3pm. Metro: Jaume I.*

Mosaics in El Palau de la Música Catalana.

The Museu Picasso holds 2,500 paintings and sculptures (p 15).

❸ ★ Carrer de Montcada/ Passeig del Born. La Ribera is at its most evocative and lively along the wonderful street lined with Renaissance palaces, including the ones that now house the Picasso Museum, and the Passeig del Born, a tree-lined promenade that's become one of the trendiest areas in old Barcelona. ⏱ *30 min. See p 31, ❷ and p 65, ❹.*

❹ ★★★ Santa Maria del Mar. A stunning 14th-century Catalan Gothic church that's neither opulent and jewel-encrusted nor home to a fabulous art collection. Instead, it's a simple and solemn, but wholly inspired, space: perfectly proportioned with three soaring naves, wide-spaced columns, and gorgeous stained-glass windows. It's the kind of place architects understandably wax poetic about. ⏱ *20 min. Pl. de Santa Maria.* ☎ *93-215-74-11. Free admission. Mon–Sat 9am–1:30pm and 4:30–8pm; Sun 9am–2pm and 5–8:30pm. Metro: Jaume I.*

The "Nation" of Catalunya

As the capital of Catalunya, Barcelona has an identity distinct from the rest of Spain. The fiercely independent streak of the Catalan people is forged of a unique history, language, and culture—prompting Catalan nationalists to refer to their semiautonomous region as *un país* (literally, a nation). The most prosperous region in Spain, Catalunya has often maintained a testy relationship with Madrid and the rest of the country. The long, insular Franco dictatorship outlawed the Catalan language, but the ancient tongue has experienced a dramatic resurgence and is now the principal language in public schools and on the streets (although in multilingual Barcelona, Spanish is spoken about as often). While some Catalan separatists continue to argue for full political independence from Spain, Catalunya has largely been exempt from the kind of deadly terrorism that ETA has waged in the Basque Country. To learn more about the Catalan people and history, visit the engaging Museu d'Història de Catalunya on the waterfront in the Palau de Mar (Pl. de Pau Vila, 3; ☎ 93-225-42-44; www.mhcat.net; 4€).

5 ★ **La Vinya del Senyor.** A hip little wine bar with much-coveted tables on a terrace at the lovely square across from Santa María del Mar, it features an excellent selection of 100 or so wines from across Spain, including two dozen by the glass, as well as Spanish ham, salami, and cheeses. *Pl. de Santa María, 5.* ☎ *93-310-33-79. $$.*

Public sculptures can be found along Barcelona's beaches.

6 ★ **kids Moll de la Fusta/ Port Vell/Barceloneta.** The boardwalk and series of esplanades along Passeig Colom called Moll de la Fusta is a local favorite for a *paseo,* or stroll. It stretches from the Columbus statue at the bottom of La Rambla and past Port Vell, the old harbor, to a giant Xavier Mariscal sculpture of a playful crayfish and colorful pop-art work, *Cap de Barcelona,* by the American artist Roy Lichtenstein. The colorful old beachfront neighborhood Barceloneta received a controversial makeover for the '92 Olympics, displacing many longtime residents, but it's still renowned for its *chiringuitos,* or informal seafood restaurants— which makes it a perfect place to stop for lunch, especially on weekends. ⏱ *1 hr. Metro: Drassanes or Barceloneta.*

7 ★★ **kids Beaches/Port Olímpic.** It wasn't long ago that no

self-respecting Barcelonan would venture down to the city's beaches, much less dream of wading into the polluted waters. The 1992 Olympics dramatically reopened the city to the Mediterranean and cleaned up the urban beaches, vastly improving water quality and transforming the long stretches of sand into a playground for city dwellers. The beaches *(platges)* are lined with palm trees, innovative public sculptures, bars, and restaurants, as well as paths for biking, in-line skating, and walking. The first major beach is Barceloneta, followed to the north by Nova Icària (the most popular, near the Port Olímpic marina and Vila Olímpica district), Bogatell, and Mar Bella (an unofficial nudist beach). Look for Frank Gehry's massive *Fish* sculpture in front of the Hotel Arts. ⏱ *2 hr. Metro: Barceloneta or Ciutadella/Vila Olímpica.*

Xavier Mariscal's crayfish at the Moll de la Fusta.

The Best **in Three Days**

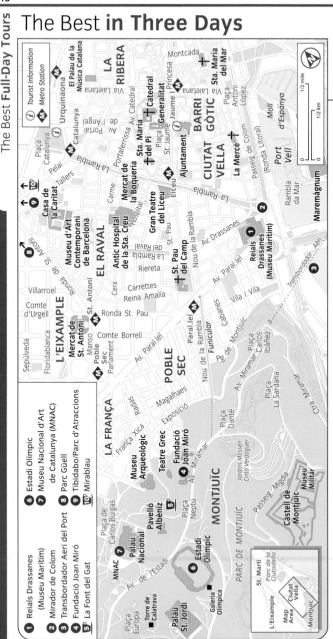

1. Reials Drassanes (Museu Marítim)
2. Mirador de Colom
3. Transbordador Aeri del Port
4. Fundació Joan Miró
5. La Font del Gat
6. Estadi Olímpic
7. Museu Nacional d'Art de Catalunya (MNAC)
8. Parc Güell
9. Tibidabo/Parc d'Atraccions
10. Mirablau

_i_ Tourist Information

Ⓜ Metro Station

Map Area

L'Eixample — Ciutat Vella — Montjuïc

St. Martí — Parc de la Ciutadella

This tour begins with Barcelona's maritime roots before exploring Montjuïc hill, site of the '92 Olympics and two spectacular art museums. In the afternoon, venture uptown to a whimsical Gaudí park and finish the day with a gorgeous bird's-eye view of the city from Tibidabo. The tour includes some great stops for kids.

START: Metro to Drassanes.

❶ ★★ kids Reials Drassanes (Museu Marítim). Barcelona's seafaring past comes to life in this rich maritime museum, located in the Reials Drassanes, or Royal Shipyards, which includes a glorious replica of a massive 16th-century vessel, the *Galería Reial*. The medieval shipyards—a collection of evocative arches, columns, and vaults that was once at water's edge and today remains magnificently intact—is where the kingdom's ships were constructed, repaired, and dry-docked. The *Santa Eulàlia* schooner (included in admission) is docked at Port Vell. This is a winner for both kids and parents. ⏱ *1 hr. Av. de les Drassanes, s/n.* ☎ *93-342-99-20. www. mmb.cat. Admission 2.50€ adults, 1.25€ seniors and children 7–16. Daily 10am–8pm. Metro: Drassanes.*

See relics from Barcelona's seafaring past at the Museu Marítim.

Mirador de Colom.

❷ kids Mirador de Colom. Though this monument to Christopher Columbus, built in 1888, has him pointing the wrong direction to the New World, it's a focal point and meeting point, dividing the lower end of the Rambla from the waterfront. An elevator takes visitors inside to a mirador for panoramic harbor views. ⏱ *30 min. Portal de la Pau, s/n.* ☎ *93-302-52-24. Admission 3€ adults, 2€ children 4–12, free for children 3 and under. May–Oct daily 9am–8:30pm; Nov–Apr daily 10am–6:30pm. Metro: Drassanes.*

❸ ★ kids Transbordador Aeri del Port. Traveling 70m (230 ft.) above the old port and across lower Barcelona up to Montjuïc hill, this aerial cable car (also called the Telefèric de Montjuïc), inaugurated in

1931, is the most unique way to travel the city. The views of the Mediterranean, La Rambla, and the grid of Barcelona rising up to the hills are unforgettable. 🕐 *30 min. Pg. Joan de Borbó, s/n, Barceloneta.* ☎ *93-328-90-03. www.barcelona busturistic.cat/web/guest/teleferic. Admission round-trip 9€ adults, 6.50€ children; one-way 6.30€ adults, 4.80€ children. Daily every 15 min. from 10:15am–7pm (until 9pm in summer). Metro: Barceloneta.*

❹ ★★ **Fundació Joan Miró.** A resolutely Catalan surrealist painter and sculptor, Miró (1893–1983) created a unique, whimsical artistic language—which to the uninitiated may look like colorful doodles—on his way to becoming one of the 20th century's most celebrated artists. In minimalist galleries bathed with natural light are several hundred of Miró's canvases, as well as a wealth of his drawings, graphics, and sculptures. A rooftop terrace and sculpture garden provides lovely views of Barcelona below. 🕐 *1½ hr. Parc de Montjuïc, s/n.* ☎ *93-443-94-70. www.fundaciomiro-bcn.org. Admission 8€ adults, 6€ students, free for children under 14. Also part of ArticketBCN joint admission. July–Sept Tues–Wed and Fri–Sat 10am–8pm; Oct–June Tues–Wed and Fri–Sat 10am–7pm; year-round Thurs 10am–9:30pm and Sun 10am–2:30pm. Bus no. 50 at Pl. d'Espanya, or Funicular de Montjuïc.*

Visit the rooftop terrace and sculpture garden at the Fundació Joan Miró.

❺ **La Font del Gat.** This resurrected *modernista* cafe and restaurant, built by the acclaimed architect Puig i Cadafalch, is ensconced in gardens of the Montjuïc hillside and makes for a relaxing spot for a coffee or beer, or even an inexpensive fixed-priced lunch. *Pg. Sta. Madrona, 28.* ☎ *93-289-04-04. $.*

❻ **Estadi Olímpic/Museu Olímpic i de L'Esport.** The setting for the majority of events during Barcelona's hosting of the 1992 Summer Olympics was Montjuïc, including the Olympic Stadium, originally built in 1929 for the World's Fair, and Arata Isozaki's sleek Palau d'Esports Sant Jordi, the indoor stadium that hosted gymnastics and volleyball events (and now also hosts concerts). Nearby are a new sports museum (Av. de l'Estadi, 60), Galería Olímpica, and the outdoor pool and diving pavilion, which overlooks the city below. 🕐 *1 hr. Av. de L'Estadi, s/n (Parc de Montjuïc).* ☎ *93-292-53-79. www.museu olimpicbcn.cat. Museum admission 4€ adults, 2.50€ students, free for seniors and children 13 and under. Oct–Mar Tues–Sat 10am–6pm, Sun 10am–2:30pm; Apr–Sept Tues–Sat 10am–8pm. Metro: Pl. de Espanya (then take the escalator from Palau Nacional), bus no. 50 at Pl. d'Espanya, or Funicular de Montjuïc.*

A piece from the Museu Nacional d'Art de Catalunya (MNAC).

❼ ★★★ Museu Nacional d'Art de Catalunya (MNAC). At the base of Montjuïc, within the domed Palau Nacional, this museum is anything but a stale repository of religious art. Its medieval collection, which includes Romanesque works salvaged from churches all over Catalunya, is unequaled; many of the superb altarpieces, polychromatic icons, and treasured frescoes are displayed in apses, just as they were in the country churches where they were found. Other highlights are paintings by some of Spain's most celebrated Old Masters, including Velázquez, Ribera, and Zurbarán, as well as nine newly acquired Picassos, exhibited in their own gallery. If it's gotten late in the day and you don't have the energy for the last two stops, you might stick around for the light-and-sound show of the **Font Màgica,** at the base of the steps up to the Palau Nacional. ⏱ 1½ hr. Palau Nacional (Parc de Montjuïc). ☎ 93-622-03-60. www.mnac.cat. Admission 8.50€ adults, free for seniors, children 16 and under, and 1st Sun of month; joint admission to Poble Espanyol 12€ (also part of ArticketBCN joint admission). Tues–Sat 10am–7pm; Sun 10am–2:30pm. Metro: Pl. de Espanya.

❽ ★★★ kids Parc Güell. Yet another of Gaudí's signature creations, this open-air park on the outskirts of the Eixample district is pure whimsy. Resembling an idiosyncratic theme park, it features a mosaic-covered lizard fountain, Hansel and Gretel pagodas, and undulating park benches swathed in broken pieces of ceramics, called *trencadís.* Gaudí carved part of the park out of a hillside, fashioning a forest of columns like tree trunks. A planned housing development that was never fully realized, the park is home to but a single house, now the **Casa Museu Gaudí,** a small museum about Gaudí's life and work (where the ascetic architect lived while working on the project). On clear days, you can see much of Barcelona laid out beneath your feet, including the spires of La Sagrada Família and the twin towers on the beach. ⏱ 1 hr. Ctra. del Carmel, 28. ☎ 93-213-04-88. www.bcn. cat/parcsijardins. Free admission to park; Casa Museu Gaudí 4€. Daily Dec–Feb 10am–6pm, Mar and Nov

Casa-Museu Gaudí in the Parc Güell.

10am–7pm, Apr and Oct 10am–8pm, May–Sept 10am–9pm. Metro: Lesseps (then a 15-min. walk uphill). Bus: 24 or 28.

❾ ★ kids Tibidabo/Parc d'Atraccions. High above Barcelona is Tibidabo Mountain, which has been a getaway destination for Barcelonans since the early 1800s for its cooler temperatures and panoramic views of the city and the ocean. The historic Tramvia Blau, or Blue Tram, carries visitors to an overlook with bars and restaurants.

Tibidabo amusement park.

Crowning Tibidabo is the odd juxtaposition of a neo-Gothic church and a 1950s-style amusement park, Parc d'Atraccions (the gentle swing ride is spectacular; it seems to suspend riders over the city). 🕐 *1–2 hr. Pl. Tibidabo, 3. ☎ 93-211-79-42. www. tibidabo.es. Parc d'Atraccions 52€ for unlimited rides, 11€ 6 rides, 9€ children under 1.2m (4 ft.), free for children under 90cm (35 in.). Summer Tues–Thurs noon–10pm, Fri–Sat noon–11pm; off-season hours vary (check website); closed most of Jan–Feb. From Pl. Kennedy (Metro: Tibidabo), the Blue Tram connects with the Funicular Tibidabo, a cable car that completes the trek to the top of the mountain (mid-Sept to the end of Apr, weekends only); round-trip 4.30€ (funicular cost refunded with park admission). A T2 Tibibus also travels from Pl. de Catalunya (2.80€) and is refunded with park admission.*

🔟 ★ Mirablau. This bar perched on Tibidabo Mountain is sedate in the late afternoon and early evening, when it's perfect to relax and contemplate all of Barcelona, stretching out to the sea beneath you. *Pl. Doctor Andreu, 2. ☎ 93-418-58-79. $$.* ●

Modernista Barcelona

1. Parc Güell
2. La Sagrada Família
3. Hospital de
   Santa Creu i Sant Pau
4. La Pedrera (Casa Milà)
5. Passeig de Gràcia
6. El Palau de la
   Música Catalana
7. Els Quatre Gats
8. Palau Güell
9. Casa Calvet

Previous page: Antoni Gaudí's Casa Batlló.

Barcelona is renowned for the wildly original *modernisme*, or Catalan Art Nouveau, style of architecture that flourished in the late 19th and early 20th centuries. Best known are the stunning works of Antoni Gaudí, but so many talented architects left their mark on Barcelona that it's a big task even to do a greatest hits tour in a single day. START: **Metro to Lessep, then a taxi or 15-min. walk uphill to Parc Güell, the first stop on the itinerary.**

1 ★★★ kids **Parc Güell.** In 1900 Gaudí's lifelong patron, the Catalan industrialist Eusebi Güell, envisioned a real-estate development in a garden setting. Although never completed, the project bears Gaudí's visionary stamp and reflects the naturalism beginning to flower in his work. The architect set out to design every detail in the park, but much of the work was in fact completed by a disciple, Josep María Jujol, best known for the park's colorful splashes of *trencadis* (designs of broken shards of ceramics). Yet the unique man-made landscape is all Gaudí. At the main entrance are fairy-tale-like gatehouses topped with chimneys resembling wild mushrooms. The covered marketplace, with an extraordinary tiled lizard fountain at the entrance, is supported by 86 Doric columns (not the 100 planned). But most famous are those sinuous, mosaic-covered benches that trace the perimeter of the plaza above. ⏱ *45 min. See p 54,* **9**.

2 ★★★ kids **La Sagrada Família.** Gaudí's most famous building is a work of unbridled ambition. He dedicated 4 decades of his life to it, and though the architect left behind no detailed plans, he expected that the cathedral—the world's largest if completed—would take several generations to finish. Gaudí envisioned 12 spires (one for each of the Apostles), a massive dome over the apse, and four additional, higher spires, as well as one central bell tower, representing the Virgin Mary. Portals in the dramatic Nativity facade represent Faith, Hope, and Charity, and biblical elements, such as the Tree of Calgary, pack the dense surface. ⏱ *45 min. See p 9,* **1**.

3 ★★ **Hospital de Santa Creu i Sant Pau.** Just a few blocks' walk from La Sagrada Família, this

Mosaic benches in the Parc Güell.

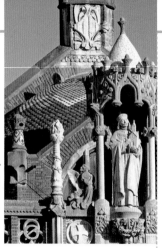

The modernista *rooftops of Sant Pau.*

hospital campus—undergoing a massive restoration in 2010, and visited only by guided tour—reveals that Domènech i Montaner (1850–1923), like Gaudí, also thought in grand terms. Hospital Sant Pau, begun in 1902, was also left unfinished at the time of its architect's death, with just 18 of a planned 48 pavilions completed (12 of those are by Domènech i Montaner, and all are classified as World Heritage monuments). The fanciful brick-and-tile pavilions feature vaulted ceilings and decorative mosaics and sculpture, techniques that reach their apex in El Palau de la Música Catalana (p 15, ❶). ⏱ *45 min. c/ Sant Antoni Maria Claret, 167–171.* ☎ *93-488-20-78. www.santpau.es. Free admission; guided tours as part of Ruta del Modernisme, 5€ adults, 3€ students, free for children 14 and under. Guided tours daily at 10:15am and 12:15pm in English, 1:15pm in Spanish. Metro: Hospital de San Pau or Sagrada Família (and 10-min. walk along Av. de Gaudí).*

❹ ★★★ **kids La Pedrera.**
Gaudí's most inspired civic work, formally named (Casa Milà) for the patron who dreamed of creating a showstopper on elegant Passeig de Gràcia, this sinuous landmark apartment block is for many the pinnacle of *modernisme.* The rooftop chimneys (which some claim represent Christians and Moors battling for Spanish turf) are spectacular, but those with an interest in architecture will be fascinated by the museum (Espai Gaudí), which exposes the splendid arches of the attic and delves into the life, times, and techniques of the architect, while the restored original apartment (El Pis) shows off its peculiar shapes, handcrafted doorknobs, and period furniture, all of Gaudí's design. ⏱ *1 hr. See p 9,* ❷.

❺ ★★★ **Passeig de Gràcia.**
This elegant shopping boulevard is ground zero for *modernisme,* the one place to see an amazing collection of *modernista* architecture without covering much distance. In fact, on a single block are pivotal buildings by Gaudí and the other two architects that make up the movement's great troika, Domènech i Montaner and Puig i Cadafalch. The competing proximity of these landmarks earned the block the nickname "Manzana de la Discòrdia" (Block of Discord). See mini-tour on following page.

El Pis apartment is refurbished to its early-20th-century look.

At the foot of La Pedrera are some *modernista* surprises: **5A** The **street tiles** on the sidewalk (trumpeting nature and ocean themes) are by Gaudí, while the white **mosaic-covered benches** that flower into ornate, **wrought-iron lampposts** are by Pere Falqués. On the same block is the design shop **5B** **Vinçon** (p 78), which occupies an elegant house built for the *modernista* painter Ramón Casas. Three blocks down is the famed **Manzana de la Discòrdia.** First take a peek at **5C** ★ **Fundació Tàpies** (p 37, **2**), just off the boulevard at c/ Aragó, 225, a museum dedicated to the Catalan artist Antoni Tàpies. Domènech i Montaner designed the erstwhile publishing headquarters in 1884. Gaudí's spectacular

5D ★★★ **Casa Batlló** (p 9, **3**), open to the public since 2004, is as stunning inside as out; it features flowing staircases, a mushroom-shaped fireplace, and a gallery with bonelike columns. **5E** ★★ **Casa Amatller** (p 10, **4**), Puig i Cadafalch's most famous building, was the first *modernista* building on the block. The exterior of carved stone is the work of a celebrated artisan, Eusebi Arnau. Domènech i Montaner's ornate **5F** ★ **Casa Lleó Morera** (p 11, **5**) is ornate but less groundbreaking than its *modernista* companions on the block, but suffers even more in comparison since commercial tenants altered the ground floor and destroyed several magnificent sculptures.

Ruta del *Modernisme*

You could easily spend days visiting *modernista* landmarks in Barcelona. If your appetite has been whetted, check out the **Ruta del Modernisme de Barcelona** (*modernisme* route) promoted by the city (www.rutadelmodernisme.com; ☎ 902-07-66-21; 12€–18€). A self-guided tour of 115 sites, it offers discounted admissions of up to 50% at both major and lesser-known buildings—everything from palaces to pharmacies. Information and discount vouchers are available at a desk in the entry of the main tourist information office on Plaça de Catalunya. Besides the highlights listed in this chapter, several other of the Route's Top 30 sites are also included in the Eixample walking tour; see p 68.

6 ★★★ **El Palau de la Música Catalana.** Domènech i Montaner designed this audacious concert hall as a home for the Orfeó Catalán (Catalan Choral Society). The interior is hallucinatory: from colored-glass canisters on staircases and a ceiling dominated by a colossal teardrop of stained glass to a stage framed by pumice busts of the composers Bach, Beethoven, and Wagner by the sculptor Pau Gargallo. Long surrounded by apartment buildings, the Palau was given some breathing space when the noted Barcelona architect Oscar Tusquets completed a tasteful extension in 2003. ⏲ *45 min. See p 15,* **1**.

The spectacular Palau de la Música Catalana.

7 ★★ **Els Quatre Gats.** A favorite hangout of Pablo Picasso, Ramón Casas, and other turn-of-the-century *modernista* bohemian intellectuals, this restaurant and cafe—one of the first commissions for the architect Puig i Cadafalch and site of Picasso's first exhibition—is the perfect stop on a *modernisme* tour of Barcelona, either for a late lunch or coffee and a pastry. *c/ Montsió, 3.* ☎ *93-302-41-40. $–$$.*

8 ★★ **Palau Güell.** Undergoing a large-scale renovation and with limited visits and hours

Picasso was a regular at Els Quatre Gats.

(10am–2:30pm), this 1888 mansion, not in the Eixample but in the much less fashionable district of El Raval, was Gaudí's first big commission from Eusebi Güell, the textile magnate who would become a lifelong confidante and patron. It's heavier and less whimsical than Gaudí's later works—on the outside it looks like a fortress—but the architect's early genius is evident in the underground stables, interconnected floors, and Moorish-style decorative skylights. On the roof is the building's crowd-pleasing surprise, a preview of what would later come with La Pedrera: a small contingent of colorful, *trencadí*-covered chimneys. ⏱ *1 hr. c/ Nou de la*

Rambla, 3–5. ☎ *93-317-39-74. Admission 3€, free for children 6 and under. Normal hours after renovation completed: Mon–Sat 10am–6:15pm. Metro: Drassanes.*

☕ ★★ **Casa Calvet.** The best way to cap a day of touring *modernista* landmarks is dinner at this upscale restaurant, in one of Gaudí's earliest (and best preserved) apartment buildings. The 1899 house features one of Barcelona's first elevators and elegant *modernista* details throughout, making for a unique dining experience. *c/ Caspe, 48.* ☎ *93-412-40-12. $$$.*

The Curious Life & Work of Gaudí

"Play the violin," the visionary architect Antoni Gaudí i Cornet (1852–1926) once told a client who was distressed to find no place for his piano in the unorthodox form of his La Pedrera apartment. Gaudí remains best known for his unfinished magnum opus, La Sagrada Família, which continues to baffle and amaze visitors more than 125 years later. Yet few fans realize that the architect's life was as eccentric as his signature works. A pious Catholic and ardent Catalan nationalist who became a religious zealot in his later years, Gaudí had a devil of an imagination but lived an ascetic life. After 1910, he devoted himself entirely to the Sagrada Família, abandoning almost all secular works, and he lived the last years of his life in the workshop of the temple to which he dedicated 44 years. He died ignominiously, run over by a street trolley; taxis refused to take him—destitute, dressed like a pauper, and unrecognizable—to a hospital.

Ciutat Vella: **Ancient Barcelona**

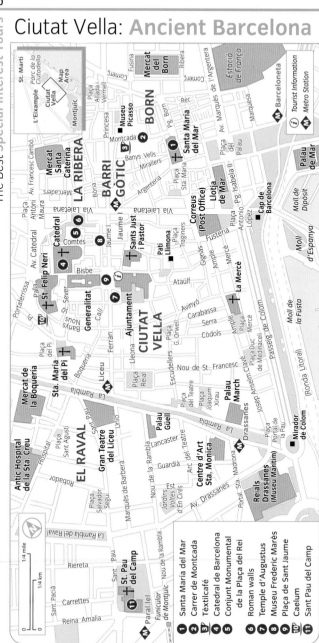

1. Santa Maria del Mar
2. Carrer de Montcada
3. Tèxtilcafé
4. Catedral de Barcelona
5. Conjunt Monumental de la Plaça del Rei
6. Roman walls
7. Temple d'Augustus
8. Museu Frederic Marès
9. Plaça de Sant Jaume
10. Caelum
11. Sant Pau del Camp

B arcelona is one of Spain's most historic cities. Founded as Barcino by the Romans in A.D. 15, it expanded outside the ancient walls—sections of which still remain—in the 11th century. Much of medieval Barcelona lives on gloriously in the Ciutat Vella (old city) quarters of Barri Gòtic and La Ribera. See the Barri Gòtic walking tour (p 60) for additional details of the Roman and medieval city, including El Call, the old Jewish Quarter. START: **Metro to Jaume I.**

❶ ★★ Santa María del Mar.
Designed by the architect Berenguer de Montagut in the mid–14th century and completed in just 5 decades, Santa María del Mar is a soaring Catalan Gothic church that once faced the Barcelona waterfront; its name ("St. Mary of the Sea") refers to its history as a place of worship for ship owners, merchants, and sailors (and wives left behind) who came to pray for safe returns. ⏱ *30 min. See p. 16,* **❹**.

❷ Carrer de Montcada. At the back entrance to Santa María del Mar, this narrow, pedestrian-only lane through the La Ribera quarter is one of the most handsome medieval streets in Barcelona. From its

Santa María del Mar is one of Barcelona's purest examples of Catalan Gothic architecture.

origins in 1148, the street became an epicenter of commercial life. From the 14th to 17th centuries, Montcada's *palaus,* or mansions, were home to wealthy and noble families, many of whom were patrons of Santa María del Mar. While many *palaus* are private, a few are occupied by museums and galleries, giving visitors a chance to see their gorgeous courtyards and massive central stone staircases. ⏱ *45 min. Metro: Jaume I. See mini-tour on following page.*

❸ Tèxtilcafé. This unexpected retreat, in the splendid medieval courtyard of the palace that houses the Museu Tèxtil i d'Indumentària, is a perfect relaxed spot either for coffee and a croissant at an outdoor table or a full, fixed-price value lunch inside. *c/ de Montcada, 12–14.* ☎ *93-268-25-98. $.*

❹ ★★★ Catedral de Barcelona. A Roman temple and later a mosque once stood on this site in the heart of the Gothic Quarter. The lush cloister, built between 1350 and 1448, continues to be home to white geese, which in the Middle Ages functioned as guard dogs, their squawks alerting priests to intruders. Beneath the ancient slabs of the stone floor lie the remains of members of the Barri Gòtic's ancient guilds. ⏱ *30 min. See p 13,* **⓬**.

❺ ★★★ kids Conjunt Monumental de la Plaça del Rei.
Plaça del Rei abuts a remaining sec-

The Best Special-Interest Tours

Carrer de Montcada — LA RIBERA

Tiny **2A Carrer de les Mosques** ("street of the flies") is reputed to be the narrowest street in Barcelona; residents are able to reach out and touch the building across the street from their windows. The 15th-century **2B Palau dels Cervelló (no. 25),** today home to a famous contemporary art gallery (Galería Maeght), maintains its original Gothic facade, while the 17th-century **2C Palau Dalmases (no. 20)** retains a Gothic chapel and richly carved Renaissance staircase and elegant arches. **2D Palau Nadal (no. 12–14),** home to the **Museu Barbier-Mueller d'Art Precolombí**—an excellent private collection of pre-Columbian art—was constructed in the 15th and

16th centuries. Next door, the 13th-to15th-century **2E Palau dels Marquesos de Lió (no. 12)** houses the **Museu Tèxtil i d'Indumentària (Textile and Clothing Museum),** which features costumes, fabric, and lace-making techniques from the 16th century to present day, and is home to a nice little cafe-restaurant. The 15th-century **2F Palau Aguilar (no. 15–23)** is today the site of the **Museu Picasso,** which it has been since 1963. Even if the art weren't inside, the museum would be worth visiting to see the extraordinary Gothic patios and staircases flanking superbly carved windows. See *p 15,* **2**.

Practical Matters: Carrer de Montcada

Museu Barbier-Mueller d'Art Precolombí. c/ de Montcada 12–14. ☎ 93-310-45-16. www.barbier-mueller.ch. Admission 3.5€ adults, 1.70€ students, free for children 15 and under. Tues–Fri 11am–7pm; Sat 10am–6pm; Sun 10am–3pm. Free on first Sun of the month. Metro: Jaume I.

Museu d'Tèxtil i d'Indumentària. c/ de Montcada 12. ☎ 93-319-76-03. www.museutextil.bcn.cat. Admission 5€ adults, 3€ seniors and students 24 and under, free for children 15 and under. Tues–Sat 10am–6pm; Sun 10am–3pm. Metro: Jaume I.

tion of the old Roman walls, and in the 1930s archaeologists unearthed ruins of Barcino, the old Roman city. The subterranean ruins (1st C. B.C.–7th C. A.D.) can be visited as part of the fine **Museu d'Història de Barcelona.** The five-story tower Mirador del Rei Martí, which rises above the square, dates to 1555, when it was built as a look-out for foreign invasions and peasant uprisings. ⏱ *45 min. Pl. del Rei, s/n.* ☎ *93-256-21-00. Admission 6€ adults, 4€ students and seniors. Oct–Mar Tues–Sat 10am–2pm and 4–9pm; Apr–Sept Tues–Sat 10am–8pm; Sun year-round 10am–8pm. Metro: Jaume I.*

⑥ ★ kids Roman walls. Barcino was a small settlement, comprising just 10 hectares (25 acres) enclosed by walls 2m (6½ ft.) thick. Several sections of the Roman walls, enlarged in the 3rd and 4th centuries A.D., remain; some of the best examples are on Plaça Ramon Berenguer, parallel to Via Laietana. To the right of the front entrance to the Catedral de Barcelona, the Portal de l'Angel's twin semicircular towers frame the entrance to carrer del Bisbe. ⏱ *15 min. Metro: Jaume I.*

⑦ ★ Temple d'Augustus. Three massive Corinthian columns, the best-preserved relics of the Roman city, are all that remain of the Temple d'Augustus, the principal temple built in the 1st century B.C. Hidden from view and lower than Barcelona's modern street level, they are one of the Barri Gòtic's great secrets. The temple once formed part of the Roman Forum dedicated to the

Geese in the cloister of Catedral de Barcelona (p 31).

emperor Caesar Augustus. *c/ del Paradis, 10 (inside Centre Excursionista de Catalunya).* ☎ *93-315-23-11. Free admission. June–Sept Mon–Sat 10am–8pm, Sun 10am–2pm; Oct–May daily 10am–2pm and 4–8pm. Metro: Jaume I.*

8 ★★ Museu Frederic Marès. Marès, a 20th-century sculptor and evidently obsessive collector, amassed one of Spain's finest private collections of medieval sculpture, from the pre-Roman to the Romanesque, Gothic, Baroque, and Renaissance eras. The collection is housed in a palace—itself worthy of study, with its handsome interior courtyards, carved stone, and expansive ceilings—just behind the Catedral. The museum will reopen in early 2011 after an extensive remodeling. ⏱ *45 min. Pl. de Sant Lú, 5–6.* ☎ *93-310-58-00. www.museumares.bcn.es. Admission 3€ adults, free for children 11 and under. Tues–Sat 10am–7pm; Sun 10am–3pm. Free Wed 3–7pm. Metro: Jaume I.*

9 ★ Plaça de Sant Jaume. The site of the city and regional governments, this stately plaza is also

Portrait bust of the Roman Emperor Nerva at the Museu d'Història (p 33).

a popular gathering place for Barcelonans during holiday celebrations and political demonstrations. The **Palau de la Generalitat,** home to the autonomous Catalunian government, dates to the 15th century, while across the square the 14th-century **Casa de la Ciutat,** built around a central courtyard, houses the municipal government. The **Saló de Cent** (Room of 100 Jurors) features immense arches, typical of the Catalan Gothic style. ⏱ *30 min. Casa de la Ciutat: Pl. de Sant Jaume, s/n.* ☎ *93-402-70-00. Free admission. Sun 11am–3:30pm. Metro: Jaume I.*

10 ★ Caelum. On the surface this appears to be simply an appealing shop selling teas, jams, olive oil, sweets, and other products made by nuns and religious orders in Spain and Europe. But downstairs in the cafe (where you can have tea, coffee, pastries, and sandwiches), in a space referred to as "the crypt," is another treat altogether: the exposed foundations of 14th-century Jewish baths (*mikves* or *mikva'ot*). *c/ de la Palla, 8.* ☎ *93-302-69-93. $.*

The Roman walls at night (p 33).

The (Hairy) Birth of a Nation

Although the Moors invaded Spain in 711 and would rule over much of its territory for 8 centuries, Catalunya only briefly succumbed to the invaders from North Africa. The Moors retreated after a defeat near the Pyrenees in 732, never establishing a lasting foothold in Catalunya. A 9th-century count with a descriptive name, Guifré el Pilós—Wilfred the Hairy—became a feudal lord and the founding father of Catalunya's independence. He founded a dynasty in 878 that ruled for nearly 500 years. Much of Spain remained under Moorish domination, but Barcelona and Catalunya were linked instead to northern Europe, a geopolitical wrinkle that formed the basis for the fiercely independent and northward-looking Catalan character. The hero of Catalunya has been mythologized in the region's flag, which features four horizontal red stripes on a yellow field (and is said to be the oldest still in use in Europe today). According to legend, the red bars were first etched in Wilfred's own blood on his golden shield (perhaps as he lay dying in battle). Scholars cast doubt on the veracity of the tale, but most Catalans believe it to be true.

⓫ ★★ Sant Pau del Camp. The oldest church in Barcelona, dating back to the 9th century, "Saint Paul of the Countryside" was once a rural church and part of a monastery, far beyond the city walls. It remains remarkably intact, with original Romanesque capitals and bases of the portal complementing sections from a rebuilding in the 11th and 12th centuries. The chapter house holds the tomb—which reads A.D. 912—of Count Guífre Borrell, son of Wilfred the Hairy (above). ⏱ *30 min. c/ de Sant Pau, 99 (El Raval).* ☎ *93-441-00-01. Admission to cloister 2€. Mon–Sat 10am–1:30pm and 4–7:30pm. Metro: Paral.lel.*

The Temple d'Augustus columns date to the 1st century b.c. (p 33).

Barcelona for Modern-Art Lovers

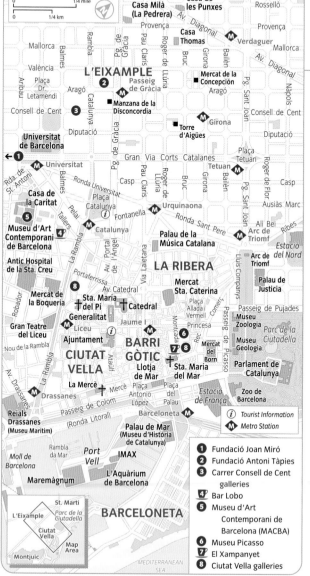

1. Fundació Joan Miró
2. Fundació Antoni Tàpies
3. Carrer Consell de Cent galleries
4. Bar Lobo
5. Museu d'Art Contemporani de Barcelona (MACBA)
6. Museu Picasso
7. El Xampanyet
8. Ciutat Vella galleries

Barcelona has a long tradition of embracing adventurous art and eccentric artists. Picasso began his career here, and the Catalans Miró, Dalí, and Tàpies all made their marks in Barcelona before becoming international superstars. Barcelona's lively art scene of museums and galleries is especially strong in contemporary and modern art, though this is a tour for those who have the stamina to take in several museums back to back. For a superb collection of Gothic art, don't miss **MNAC** (p 21, **7**). START: **Metro to Espanya (or funicular to Montjuïc).**

1 ★★★ **Fundació Joan Miró.** Miró, born in rural Catalunya in 1893, became one of the 20th century's most important artists. His whimsical and enigmatic abstract forms expressed complex themes, including sexuality, Catalan national identity, and opposition to the Spanish Civil War. Miró himself donated 11,000 works to the museum. Pivotal works include the 1970s tapestry *Tapis de la Fundació; L'Estel Matinal*, part of the Constellation Series; and mid-century sculptures, including *Sun Bird* and *Moon Bird*. The museum's audioguide is especially insightful. ⏲ *1 hr. See p 20, **4**.*

2 ★★ **Fundació Antoni Tàpies.** One of Spain's great artists of the 20th century is the abstract expressionist Antoni Tàpies, born in Barcelona in 1923. Tàpies is known for his collage and mixed-media "matter" paintings that incorporate earth, sand, and even pedestrian items such as socks into large canvasses. His work is replete with politically charged and religious imagery, as well as graffiti-like words and insignias. After a 2-year renovation, the museum reopened in early 2010. The giant tangle of steel on the roof of this emblematic *modernista* building, designed by Domènech i Montaner, is the artist's once-controversial sculpture (now accepted by most Barcelonans) called Cloud and Chair. ⏲ *45 min. c/ Aragó, 255.* ☎ *93-487-03-15. www.*

fundaciotapies.org. Admission 6€ adults, 4€ students. Tues–Sun 10am–8pm. Closed Mon, Dec 25–26, and Jan 1–6.

3 **Carrer Consell de Cent.** This leafy Eixample street, between Passeig de Gràcia and Muntaner, is one of the most frequented in Barcelona for its contemporary art galleries. Among the galleries to keep an eye out for: **Sala Dalmau** (no. 349; ☎ 93-215-45-92); **Jordi Barnadas** (no. 347; ☎ 93-215-63-65); **Senda** (no. 337; ☎ 93-487-67-59); **Galería René Metras** (no. 331; ☎ 93-487-58-74); **Galería Llucià Homs** (no. 315; ☎ 93-467-71-62); **Galería Carles Tache** (no. 290; ☎ 93-487-88-36); **Ambit** (no. 282; ☎ 93-488-18-00); and **Galería Eude** (no. 278; ☎ 93-487-93-86). ⏲ *1 hr. Metro: Pg. de Gràcia.*

The sculpture Cloud and Chair sits atop the Fundacio Antoni Tàpies.

The Carles Tache gallery.

4 **Bar Lobo.** This cool tapas bar is decorated with graffiti murals and the kind of concert posters and ads that usually litter city walls. It's great for lunchtime snacks or late-night drinks. *c/ Pintor Fortuny, 3.* ☎ *93-481-53-46. $–$$.*

5 ★ **Museu d'Art Contemporani de Barcelona (MACBA).** This gleaming white 1995 Richard Meier design remains a stark contrast in the emerging Raval quarter, but the Museum of Contemporary Art is continually expanding its permanent collection of works by Calder, Basquiat, and Klee, as well as major Catalan artists such as Tàpies and Miquel Barceló. ⏲ *45*

Sunlight provides brilliant, natural interior lighting at MACBA.

min. *Pl. dels Angels, 1.* ☎ *93-412-08-10. www.macba.es. Admission 7.50€ adults, 6€ students, free for seniors and children 13 and under (also part of ArticketBCN joint admission). Mon and Wed–Fri 11am–7:30pm; Sat 10am–8pm; Sun 10am–3pm. Metro: Catalunya or Universitat.*

6 ★★★ **Museu Picasso.** Picasso (1881–1973) donated 2,500 paintings and sculptures to this museum, the largest representation of his work in Spain, in 1970. While especially strong on the artist's early development, including his Blue and Rose periods (Picasso's early talents for traditional portraiture and figurative painting are a revelation), the highlight is his playful series of 59 paintings based on Velázquez's seminal work *Las Meninas*. Also of note are *The Harlequin* and the young artist's sketch notebooks of Barcelona street scenes. Picasso fans should not miss the new gallery of nine works, including *Woman in Hat and Fur Collar,* at the superb **MNAC** (p 21, **7**) on Montjuïc hill. ⏲ *1 hr. See p 15,* **2**.

7 **El Xampanyet.** A wonderful throwback, this classic and gregarious *cava* bar serves its sparkling wine (here, more a fizzy white wine than *cava*) in '50s-style glasses. An excellent selection of Catalan cheeses, salamis, and more is on offer. *c/ de Montcada, 22.* ☎ *93-319-70-03. $.*

Barcelona's Outdoor Sculpture

Not all of Barcelona's great art is behind museum doors; the city is full of outdoor sculpture. If you arrive by air, you may first see Joan Miró's giant **mosaic mural** (1970) outside Terminal B at the Barcelona Airport. Look also for the great Basque sculptor Eduardo Chillida's *Topos V* in Plaça del Rei; Roy Lichtenstein's *Cap de Barcelona* (1992) at the intersection of Moll de la Fusta and Vía Laietana; Antoni Tàpies's glass-enclosed *Homage to Picasso* (1983) on Passeig Picasso, at the entrance to Parc de la Ciut-

Antoni Tàpies's Homage to Picasso.

adella; Miró's *Woman and Bird* (1982) in Parc Joan Miró, near Estació de Sants; *Pla de l'Ós,* the Miró mosaic underfoot on La Rambla (across from the Teatre Liceu opera house); and a couple for the kids, Xavier Mariscal's **giant crayfish** on Moll de la Fusta and Frank Gehry's monumental *Fish* sculpture on the beach at Vila Olímpica in front of Hotel Arts.

❽ Ciutat Vella galleries.

Although the bulk of contemporary and modern art galleries are in L'Eixample, those in the old city pose a dramatic contrast to the ancient surroundings. The Barri Gòtic streets Petritxol and Palla mix art galleries in with boutiques and antiques dealers. Galleries worth seeking out are **Galeria Maeght** (c/ de Montcada, 25; ☎ 93-310-42-45); **Artur Ramón Espai Contemporani** (c/ de la Palla, 10; ☎ 93-301-16-48); **Trama** (Petritxol, 8; ☎ 93-317-48-77); and the city's oldest gallery, **Sala Parés** (Petritxol, 5; ☎ 93-318-70-08). ⏱ *1 hr. Metro: Jaume I.*

Inside the Museu Picasso.

Barcelona for Design & Architecture Fans

1. CaixaForum
2. Pavelló Mies van der Rohe
3. Palau d'Esports Sant Jordi
4. Transbordador Aeri del Port
5. Vila Olímpica
6. Cuines de Santa Caterina
7. Mercat de Santa Caterina
8. Museu d'Art Contemporani de Barcelona (MACBA)
9. Casa de la Caritat
10. L'Eixample shopping
11. Suites Avenue
12. Moovida

Plaça Francesc Macià
LES CORTS
Av. Diagonal
Av. Sarrià
Buenos Aires
Av. Josep Tarradellas
Londres
Paris
Còrsega
Ecola Industriel
Rosselló
Hospital Clinic
Provença
Viladomat
Comte d'Urgell
Mallorca
Av. Roma
València
L'EIXAMPLE
Aragó
Villarroel
Casanova
Muntaner
Aribau
Creu Coberta
Parc de Joan Miró
Consell de Cent
Ctra. de la Bordeta
Plaça Toros Las Arenas
Diputació
Gran Via Corts Catalanes
Plaça Espanya
Gran Via Corts Catalanes
Sepúlveda
Plaça Univers
Av. Paral·lel
Mistral
Floridablanca
Ronda de St. Antoni
Poble Espanyol
Plaça de Carlos Buigas
Tamarit
Mercat de St. Antoni
MACBA
LA FRANÇA
Manso
EL RAVAL
MNAC
Palau Nacional
Museu Arqueològic
Parlament
Ronda St. Pau
La Rambla del Raval
Palau St. Jordi
Av. de l'Estadi
Fundació Joan Miró
Exposició
POBLE SEC
Av. Paral·lel
Estadi Olímpic
Plaça Neptú
Nou de la Rambla
Av. Drassanes
MONTJUÏC
Av. Miramar
Reials Drassanes (Museu Marítim)
PARC DE MONTJUÏC
Plaça Carlos Ibáñez
Transbordador Aeri
Castell de Montjuïc
Museu Militar
Ronda Litoral
World Trade Center
Moll de la Costa
Moll de Ponent

0 — 1/2 mile
0 — 1/2 km

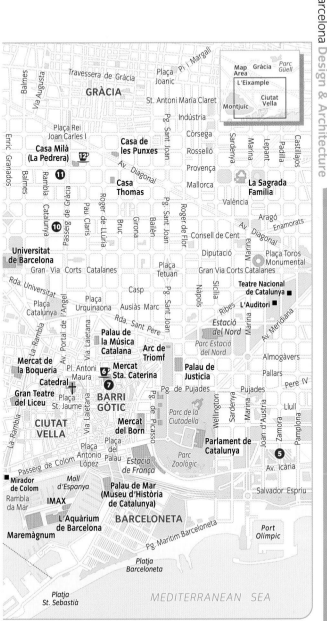

Balmes
Via Augusta
Travessera de Gràcia
Plaça Pi i Margall
Joanic
GRÀCIA
St. Antoni Maria Claret
Map Area
Gràcia
Parc Güell
L'Eixample
Montjuic
Ciutat Vella
Indústria
Enric Granados
Plaça Rei Joan Carles I
Pg. Sant Joan
Còrsega
Sardenya
Marina
Lepant
Padilla
Castillejos
Casa Milà (La Pedrera) 12
Casa de les Punxes
Rosselló
Av. Diagonal
Provença
La Sagrada Família
11
Balmes
Casa Thomas
Mallorca
Rambla Catalunya
Passeig de Gràcia
Roger de Llúria
Pau Claris
Bruc
Girona
Bailèn
Pg. Sant Joan
Roger de Flor
València
Aragó
Enamorats
10
Av. Diagonal
Marina
Consell de Cent
Universitat de Barcelona
Gran Via Corts Catalanes
Diputació
Plaça Toros Monumental
Rda. Universitat
Plaça Tetuan
Gran Via Corts Catalanes
Plaça Catalunya
Casp
Sicília
Nàpols
Teatre Nacional de Catalunya ■
Plaça Urquinaona
Ausiàs Marc
Pg. Sant Joan
Ribes
L'Auditori ■
La Rambla
Rda. Sant Pere
Estació del Nord
Av. Meridiana
Av. Portal de l'Àngel
Via Laietana
Palau de la Música Catalana
Arc de Triomf
Marina
Parc Estació del Nord
Almogàvers
Mercat de la Boqueria
Pl. Antoni Maura
6
Mercat Sta. Caterina
Palau de Justicia
Pallars
Pere IV
Catedral ✝
7
Pg. de Pujades
Pujades
Gran Teatre del Liceu
Plaça St. Jaume
BARRI GÒTIC
Wellington
Sardenya
Marina
Joan d'Àustria
Llull
CIUTAT VELLA
Mercat del Born
Pg. de Picasso
Parc de la Ciutadella
Zamora
Pamplona
La Rambla
Plaça Antonio López
Plaça del Palau
Estació de França
Parlament de Catalunya
5
Passeig de Colom
Parc Zoològic
Av. Icària
■ **Mirador de Colom**
Moll d'Espanya
Palau de Mar (Museu d'Història de Catalunya)
Salvador Espriu
Rambla da Mar
IMAX
L'Aquàrium de Barcelona
BARCELONETA
Port Olímpic
Maremàgnum
Pg. Marítim Barceloneta
Platja Barceloneta
Platja St. Sebastià
MEDITERRANEAN SEA

Though visitors flock to Barcelona for its *modernista* architecture and picturesque Gothic Quarter, the forward-looking Catalan capital is also a favorite with fans of contemporary architecture and design. The 1992 Olympic Games provided a huge impetus for adventurous urban planning projects. As the dean of Harvard's Graduate School of Design proclaimed, "Unlike many other cities, Barcelona seems to have chosen architecture and urbanism as its most conspicuous, long-lasting, and crowning glory." From the new Ricardo Bofill terminal at El Prat airport to the emerging El Raval neighborhood, cutting-edge design is everywhere in Barcelona. **START: Metro to Plaça Espanya.**

❶ ★ CaixaForum. The 2002 conversion of a 1911 red-brick *modernista* textile factory (by Puig i Cadafalch), by the Japanese architect Arata Isozaki and three others, transformed it into a brilliant new art exhibition space. It's a terrific synthesis of Barcelona's dominant design motifs—*modernista* and cutting-edge contemporary—and a terrace on the roof provides great views of the Palau Nacional, home to the Museu Nacional d'Art de Catalunya, and Montjuïc hill (p 21, ❼). ⏱ *30 min. Av. Marquès de Comillas, 6–8.* ☎ *93-476-86-00. www.fundacio. lacaixa.es. Free admission. Tues– Sun 10am–8pm (Sat until 10pm). Metro: Pl. Espanya.*

❷ ★★ Pavelló Mies van der Rohe. The famous minimalist German architect created this steel, glass, and marble structure as the German Pavilion for the 1929 World's Fair. Considered a classic of 20th-century design, it is recognized for its pure, precise lines. The interior holds little save van der Rohe's original Barcelona Chair, today a much-reproduced icon of modern design. The pavilion, unceremoniously banished from the city after the Fair, was returned to its original location in 1985 after prominent architects petitioned the city. ⏱ *30 min. Av. Marquès de Comillas, s/n.* ☎ *93-423-40-16. www.miesbcn. com. Admission 4.50€ adults, 2.30€*

The Pavelló Mies van der Rohe is considered a classic of 20th-century design.

Frank Gehry's Fish *sculpture at the Vila Olimpica.*

students, free for children 17 and under. Daily 10am–8pm. Metro: Pl. Espanya.

❸ Palau d'Esports Sant Jordi.

Arata Isozaki's sleek indoor sports stadium held gymnastic, volleyball, and basketball events during the '92 Olympics. When it was first opened to the public, some 50,000 Barcelonans turned out to see the new addition to Montjuïc's Olympic Ring. Today it hosts both sporting events and concerts. Lording over it is the once-despised **Telefónica communications tower**, also built for the '92 Olympics, by the famed architect from Valencia, Santiago Calatrava. The tower's base is decorated with broken ceramic tiles, an homage to Gaudí. ⏱ *30 min. Av. del Estadi, s/n (Parc de Montjuïc). Metro: Pl. Espanya (then take the escalator from Palau Nacional); alternatively, take bus no. 50.*

❹ ★ kids Transbordador Aeri del Port. A great way to appreci-

ate the layout of Barcelona, especially L'Eixample's grid designed by Ildefons Cerdà in 1859, is to take the aerial cable car from Montjuïc down to the port area and Barceloneta. See p 19, ❸.

❺ ★ Vila Olímpica. The award-

winning urban-design project that revamped the waterfront created an entirely new neighborhood of apartment buildings, gardens, and large public sculptures, by a host of both celebrated and young architects, designers, and artists. The apartment blocks first housed Olympic athletes before being turned over to private buyers, and in the years since, Vila Olímpica has become a fashionable neighborhood. The waterfront's twin towers, among Barcelona's only skyscrapers (one is Hotel Arts, the other an office complex), were initially polemical, but their presence is now widely accepted. In front of Hotel Arts is Frank Gehry's massive, metal-lattice *Fish* sculpture, which appears to glow in the afternoon sun. ⏱ *45 min. Metro: Ciutadella–Vila Olímpica.*

The Antoni Llena sculpture David and Goliath *in front of the Hotel Arts.*

Architecture Superstars

For design-crazy sorts who can't get enough, a number of relatively recent contributions to Barcelona's urban landscape are by celebrated architects in the zone north of Vila Olímpica, near Plaça de les Glòries. Pritzker prizewinner Rafael Moneo built the sleek white concert hall **L'Auditori** (c/ Lepant, 150), while nearby the glass-fronted **Teatre Nacional de Catalunya** (Pl. de les Arts, 1) is by Barcelona native Ricardo Bofill. Fast becoming a symbol of the city is Jean Nouvel's **Torre Agbar** (Av. Diagonal, 209–211), a tall (142m/465 ft.), phallic skyscraper that's illuminated at night with the blue and red of Barça, the local *fútbol* (soccer) team. Several blocks west (along Ronda St. Martí at Felip II) is Santiago Calatrava's **Pont Bac de Roda,** a white, arching bridge and work of stellar engineering by the man who has quickly become Spain's most famous architect, with projects in place across the globe.

6 ★★ **Cuines de Santa Caterina.** This cool tapas bar and restaurant makes the best of its privileged location inside the market and offers the freshest of seafood and vegetables, and inexpensive wines by the glass or carafe. It's a great spot for an array of small plates. *Av. Francesc Cambó, 16.* ☎ 93-268-99-18. $–$$.

7 ★★ **Mercat Santa Caterina.** The 2005 remodeling of this 1848 city food market—the first covered market in Barcelona—is renowned for its colorful and undulating mosaic-tile roof. The project was the work of the celebrated firm of Enric Miralles and Benedetta Tagliabue. ⏱ *30 min. Av. Francesc Cambó, 16. www.mercatsantacaterina.net. Mon 7:30am–2pm; Tues–Wed and Sat 7:30am–3:30pm; Thurs–Fri 7:30am–8:30pm.*

8 ★ **Museu d'Art Contemporani de Barcelona (MACBA).** Much like the way that Frank Gehry's Guggenheim Bilbao stimulated the arts and urban development in that Basque city, Richard Meier's MACBA has been the impetus for updating and integrating the Raval district. Art galleries, boutiques, bars,

The colorful, wavelike roof of Mercat Santa Caterina.

The Richard Meier–designed Museu d'Art Contemporani de Barcelona (MACBA).

and restaurants, as well as new hotels and apartment buildings, have followed, displacing many longtime residents but overall making the northern section of the neighborhood safer and more attractive. ⏱ *45 min. See p 38,* **5**.

9 ★ **Casa de la Caritat.** One of the first projects undertaken in the revamping of the formerly marginal Raval district was the conversion of this 13th-century convent and charity hospital into an art and culture space. Two avant-garde Catalan architects, Albert Viaplana and Helio Piñón, gave the Centre de Cultura Contemporània de Barcelona (CCCB) an angled wall of glass that reflects neighborhood rooftops and the Mediterranean Sea. ⏱ *45 min. c/ de Montalegre, 5–9.* ☎ *93-306-41-00. www.cccb.org. Tues–Sun 11am–8pm (Thurs until 10pm). Admission 4.50€, seniors and students 3.40€; free for children 15 and under and 1st Wed of every month. Metro: Catalunya or Universitat.*

10 ★ **L'Eixample Shopping.** A day of design for the fashion-conscious would be senseless without at least a couple of stops at Barcelona's renowned design emporiums. **Vinçon** (Passeig de Gràcia, 96) is a local institution for housewares, lamps, and furniture, all selected for their innovative design. Also visit the shops of

Catalan fashion designers **Josep Font** (c/ Provença, 304), **Antonio Miró** (c/ Consell de Cent, 349), and **Armand Basi** (Pg. de Gràcia, 49), three of the hippest clothiers in town. ⏱ *45 min. Metro: Pg. de Gràcia or Provença. See p 73.*

11 ★ **Suites Avenue.** It seems there's always a new building by an important international architect creating a buzz in Barcelona. The newest talked-about entry is this hotel facade by the famed contemporary Japanese architect Toyo Ito. The undulating stainless-steel facade mimics the waves of Gaudí's La Pedrera, which is right across the street, and is a fascinating addition to the *modernista* structures lining elegant Passeig de Gràcia. Architecture buffs will dig the expansive views of La Pedrera from the apartments here. ⏱ *15 min. Pg. de Gràcia, 83. Metro: Pg. de Gràcia or Provença.*

12 ★ **Moovida.** In the lobby of the high-design Hotel Omm, a hot spot with fashionable types, is the informal and less pricey cousin to Moo, the ultra-hip restaurant of the Roca brothers. It won't break the bank, and you can just have a drink or order a few tapas if you want. *c/ Rosselló, 265–269.* ☎ *93-445-40-00. $$.*

Gourmet Barcelona

0 1/2 mile
0 1/2 km

i Tourist Information
Ⓜ Metro Station

Casa Milà (La Pedrera)
Casa de les Punxes
Casa Thomas
Av. Diagonal
Verdaguer

Provença
Rambla de Catalunya
Pg. de Gràcia
Pau Claris
Roger de Llúria
Bruc
Girona
Bailèn

Mallorca
València
L'EIXAMPLE
Aragó
Plaça Dr. Letamendi
Consell de Cent
Diputació

Passeig de Gràcia
Manzana de la Disconcordia
Mercat de la Concepció
Aragó
Torre d'Aigües
Girona

Universitat de Barcelona

Gran Via Corts Catalanes
Plaça Tetuan
Tetuan

Universitat
Ronda Universitat
Plaça Catalunya
Casp
Urquinaona
Ronda Sant Pere
Ausiàs Marc
Arc de Triomf

Museu d'Art Contemporani de Barcelona
EL RAVAL
Mercat de la Boqueria
Palau de la Música Catalana
LA RIBERA
Mercat Sta. Caterina
Arc de Triomf
Estació del Nord
Palau de Justicia

Sta. Maria del Pi
Generalitat
Catedral
Jaume I
BARRI GÒTIC
Mercat del Born
Sta. Maria del Mar
Passeig de Pujades
Museu Zoologia
Museu Geologia
Parc de la Ciutadella
Parlament de Catalunya

Gran Teatre del Liceu
Liceu
Ajuntament
CIUTAT VELLA
La Mercè
Llotja de Mar
Drassanes
Reials Drassanes (Museu Marítim)
Passeig de Colom
Barceloneta
Palau de Mar (Museu d'Història de Catalunya)
Estació de França
Zoo de Barcelona

Port Vell
Moll d'Espanya
IMAX
BARCELONETA
Ronda Litoral
Maremàgnum

St. Martí
L'Eixample
Parc de la Ciutadella
Ciutat Vella
Montjuic
Map Area

1 Crustó
2 Colmado Quilez
3 Cacao Sampaka
4 La Cuina d'en Garriga
5 Granja Viader
6 Mercat de la Boqueria
7 El Quim de la Boqueria
8 Carrer Petritxol
9 La Pineda
10 Mesón del Café
11 Formatgeria La Seu
12 E & A Gispert
13 Vila Viniteca/La Teca
14 Mercat de la Barceloneta
15 Els Fogons de la Barceloneta

With its rise as a foodie capital, Barcelona now rivals San Sebastián and even Paris. Barcelona's innovative dining scene and the ever-escalating fame of Ferran Adrià, of El Bulli restaurant, are prompting food pilgrims to discover the coolest culinary stops in the Catalan capital. Besides haute-cuisine restaurants and chef-driven tapas bars, you'll find scores of old-school *colmados* (grocery stores), inventive chocolatiers, and gourmet food and wine shops. Strap on your feed bag, but note that on Mondays several shops are closed (and on Sundays La Boquería market is), and some places (like Granja Viader) have odd hours, closing for long stretches of the afternoon. START: **Metro to Liceu.**

1 ★ **Crustó.** Start your day off with some incredible baked goods and artisanal breads from this rustic yet modern bakery/cafe, prized by chefs and gourmands as one of the finest in the city. It's low-key but always swarmed with locals, leaving the buzz to competitors like (admittedly very cool-looking) Barcelona-Reykjavik (Doctor Dou, 12; Raval). ⏲ *20 min. c/ València, 246.* ☎ *93-487-05-51. www.crusto.es. Metro: Pg. de Gràcia.*

Colmado Quílez is an old-school Barcelona grocery store.

Gourmet Tip

For more suggestions on where to buy and eat your favorite gourmet items, see also "The Best Shopping," p 71, and "The Best Dining," p 93.

2 ★★ **Colmado Quílez.** This 1908 grocery store and wine shop, the most famous *colmado* in Barcelona, is a charming throwback. Floor-to-ceiling shelves are stocked with gourmet packaged goods, while back rooms stock wines from across Spain and even 300 types of beer. You have to select your item, pay for it, and get a ticket before picking up the goods. ⏲ *20 min. Rambla de Catalunya, 63.* ☎ *93-215-23-56. www.lafuente.es. Metro: Pg. de Gràcia.*

3 ★★ **Cacao Sampaka.** Best described as designer chocolate, with items categorized into "collections," such as "flowers and herbs," and so on. Repair to the bar/cafe for delicious hot chocolate, pastries, and sandwiches. ⏲ *30 min. c/ Consell de Cent, 292.* ☎ *93-272-08-33. Metro: Pg. de Gràcia.*

4 ★★ **La Cuina d'en Garriga.** Helen Garriga's gourmet temple dedicated to all things culinary stocks carefully selected Catalan foodstuffs from the city's finest independent purveyors, such as artisanal bread, and sought-after appliances and items for the kitchen. Sample the goods at the tasting room in back. ⏲ *20 min. c/ Consell de Cent, 308.* ☎ *93-215-72-15. Metro: Pg. de Gràcia.*

5 ★ **Granja Viader.** Although the old neighborhood of El Raval has seen a huge amount of upheaval, this place with marble-topped tables has resisted change. A gloriously authentic *granja*, or "milkbar," (the oldest in Barcelona, since 1870), it's known for thick chocolate drinks such as *xocolata desfeta* and the original *cacaolat*, a bottled chocolate drink famous throughout Spain. c/ *Xuclà, 4–6.* ☎ 93-318-34-86. www.granjaviader.cat. $.

Granja Viader.

6 ★★★ **Mercat de la Boquería.** Spain's largest food market is a gastronomic paradise. The market, just off La Rambla, dates to 1840; today it has more than 300 stalls stocked with eye-popping displays of salted fish, exotic fruits, wild mushrooms (*ceps* and *bolets*), and more. You can eat, too, at the gourmet kiosks El Quim and Bar Pintxo, as well as a couple of restaurants in the back. ⏱ *1 hr. See p 12,* **9**.

7 ★★ **El Quim de la Boquería.** Quim has been at the helm of this bustling kiosk bar *(taburete)* within La Boquería food market nearly a

quarter-century. Prized by fellow chefs and foodies-in-the-know, it's a place for fresh grilled seafood and tapas of the highest order. *La Rambla, 91 (parada no. 584/585).* ☎ *93-301-98-20. $$. See p 102.*

8 **Carrer Petritxol.** One of the Gothic Quarter's most atmospheric streets is lined with *granjas*, or milk bars, *xocolaterias*, and *pastisserias*, all tempting the taste buds. ⏱ *25 min. Metro: Liceu.*

9 ★ **La Pineda.** This tiny charcuterie storefront, in business since 1930, is where I tasted my first real

A few of the bountiful offerings at La Boquería.

Spanish ham. It is jampacked with jamón Serrano, chorizos, cheeses, wines, olive oils, canned goods, and other gourmet products. If you're lucky enough to score one of the few marble-topped tables and not too full from previous stops, dive into a selection of tapas. ⏲ 15 min. c/ del Pi, 16. ☎ 93-302-43-93. Metro: Liceu.

Some of the wares at E&A Gispert.

10 **Mesón del Café.** This tiny, century-old place is just ineffably cool. Locals drop in at all hours for superb *cortado,* but after several gourmet stops, go for a mean *picardia* (coffee with layers of condensed milk and whiskey). c/ Llibreteria, 16. ☎ 93-315-07-54. $.

11 ★ **Formatgeria La Seu.** A Scotswoman passionate about artisanal Spanish farmhouse cheese runs this cool cheese shop, which stocks a couple dozen mostly unpasteurized cheeses from across Catalunya and Spain (formal tastings, breakfast, and lunch are offered). ⏲ 30 min. c/ d'Augeria, 16. ☎ 93-412-65-48. www.formatgeria laseu.com. Metro: Jaume I.

12 ★★ **E&A Gispert.** One of the oldest continuously running shops in Barcelona (since 1851) sells coffee and teas, dried fruits and nuts, honey and jams, and traditional Catalan *torrón* desserts, as well as gift baskets and other artisanal and organic products. Possibly the most redolent place you'll ever poke your nose into, the shop retains the original one-piece counter and wood shelves and still uses a spectacular 150-year-old, wood-burning nut roaster—the only one of its kind in Europe. ⏲ 30 min. c/ dels Sombrerers, 23. ☎ 93-319-73-35. www.casa gispert.com. Metro: Jaume I.

13 ★★ **Vila Viniteca/La Teca.** From cult wines like Pingus to small-yield Priorats, including plenty of bottles you can't get outside Spain, this is Barcelona's wine temple, with more than 6,000 choices. Check out scheduled *catas* (wine tastings) at www.vilaviniteca.es. Don't miss the little gourmet shop, La Teca, next door. ⏲ 30 min. c/ Agullers, 7. ☎ 93-268-32-27. Metro: Jaume I.

14 **Mercat de la Barceloneta.** Redesigned, just like much of the formerly blue-collar and fishermen's neighborhood that surrounds it, this covered food market has a new spring in its step, and like Mercat de Santa Caterina and La Boquería, is also a great place to sit down for lunch or dinner once you've checked out all the fresh fish, meats, and produce inside. ⏲ 30 min. Pl. de la Font, 1. ☎ 93-221-64-71. Metro: Barceloneta.

15 ★★ **Els Fogons de la Barceloneta.** Within the food market, and spilling out onto the newly designed square that's opened up this section of the barrio, this cool seafood and tapas joint, with a modern industrial look, is the baby sister of the Michelin-starred restaurant Lluçanes. Pl. de la Font, s/n. ☎ 93-224-26-26. Metro: Barceloneta. $$.

Barcelona with Kids

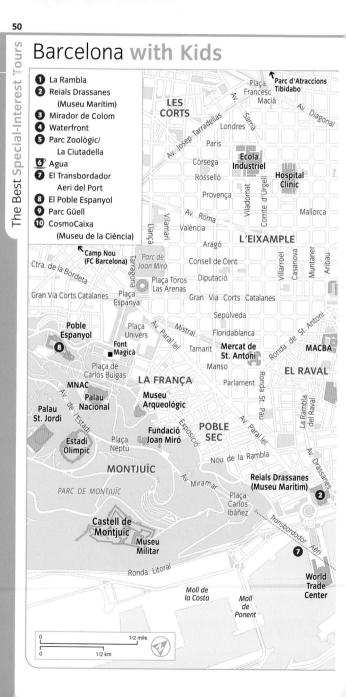

1 La Rambla
2 Reials Drassanes
   (Museu Marítim)
3 Mirador de Colom
4 Waterfront
5 Parc Zoològic/
   La Ciutadella
6 Agua
7 El Transbordador
   Aeri del Port
8 El Poble Espanyol
9 Parc Güell
10 CosmoCaixa
   (Museu de la Ciència)

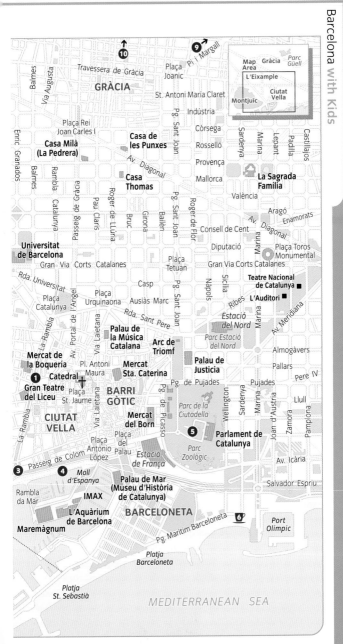

Map Area — Gràcia — Parc Güell — L'Eixample — Ciutat Vella — Montjuïc

Travessera de Gràcia
Plaça Joanic
Pi i Margall
GRÀCIA
St. Antoni Maria Claret
Indústria
Balmes
Via Augusta
Plaça Rei Joan Carles I
Casa Milà (La Pedrera)
Casa de les Punxes
Còrsega
Rosselló
Provença
Mallorca
Sardenya
Marina
Lepant
Padilla
Castillejos
Enric Granados
Balmes
Rambla Catalunya
Passeig de Gràcia
Pau Claris
Roger de Llúria
Bruc
Girona
Bailén
Pg. Sant Joan
Roger de Flor
Av. Diagonal
Casa Thomas
La Sagrada Família
València
Consell de Cent
Aragó
Enamorats
Av. Diagonal
Universitat de Barcelona
Gran Via Corts Catalanes
Diputació
Gran Via Corts Catalanes
Marina
Plaça Toros Monumental
Rda. Universitat
Plaça Catalunya
Av. Portal de l'Angel
Plaça Urquinaona
Rda. Sant Pere
Casp
Ausiàs Marc
Plaça Tetuan
Pg. Sant Joan
Nàpols
Sicília
Ribes
Teatre Nacional de Catalunya ■
L'Auditori ■
La Rambla
Palau de la Música Catalana
Arc de Triomf
Estació del Nord
Parc Estació del Nord
Av. Meridiana
Almogàvers
Pallars
Mercat de la Boqueria
Catedral ✝
Gran Teatre del Liceu
Pl. Antoni Maura
Plaça St. Jaume
Mercat Sta. Caterina
BARRI GÒTIC
Via Laietana
Pg. de Picasso
Pg. de Pujades
Palau de Justicia
Parc de la Ciutadella
Wellington
Sardenya
Marina
Joan d'Austria
Pujades
Pere IV
Llull
Zamora
Pamplona
Av. Portal de l'Angel
CIUTAT VELLA
La Rambla
Passeig de Colom
Plaça Antonio López
Mercat del Born
Plaça del Palau
Estació de França
Parc Zoològic
Parlament de Catalunya
Av. Icària
Salvador Espriu
Moll d'Espanya
IMAX
L'Aquàrium de Barcelona
Maremàgnum
Palau de Mar (Museu d'Història de Catalunya)
BARCELONETA
Rambla da Mar
Pg. Marítim Barceloneta
Port Olímpic
Platja Barceloneta
Platja St. Sebastià
MEDITERRANEAN SEA

① ③ ④ ⑤ ⑥ ⑨ ⑩

Sophisticated Barcelona might seem like a city just for grown-ups, but it has plenty to offer children of all ages. Much of the fun is outdoors, from La Rambla's amusing, costumed mimes and Gaudi's whimsical park to the family-oriented waterfront and zoo in the city's largest green space. Kids are sure to love the aerial cable car from the port to Montjuïc and the antique Blue Tram that climbs the hill to Tibidabo, but you might want to tackle this tour over 2 days, leaving Parc Güell and Poble Espanyol for tomorrow.

START: Metro to Plaça de Catalunya.

① ★★★ **La Rambla.** You'll need to watch your kids closely amid the throngs, but La Rambla's human theater is enhanced by creative human statues—from Roman soldiers to mummies—that spring to life for a coin or two. ⏲ *45 min. See p 11,* ⑧.

② ★★ **Reials Drassanes (Museu Marítim).** Older kids will love the magnificent ships at this seafaring museum, housed in stunning medieval shipyards. ⏲ *1 hr. See p 19,* ①.

A performer on La Rambla.

③ **Mirador de Colom.** Take the elevator to the top of this Christopher Columbus monument overlooking the old port for fantastic views. ⏲ *30 min. See p 19,* ②.

④ ★★ **Waterfront.** On the other side of the cool, pedestrian-only **Rambla del Mar** drawbridge are excellent options for families: **L'Aquàrium,** a huge, well-designed aquarium with a glass-enclosed tunnel that produces the effect of fish, eels, and sharks swimming around and over wide-eyed visitors; a traditional **carousel** for younger children; and **Maremàgnum** shopping mall, with lots of shops geared toward kids. You can also board double-decker swallow boats, **Las Golondrinas,** to cruise the harbor, or stroll along the

View marine life galore at L'Aquàrium.

Evening Entertainment for Families

If kids and parents are both raring to go at night, consider these options:

The nostalgic amusement park **Parc d'Atraccions Tibidabo,** with a magnificent chair ride that appears to dangle high above the city below. See p. 22, ❾.

Font Màgica, the colorful, dancing fountains set to pop tunes at the base of Montjuïc (Pl. Carles Buïgas, 1; May–Oct Thurs–Sun every half-hour between 9:30 and 11:30pm, Oct–Sept Fri–Sat every half-hour between 7 and 8:30pm; free admission; Metro: Pl. Espanya).

IMAX Port Vell theatre (Moll de Espanya; ☎ 93-225-11-11; www. imaxportvell.com; admission 8.10€–12€; Metro: Drassanes).

A match of Barcelona's hugely popular *fútbol,* or soccer, team, "Barça," at **FC Barcelona/Camp Nou,** c/ Aristides Maillol, s/n (☎ 93-496-36-00; www.fcbarcelona.com). Tickets (available online) start at 30€. Visits to the Camp Nou stadium and museum are also available, 14€ children, 17€ adults. Metro: Collblanc.

Moll de la Fusta boardwalk; there's a sculpture of a giant, cartoon-like crayfish waiting for kids at the end. 🕐 *2 hr. L'Aquàrium:* ☎ *93-221-74-74. www.aquariumbcn.com. Admission 17€ adults, 14€ seniors, 12€ children 4–12 and students, free for children 3 and under. July–Aug daily 9:30am–11pm; Sept–June Mon–Fri 9:30am–9pm, Sat–Sun 9:30am–9:30pm. Metro: Drassanes. Also see p 89.*

❺ ★★ **Parc Zoològic/La Ciutadella.** Barcelona's largest city park is a great place for kids to unwind, with a large pond and rowboats, a massive Gaudí-designed fountain, and a vintage greenhouse. But the zoo is probably the main draw. Although its star attraction, an albino gorilla, passed on a few years ago, several of his (non-albino) offspring are here, as well as llamas, lions, bears, hippos, and a large primate community—most are not behind bars, but kept in their

"enclosures" by a slightly more humane moat. 🕐 *1 hr. Parc de la Ciutadella.* ☎ *902-45-75-45. www. zoobarcelona.cat. Admission 16€ adults, 9.60€ students and children 3–12, 8.40€ seniors. Summer daily*

Parc de la Ciutadella is one of Barcelona's most popular green spaces.

10am–7pm; off season daily 10am–5/6pm. Metro: Ciutadella or Arc de Triomf.

 **Agua.** Near Port Olímpic and the beach is this informal and good-value restaurant with outdoor tables overlooking the water. The Mediterranean menu features seafood and risottos, with plenty of items for the kids, and you can just get some small plates and drinks and feast your eyes on the beach. *Pg. Marítim de la Barceloneta, 30.* ☎ *93-225-12-72. $–$$.*

⑦ ★★ El Transbordador Aeri del Port. Taking the aerial cable car from Barceloneta high above the port and city on the way up to Montjuïc is like a theme-park ride for kids. *See p 19,* **③**.

⑧ ★ El Poble Espanyol. Created for the 1929 Barcelona International Exhibition, this re-creation of a Spanish village contains 100-plus styles of architecture from across Spain, with emblematic mansions, churches, streets, and squares reduced to scale. Though purists may find it well-meaning kitsch, it's a fun and instructive place for families and a great introduction to the country's architectural diversity—a taste of Spain's whitewashed Andalusian alleyways, small-town plazas,

CosmoCaixa.

and Renaissance palaces. ⏱ *1 hr. Av. Marqués de Comillas, s/n (Parc de Montjuïc).* ☎ *93-508-63-00. www.poble-espanyol.com. Admission 8.50€ adults, 6.50€ seniors and students, 5.50€ children 4–12, free for children 3 and under; 20€ family ticket, 5€ night ticket; joint admission to MNAC 12€. Mon 9am–8pm; Tues–Thurs 9am–2am; Fri 9am–4am; Sat 9am–5am; Sun 9am–midnight. Metro: Espanya, then 10-min. walk uphill, or bus no. 13 or 50 from Pl. de Espanya.*

⑨ ★★★ Parc Güell. Gaudí's wildly imaginative park is mostly playground, and kids love it. Stone columns look like trees, gatehouses look transported from Hansel and Gretel, and the gurgling, mosaic-covered lizard fountain simply looks adorable. It's a great place for hide-and-seek. On a clear day, you can see past the spires of La Sagrada Família all the way to the beach. ⏱ *1 hr. See p 25,* **①**.

⑩ ★★★ CosmoCaixa (Museu de la Ciència). One of the biggest and best science museums anywhere, this learning center is high-tech, hands-on, and a blast for kids. In an original *modernista* building with a daring underground extension, the huge museum features thrilling exhibitions like "The Flooded Forest," a living Amazonian rainforest with over 100 species of animal and plant life (kids are encouraged to pick up and touch frogs, spiders, and other fauna). The 3-D planetarium and cool Geological Wall are also big draws. ⏱ *1½ hr. c/ Teodor Roviralta, 55.* ☎ *93-212-60-50. obrasocial.lacaixa.es. 3€ Planetarium and other activities, 2€ supplement; 2€ children 8–16; free for children 7 and under and seniors. 1st Sun every month free admission. Tues–Sun 10am–8pm. FGC: Av. Tibidabo (then 10-min. walk). Bus: 17, 22, 58, or 73.* ●

3 The Best
Neighborhood Walks

La Rambla

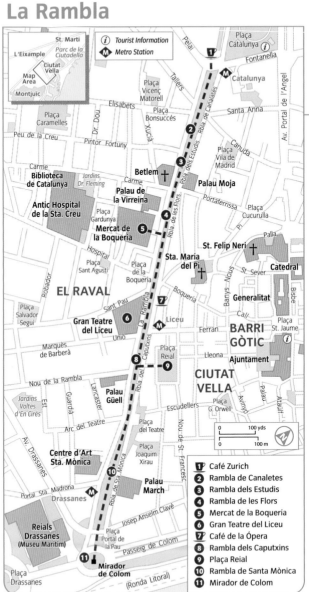

- ⓘ Tourist Information
- Ⓜ Metro Station

1. Café Zurich
2. Rambla de Canaletes
3. Rambla dels Estudis
4. Rambla de les Flors
5. Mercat de la Boqueria
6. Gran Teatre del Liceu
7. Café de la Ópera
8. Rambla dels Caputxins
9. Plaça Reial
10. Rambla de Santa Mònica
11. Mirador de Colom

Previous page: A couple strolls through La Ribera.

s there a finer boulevard for strolling in the world? Victor Hugo proclaimed La Rambla "the most beautiful street in the world," while the Spanish poet Federico García Lorca said it was the "only street he wished would never end." The tree-shaded, pedestrian-only promenade stretches nearly 2km (1.2 miles) down a gentle slope from the city's hub, Plaça de Catalunya, to the waterfront. To the left (as you walk down it) is the Barri Gòtic; to the right is El Raval, an emerging artsy neighborhood. START: **Metro to Plaça de Catalunya.**

1 **Café Zurich.** At the very top of La Rambla, to the west of Plaça de Catalunya (and at the base of El Triangle shopping mall), is this terrace cafe, the best spot in the city for people-watching and a jolt of coffee before you start your stroll. The cafe was much more atmospheric before it was rebuilt and sanitized a few years back (the mall's to blame), but it remains a pivotal reference point in Barcelona. *Pl. Catalunya, 1.* ☎ *93-317-91-53. $.*

The Font de Canaletes.

2 **Rambla de Canaletes.** The beginning of La Rambla usually swarms with people, particularly on game days of Barça, the local football (soccer) club. Kiosks sell foreign newspapers and magazines, and the first of La Rambla's celebrated mimes, or "human statues," begin to appear. The rotating cast of flamboyant characters includes opera singers, bearded nuns, and Roman

La Rambla? Les Rambles? Las Ramblas?

The name La Rambla is derived from Arabic, signifying a dry riverbed—which is what this spot was until the 14th century, when Barcelonans began to populate the area. The stream was soon paved over, and it developed into a pedestrian-only boulevard. Some call it by the plural name, Les Rambles (Las Ramblas in Spanish), since in fact it comprises five distinct sections with individual names. However, they all blend together so seamlessly that most Barcelonans call the whole stretch by the singular, La Rambla. It's most crowded just before the lunch hour and in the early evening, but it's never deserted. In the wee hours it's the haunt of a sometimes motley mix of early morning newspaper sellers, street sweepers, and party animals stumbling back to their apartments and hotels.

Springtime throngs strolling popular La Rambla boulevard.

soldiers, all vying for a few coins. The 19th-century Font (fountain) de Canaletes is said to convert anyone who drinks from it into a lifelong resident of Barcelona.

3 ★★ kids **Rambla dels Estudis.** Hear that squawking? Popularly called Rambla dels Ocells ("of the birds"), this section becomes an outdoor aviary, with parakeets, parrots, and other winged creatures in cages for sale. At the end of the day, vendors simply board up the stalls, and the birds remain overnight.

4 ★★ kids **La Rambla de les Flors.** Birds are replaced by flowers in this section, officially La Rambla de Sant Josep. Keep an eye out, to your right, for the *modernista* chocolate shop, **Escribà** (Antiga Casa Figueres, La Rambla, 83), one of the oldest chocolatiers in Barcelona. Another notable *modernista* building to look for is the **Farmacia Genové** (no. 77). **Palau de la Virreina** (no. 99), a grand, late-18th-century palace built for the widow of the viceroy of colonial Peru and today a museum hosting rotating contemporary art exhibits, is also worth a look.

5 ★★★ **Mercat de La Boquería.** Set back from La Rambla, on the right side, is a constant in the life of Barcelonans: Mercat de Sant

Josep, better known as La Boquería. This bustling 19th-century covered market overflows with gastronomic delights. Longtime shoppers and merchants greet each other by name and shout across the aisles. The market opens before dawn, and the best shoppers know to arrive early (note that it's closed Sun, though). *La Rambla, 91–101.* ☎ *93-318-25-84.*

6 ★★ **Gran Teatre del Liceu.** The midpoint and heart of the

A vendor clips her flowers on La Rambla de les Flors.

Ramblas is the bustling intersection Pla de la Boquería, with a **Joan Miró mosaic** underfoot. One of Europe's great opera houses, the **Liceu** (lee-*say*-oo), is to the right. Since 1874 it has been home to all the Catalan greats, including Montserrat Caballé and Josep Carreras. Gutted by fire in 1994 (its third), it reopened after a restoration added high-tech improvements but preserved its soul. *La Rambla, 51–59.* ☎ *93-485-99-14. www.liceu barcelona.com. Guided tours (70 min.), including the private Cercle del Liceu, daily at 10am. Admission 8.70€, free for children under 10. Unguided tours (no entry to the Cercle del Liceu) daily at 11:30am, noon, and 12:30pm and 1pm. Admission 4€, free for children 9 and under.*

7 ★ **Café de la Ópera.** This Belle Epoque cafe is a longtime gathering spot for operagoers and literary types and now a hangout for young people, tourists, gays, and old-timers. A good spot for coffee, beers, and snacks during the day, it gets more animated at night. *La Rambla, 74.* ☎ *93-317-75-85. $.*

8 ★ **Rambla dels Caputxins.** As the Rambla descends down a slight incline, so does its reputation. But you'll also find some of the Rambla's best entertainment—jugglers, tarot-card readers, more mimes, and street artists whipping out portraits and caricatures. On the right is **Hotel Oriente;** it was Hemingway's favorite place to stay in Barcelona. Nearby is **Palau Güell,** a Gaudí-designed mansion built in 1885. The

high-Gothic palace can and should be visited; make sure to see the impressive tiled chimneys on the rooftop.

9 ★ **Plaça Reial.** Across La Rambla and down a short passage is a pretty, arcaded square with a central fountain and soaring palm trees. Once home to a convent and later the haunt of junkies and thieves, today it is greatly cleaned up, and full of bars, cafes, and restaurants pushing legal stimulants.

10 ★ **Rambla de Santa Mònica.** The final section leads down to the harbor. Though the sleek **Centre d'Art Santa Mònica** hosts contemporary art exhibits, this zone is the least savory part of La Rambla (the maze of small and still-scruffy streets to the right, or west, comprise Barcelona's once-notorious Barri Xino, or Chinatown). The **Drassanes Reials,** beautifully vaulted medieval shipyards and home to the excellent **Museu Marítim,** are the highlight of La Rambla before you arrive at the waterfront. *See p 19,* **1**.

11 **Mirador de Colom.** Marking the end of the Rambla and the start of the waterfront is a statue honoring Christopher Columbus. Though he is ostensibly indicating the way to the New World, snarky observers like to point out that Columbus is actually looking towards Mallorca rather than the Americas. Columbus is reputed to have come to Barcelona after his maiden journey to the Americas to meet with the Catholic monarchs Isabel and Ferdinand. *See p 19,* **2**.

The Hotel Oriente was Hemingway's favorite Barcelona hotel.

Barri Gòtic

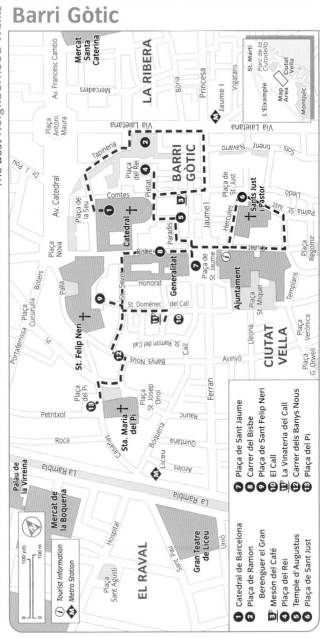

1 Catedral de Barcelona
2 Plaça de Ramon Berenguer el Gran
3 Mesón del Café
4 Plaça del Rei
5 Temple d'Augustus
6 Plaça de Sant Just
7 Plaça de Sant Jaume
8 Carrer del Bisbe
9 Plaça de Sant Felip Neri
10 El Call
11 La Vinateria del Call
12 Carrer dels Banys Nous
13 Plaça del Pi

The Barri Gòtic, or Gothic Quarter, is where Barcelona was born, and it remains the heart of the city. It includes remnants of Barcelona's 2,000-year-old Roman past, as well as the medieval Jewish district, El Call, and is a joy to wander. Its labyrinth of narrow, cobblestone streets are lined with palaces, convents, and churches and a thriving collection of bars, restaurants, and chic shops. START: **Metro to Jaume I.**

Plaça Ramon Berenguer.

❶ ★★ Catedral de Barcelona.

The Barri Gòtic has long been known as the "Cathedral Quarter," so this is the logical place to start. Locals gather at the **Plaça Nova** ("new square," dating from 1358!) in front of the cathedral to perform the *sardana*, a Catalan folk dance (Sun mornings and national holidays). To the right of the main entrance to the cathedral is the **Portal de Bisbe,** semicircular twin towers and one of three gateways to the walled settlement of Roman Barcino (4th c. A.D.). *See p 13,* ⓬.

❷ ★★ Plaça de Ramon Berenguer el Gran.

In this square is one of the largest surviving sections of the second Roman wall, dating to the 4th century A.D. The equestrian statue is of the 12th-century hero who extended the reign of independent Catalunya. Rising above the wall are the 14th-century Palau Reial Major

(Royal Palace), Santa Àgata chapel, and a Gothic tower. These are all best seen from Plaça del Rei, which you'll visit shortly. *Via Laietana, s/n.*

❸ ★★ Mesón del Café.

A tiny, charming cafe that dates back to 1909, this is the kind of good-vibes spot where some neighborhood folks stop by every day for some of the city's best coffee. Belly up to the bar or see if you can score a table in back. *c/ Llibreteria, 16.* ☎ 93-315-07-54. $.

❹ ★★★ Plaça del Rei.

This noble and austere square is the most beautiful part of the Barri Gòtic. Here you'll find subterranean Roman ruins and the medieval Royal Palace where Los Reyes Católicos (Catholic Monarchs) are said to have received Columbus on his return

Mirador del Rei Martí (King Martin's Watchtower) rises above the Plaça del Rei.

A bike rider in the Barri Gòtic.

from the New World in 1493. The sculpture in the square, *Topos V*, is by the Basque sculptor Eduardo Chillida, one of Spain's great 20th-century artists. *See p 13,* **⓭**.

⑤ ★★ Temple d'Augustus. *See p 33,* **⑦**.

⑥ ★★ Plaça de Sant Just. This quiet, diminutive square is one of the most representative and unadulterated of medieval Barcelona. The **Església dels Sants Just i Pastor,** a church begun in 1342, features a single nave in the Catalan Gothic style. It's usually open only for Sunday Mass. The Gothic fountain in the square dates to 1367. **Palau Moxó,** a seigniorial mansion across the square, was added in 1700.

⑦ ★ Plaça de Sant Jaume. An important crossroads during the Roman era, this broad square has been the political epicenter of Barcelona for more than 5 centuries. On one side is the **Palau de la Generalitat.** Across from it is the 14th-century **Ajuntament,** Barcelona's Town Hall. *See p 34,* **⑨**.

⑧ ★★ Carrer del Bisbe. One of the loveliest streets in the Gothic Quarter, the former principal artery of the Roman city connects the cathedral to Plaça Sant Jaume. On

The walkway above carrer del Bisbe was added in 1928.

El Caganer in a Manger

Barcelona's annual nativity crafts fair and Christmas market in the square in front of the cathedral features one traditional folkloric figure that in recent years has taken on all kinds of modern permutations. It is *el caganer.* Placed in nativity scenes, the small figure, traditionally donning a red peasant's cap, is depicted squatting and defecating. El caganer symbolizes Catalans' ties to the land and the hope for continued fertility. With an eye toward young consumers and tourists, today el caganer is not limited to peasant figures. You'll also see figurines of priests, nuns, Bart Simpson, local and international politicians, and more—all squatting and fertilizing the earth.

one side are the **Cases dels Canonges**, a series of 14th-century Gothic palaces. On the other is the **Palau de la Generalitat,** home to the Regional Government of Catalunya. Notice the rooftop gargoyles watching over the street action below. Arching over the lane is a bridge of carved stone, which only looks to be Gothic; it was added in 1928.

⑨ ★★★ Plaça de Sant Felip Neri. Down a tiny passageway off carrer Sant Sever (home to an extraordinary, if rarely open Baroque chapel) is one of the most tranquil and poetic spots in the Ciutat Vella. It was once the site of a parish cemetery and the specter of the dead lingers. Behind the gurgling fountain is a reminder of Spain's not-too-distant violence: The walls of the 17th-century church are scarred by Civil War bombs that killed 42 people in 1938.

⑩ ★ El Call. Carrer del Call leads into the warren of small streets that once comprised the Call, or Jewish Quarter, in medieval Barcelona (until the Jews were expelled from Spain in 1492). Only a few important vestiges of the community remain. The **Sinagoga Medieval de Barcelona** claims to be the oldest synagogue in Spain (based on a royal document from 1267). A nearby medieval Hebrew inscription marking a death in A.D. 692 reads, "Rabbi Samuel Hassareri, may his life never cease." ⏱ *30 min. c/ Marlet, 5.* ☎ *93-317-07-90. www.calldebarcelona.org. Admission 2€. Mon–Sat 11am–6pm; Sun 11am–3pm.*

⑪ La Vinateria del Call. This romantic little spot in the heart of the ancient Jewish Quarter is the perfect nook to duck into for local wines and Catalan tapas, such as cured meats and cheeses. *c/ Sant Domènech del Call, 9.* ☎ *93-302-60-92.*

⑫ ★ Carrer dels Banys Nous. This atmospheric street (named for the location of the "new baths," dating from the 12th century) follows the line of the old Roman wall and today is known as *el carrer dels antiquaris*—the street of antiques dealers. No. 10, now S'Oliver, a furniture store, was the site of Jewish baths for men.

⑬ ★★ Plaça del Pi. A trio of pretty, contiguous plazas surrounds the 15th-century church **Santa Maria del Pi,** known for its rose window. **Plaça de Sant Josep Oriol** adjoins Plaça del Pi and, behind the church, tiny **Placeta del Pi.** The squares are recognized for the unusual *sgraffito* decorative technique on the plaster facades of several buildings, an 18th-century style imported from Italy. But the leafy squares are most popular for the weekend artisans' market and open-air cafe-bars, making this an excellent place to while away the hours and finish a walking tour.

A relic from Barcelona's El Call (Jewish Quarter).

La Ribera

M Metro Station

0   100 yds
0   100 m

Ortigosa   Trafalgar

Comtal

El Palau de la
Música Catalana

Sant Pere de
les Puel.les

Arc de Triomf **M**

St. Pere Més Alt

Plaça
Lluís Millet

Plaça de
St. Pere

Arc de
Triomf

Montsió

Via Laietana

Dr. J. Nou

Verdaguer

St. Pere Mitjà

St. Pere Més Baix

St. Jaume Giralt

Rec Comtal

Lluís Companys

Plaça
Antoni
Maura

Av.
Catedral

Av. Francesc Cambó

Plaça
Marquilles

Portal Nou

Pg. de Picasso

Mercaders

Mercat
Santa
Caterina

Plaça
St. Augustí
Vell

Comerç

Plaça
del
Rei

Via Laietana

Bòria

LA RIBERA

Corders

Plaça
Allada i
Vermell

Museu
Zoologia

Assaonadors

Museu de
la Xocolata

Princesa

Jaume I **M**

Princesa

Museu
Geologia

CIUTAT
VELLA

Banys Vells

Montcada

Museu
Picasso

Rec

Fusina

Paseig de Picasso

Argenteria

Miralles

BORN

Mercat
del Born

Santa María
del Mar

Pg. Born

Mosques

Comerç

Jardins de
Fontseré
i Mestre

Plaça
Sta. María

Esparteria

Rec

Ribera

Gignàs

Fustería

Correus
(Post Office)

Plaça
Olles

Comerç

Llotja
de Mar

Plaça
del Palau

Av. Marquès de l'Argentera

Passeig de Circumval lació

Zoo de
Barcelona

Estació
de França

Parc
Zoològic

Marquesa

M Barceloneta

Plaça
Pau Vila

Ronda Litoral

Balboa

St. Martí

Ginebra

L'Eixample

Parc de la
Ciutadella

BARCELONETA

Map
Area

Ciutat
Vella

La Maquinista

Montjuïc

1 Carrer de l'Argenteria
2 Santa María del Mar
3 Fossar de les Moreres
4 Passeig del Born
5 Antic Mercat del Born
6 Passeig de Picasso
7 Carrer del Comerç
8 Montiel Espai Gastronòmic
9 Carrer de Montcada
10 Carrer dels Sombrerers
11 La Ribera fashion boutiques
12 Capella del Marcús
13 Mercat Santa Caterina
14 Sant Pere de les Puel.les
15 El Palau de la
     Música Catalana

As maritime commerce grew in the 13th and 14th centuries, Barri de la Ribera ("neighborhood of the waterfront," reflecting a time when the shoreline reached this far), became a populous residential neighborhood for the merchant class. Until recently the quarter was known principally for its great church, Santa Maria del Mar, and the much-frequented Museu Picasso. But in the last decade, La Ribera (and particularly the zone within it called "El Born") has become the city's most fashionable district, exploding with bars, restaurants, and boutiques. Though it can get rowdy late at night, it still retains its medieval character. START: **Metro to Jaume I.**

❶ Carrer de l'Argenteria.
Leave behind the congestion of Vía Laietana, a thoroughfare cut through the Ciutat Vella in the 1930s, for the foot traffic of the "street of silversmiths," a name dating to the 16th century. Fashion boutiques, bars, tapas restaurants, and hotels have taken over, but take a detour onto carrer Grunyí or carrer Rosic, for example, and you'll glimpse the old Ribera district.

❷ ★★★ Santa Maria del Mar.
I am powerless to pass by without taking at least a quick, always-inspiring spin through—for the thousandth time—this extraordinarily graceful 14th-century Catalan Gothic church. It's the kind of contemplative place that should clear your head before you continue through this bustling neighborhood. *See p 16,* **❹**.

❸ Fossar de les Moreres. An eternal flame burns on a small square around the right side of the main entrance to Santa María del Mar. It commemorates the royal sacking of Barcelona on September 11, 1714, which marked the end to the Spanish War of Succession. The king, Felipe V, then outlawed Catalan culture and its institutions, including the Catalan language. The date, 9/11 (or 11/9 in Spain), is now celebrated as the National Day of Catalunya. From here, duck into the tiny passageway carrer de Malcuinat (literally, "poorly cooked")

Santa Maria del Mar.

and walk out to **Plaça de les Olles** and back to Passeig del Born, along carrer de la Vidreria, just to get a feel for this part of the quarter that leads to the waterfront.

❹ ★★ Passeig del Born. This wide and elegant tree-lined promenade, with its stone benches, is a good place for a breather. Once the site of medieval jousting tournaments, it became the main square and heart of the city during Barcelona's seafaring heyday (13th–18th c.). Today apartment dwellers in its Gothic mansions are more commonly up in arms against the busy outdoor cafes and late-night bars that populate the ground floors and every side street leading off the *passeig*.

A bustling scene on Passeig del Born (p 65).

⑤ Antic Mercat del Born. At the end of Passeig del Born is the old Ribera covered market, with its distinctive wrought-iron roof. Constructed in 1876, it has been abandoned for years, as authorities have deliberated its potential uses. However, since it was found to sit on medieval archaeological remains, plans are for it to become a museum and/or cultural center.

⑥ Passeig de Picasso. This avenue borders the western edge of Parc de la Ciutadella, the largest green space in downtown Barcelona.

Here you'll find Antoni Tàpies's 1981 sculpture, *Homenatge a Picasso*, a glass cube containing a cubist-like assemblage of running water and furniture. A bit farther up are the Museu de Geologia and Museu Zoologia (Museums of Geology and Zoology; see p 86, ②), the latter designed by Domènech i Montaner, and the L'Hivernacle, a 19th-century greenhouse.

⑦ Carrer del Comerç. This street, bending around the edges of La Ribera, is one of many that have been inundated with shops and restaurants—not surprisingly, given its name, Commerce Street. The **Museu de la Xocolata** is found at Comerç, 36. The street parallel to Comerç, **carrer del Rec,** is flush with designer clothing and furniture boutiques.

⑧ ★ Montiel Espai Gastronòmic. This attractive little gourmet food store–cum–informal restaurant serves Catalan and Spanish standards, including *jamón de Jabugo* (Iberian ham), *pa amb tomàquet* (peasant bread with rubbed tomatoes and olive oil), Catalan sausages, and local wines. Have a

Archaeological remains in the Mercat del Born.

out of the Roman city (today c/ dels Carders). *Pl. Marcús, s/n.*

⑬ ★★ Mercat de Santa Caterina. This colorfully reimagined covered market has become a hit with foodies and architecture fans. *See p 44,* ⑦.

⑭ Sant Pere de les Puel.les. Little remains of the original (A.D. 945) church and Benedictine monastery, although you can still see a section of the 10th-century Greek-cross floor plan, lone surviving bell tower, and a few Corinthian capitals beneath the 12th-century dome of the heavily restored Romanesque church. Visiting hours are very limited. *c/ Lluís el Piadós, 1.* ☎ *93-268-07-42. Free admission. Tues and Thurs 6:30–8:30pm.*

⑮ ★★★ El Palau de la Música Catalana. If you haven't already had a chance to tour this extraordinary concert hall, Domènch i Montaner's masterpiece, this would be the time to do it. *See p 15,* ①.

The carrer de les Mosques.

selection of tapas or the good-value fixed-price lunch. *c/ Flassaders, 19.* ☎ *93-268-37-29. $.*

⑨ ★★★ Carrer de Montcada. Famous for its collection of stately Gothic mansions and Museu Picasso, this elegant avenue is a joy to stroll. Don't miss the incredibly narrow and poetically named **carrer de les Mosques** ("street of the flies"). *See p 31,* ②.

⑩ Carrer dels Sombrerers. Just off carrer de Montcada, and flanking Santa María del Mar, is this small and atmospheric street, formally named "St. Anthony of the Hat Makers." **E&A Gispert** (see p 49, ⑫), at no. 23, is a wonderful old epicurean shop with a 150-year-old roasting oven.

⑪ ★ La Ribera fashion boutiques. Off carrer de la Princesa is a series of alleyways that have given over to a handful of chic designer boutiques, typifying the neighborhood's stunning transformation. Make a brief detour along carrers Carassa and Vigatans before returning to Princesa.

⑫ ★ Capella del Marcús. Worth a look is this small Romanesque chapel, built in 1166 next to what was once the main thoroughfare in and

El Palau de la Música Catalana.

L'Eixample

1 Casa Calvet
2 Passatge de Permanyer
3 Pati de les Aigües
4 Queviures J. Murrià
5 Casa Thomas
6' Cor Caliu
7 Casa de les Punxes
8 Palau del Baró de Quadras

(i) Tourist Information
Ⓜ Metro Station

L'Eixample is an area best known for its extraordinary collection of late-19th and early-20th-century *modernista* (Catalan Art Nouveau) buildings, which earned it the nickname El Quadrat d'Or (the Golden Square). This tour takes you off the Eixample's well-trodden path. If you have time and energy at the end of this tour, you should tack on a stroll down Passeig de Gràcia or pedestrian-only Rambla de Catalunya, both of which lead back to Plaça de Catalunya. START: **Metro to Urquinaona.**

Dinner at Casa Calvet allows for a sneak peak inside the remarkable building.

❶ **Casa Calvet.** Antoni Gaudí's 1899 apartment building, one of his first commissions, is an understated work, best appreciated for its wrought-iron and sculptural details. The building saw the installation of Barcelona's first elevator, which has an impressively embellished cupola. A top-flight restaurant, Casa Calvet, inhabits the first floor—originally a textile shop designed by Gaudí—allowing architectural and gastronomic enthusiasts an enticing look up-close at an important early work of Gaudí. *c/ Caspe, 48. See p 29,* ❾.

❷ ★ **Passatge de Permanyer.** This inner courtyard, with a brick water tower in the center, is now open to the public. You'll find this lovely side street off Roger de Llúria, between Diputació and Consell de Cent. It is home to a small community of impeccable town houses and English-style gardens, tucked behind an engraved iron gate. It is perhaps the finest example of what Ildefons Cerdà, who designed L'Eixample, had in mind for the district.

❸ **Pati de les Aigües.** In the next block along Diputació, between Roger de Llúria and Bruc, this inner courtyard with a brick water tower in the center has been reclaimed and opened to the public. It's one of the few opportunities to view the central courtyards of the original

The charming Passatge de Permanyer.

The castlelike Casa de les Punxes is hard to miss.

Eixample apartment buildings as Cerdà intended—as open, green public spaces. Most have been built over or otherwise appropriated by private interests. *c/ Roger de Llúria, 56.* ☎ *93-424-38-09.*

❹ ★★ Queviures J. Murrià. This wonderful, old-school *colmado* (grocery or packaged-goods store) has remained in the same family for 150 years. *See p 81.*

❺ ★★ Casa Thomas. Just down carrer Mallorca is this spectacular house (1895–98) by Domènech i Montaner. Originally just two floors, it was expanded in 1912. It now houses a furniture store, Favorita, so feel free to enter and wander among the two floors of this seminal building. *c/ Mallorca, 291–293.* ☎ *93-476-57-21.*

❻ Cor Caliu. An attractive corner restaurant-bar, this surprisingly elegant spot is perfect for coffee, a beer, or tapas in the front bar, or a full meal in the restaurant at back. It's a longtime neighborhood favorite. *c/ Roger de Llúria, 102.* ☎ *93-208-20-29. $$.*

❼ Casa de les Punxes. Also called Casa Terrades, or "House of Spikes," for its sharp turrets, this massive and eccentric 1905 house is one of Josep Puig i Cadafalch's and *modernisme's* most prized buildings. It's a neo-Gothic, fairy tale and castlelike mansion with distinctive features, such as three separate entrances (built for each of the family's daughters), outer walls facing all four points of the compass, and patriotic ceramic motifs. *Av. Diagonal, 416–420.*

❽ Palau del Baró de Quadras. This 1904–06 mansion, by Puig i Cadafalch—now operated by Casa Asia, an Asian cultural foundation, and open to visitors—is a great example of the architect's creativity. The interior's Moorish-style ceiling, carved wood, and leaded glass are sumptuous, and from the top-floor terrace are terrific views of Casa de les Punxes, echoing the spires of La Sagrada Família in the background. *Av. Diagonal, 373.* ☎ *93-368-08-36. www.casaasia.es. Free admission. Tues–Sat 10am–8pm; Sun 10am–2pm.* ●

Palau del Baró de Quadras was designed by Puig i Cadafalch.

Shopping Best Bets

Best **Dreamy Antiques**
★★ L' Arca de l'Aviva, *c/ Banys Nous, 20 (p 76)*

Best **Hip Designer Clothing (Men's)**
★★ Antonio Miró, *c/ Consell de Cent, 349 (p 78)*

Best **Drop-Dead-Gorgeous Designer Clothing (Women's)**
★★★ Josep Font, *c/ Provença, 304 (p 79);* and ★★ Nunita, *c/ del Rec, 6 (p 79)*

Best **Creative Leather Goods**
★★★ Lupo Barcelona, *c/ Mallorca, 257, bajos (p 81);* and ★★ Iriarte Iriarte, *c/ Esquirol, 1 (p 81)*

Best **Shop for Slaves to Design**
★★★ Vinçon, *Pg. de Gràcia, 96 (p 78)*

Best **Barcelona Souvenirs**
★★ Vaho Gallery Barcelona, *Pl. Sant Josep Oriol, 3 (p 80);* and ★ BCN Original Shops, *c/ Citutat, 23 (p 80)*

Best-**Smelling Gourmet Food**
★★★ E&A Gispert, *c/ dels Sombrerers, 23 (p 49,* **12***)*

Best **Wine Cellar Fantasy Shop**
★★★ Vila Viniteca, *c/ Agullers, 7 (p 49,* **13***)*

Best **Dip into Old-World Barcelona**
★★ Herbolisteria del Rei, *c/ del Vidre, 1 (p 82)*

Best **Vintage Finds**
★ Blow by Le Swing, *c/ Notariat, 3 (p 79)*

Best **Old-City Spot for an Antiques Stroll**
★★ Carrer de la Palla; and
★★ Carrer Banys Nous

Best **Mall for Kids**
Maremàgnum, *Moll d'Espanya, 5 (p 78)*

Most **Theatrical Clothing Boutique**
★★★ Natalie Capell Atelier de Moda, *c/ Carassa, 2 (p 79)*

Best **Products by Nuns & Priests (or Best Archaeological Surprise in a Store)**
★★ Caelum, *c/ de la Palla, 8 (p 80)*

Best **Catalan Goodies for Foodies**
★★ Colmado Quilez, *Rambla de Catalunya, 63 (p 47,* **2***);* and ★★ La Cuina d'en Garriga, *c/ Consell de Cent, 308 (p 47,* **4***)*

Best **Unpronounceable T-Shirt Shop**
★★ Kukuxumusu, *c/ L'Argenteria, 69 (p 80)*

Previous page: Shoes on display at Camper. This page: Fresh roasted nuts at E&A Gispert.

L'Eixample Shopping

Ciutat Vella & Waterfront Shopping

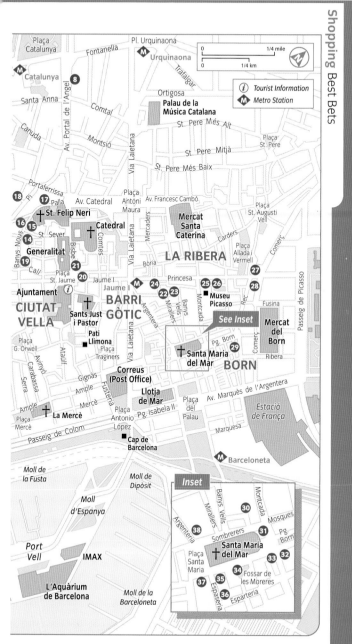

Barcelona Shopping A to Z

Art & Antiques

Bulevard dels Antiquaris

L'EIXAMPLE   An indoor mall containing some 70 small shops of art and antiques. Stall owners set their own hours, which can be wildly inconsistent. *Pg. de Gràcia, 55.* ☎ *93-215-44-99. www.bulevarddels antiquaris.com. Metro: Pg. de Gràcia. Map p 73.*

★ **Heritage** BARRI GOTIC   A theatrical-looking shop, stuffed with old costumes, jewelry, and Spanish shawls. It's worth a snoop under the proprietor's watchful eye. *c/ Banys Nous, 14.* ☎ *93-317-85-15. MC, V. Metro: Jaume I. Map p 74.*

★★ **Iguapop** LA RIBERA   From the works of modern and pop artists to fashion and art books, this place (also an indie concert promoter) is one-stop shopping for downtown *au courant* artheads. *c/ Comerç, 15.* ☎ *93-310-07-35. MC, V. Metro: Arc de Triomf. Map p 74.*

★★ **L' Arca de l'Avia** BARRI GOTIC   Antique lace, linens, and curtains, as well as handkerchiefs

Theatrical treasures abound at Heritage.

and other textiles from the 18th to early 20th centuries are found at this uniquely lovely shop, where some of the period clothing for the movie *Titanic* was purchased. *c/ Banys Nous, 20.* ☎ *93-302-15-98. www.larcadelavia.com. MC, V. Metro: Liceu. Map p 74.*

★★ **Sala d'Art Artur Ramón** BARRI GOTIC   A top antiques and art dealer and longtime family gallery known for its 19th- and 20th-century paintings, sculptures, engravings, and decorative arts. *c/ de la Palla, 23.* ☎ *93-302-59-70. AE, DC, MC, V. Metro: Jaume I. Map p 74.*

Books

Casa del Llibre L'EIXAMPLE   A large bookshop covering the gamut of titles, including English and foreign-language books. *Pg. de Gràcia, 62.* ☎ *93-272-34-80. MC, V. Metro: Pg. de Gràcia. Map p 73.*

★★ **Galería Ras** RAVAL   Part art gallery, part bookstore, this slick spot near MACBA is a fantastic stop for design hounds searching for photography, architecture, and graphic design books of all kinds. *c/ Dr. Dou, 10.* ☎ *93-412-71-99. MC, V. Metro: Pg. de Gràcia. Map p 74.*

★★ **LAIE** L'EIXAMPLE   With a cafe and nice stock of English-language books, including literature, travel maps, and guides, LAIE's a favorite with foreigners resident in Barcelona. *c/ Pau Claris, 85.* ☎ *93-318-17-39. MC, V. Metro: Urquinaona. Map p 73.*

Ceramics & Pottery

1748 Artesana i Coses EL BORN   Near Museu Picasso, this crowded ceramics shop stocks largely inexpensive pottery and porcelain from

Ceramics, like these at 1748 Artesana i Coses, make great souvenirs and gifts.

all over Spain (and Portugal). *Pl. de Montcada, 2.* ☎ *93-319-54-13. AE, MC, V. Metro: Jaume I. Map p 74.*

★ **Itaca** BARRI GOTIC   On hand is handmade pottery from Spain, Portugal, Mexico, and Morocco. Pieces are simple but well conceived, and there are a number of Gaudiesque objects fashioned with *trencadis* (broken ceramic tiles). *c/ Ferran, 26.* ☎ *93-301-30-44. MC, V. Metro: Liceu. Map p 74.*

Cosmetics

★★ **La Galería de Santa María Novella** LA RIBERA   This is the Barcelona outlet of a famed Florence apothecary, the oldest in the world. The perfumes and soaps are extraordinary, and the packaging delightfully antiquated. *c/ Espasería, 4–8.* ☎ *93-268-02-37. MC, V. Metro: Jaume I. Map p 74.*

★ **Regia** L'EIXAMPLE   This high-end cosmetics shop has a treat: a museum (free admission) with 5,000 examples of perfume bottles and flasks dating back as far as ancient Greece, including a cool bottle by Salvador Dalí. *Pg. de Gràcia, 39.* ☎ *93-216-01-21. AE, MC, V. Metro: Pg. de Gràcia. Map p 73.*

Department Stores/ Shopping Centers

El Corte Inglés PLAÇA DE CATALUNYA   Spain's largest department-store chain sells everything from wine and music to furnishings and fashion. You'll also find a restaurant, travel agent, and excellent supermarket (Plaça de Catalunya branch only). *Pl. de Catalunya, 14.* ☎ *93-306-38-00. AE, DC, MC, V. www.elcorteingles.es. Metro: Catalunya. Map p 73.*

El Triangle PLAÇA DE CATALUNYA   This large white elephant occupies a good chunk of Plaça de Catalunya

Prime Shopping Zones

Barcelona's elegant **Passeig de Gràcia** is home to some of the most fashionable and expensive retail space in Spain. Pedestrian-only **Rambla de Catalunya,** which runs parallel to Passeig de Gràcia, is like an open mall of stores, perfect for strolling, and the cross streets between the two are loaded with interesting shops of all kinds—particularly València, Provença, and Consell de Cent, the last known for its art galleries. The long boulevard **Avenida Diagonal** is the site of many high-end furnishings and fashion boutiques. In the **Ciutat Vella,** the main streets Portal d'Angel, Portaferrisa, and Ferrán are packed with clothing stores and young shoppers. Small boutiques and one-of-a-kind retailers are tucked in the neighborhoods **El Born** and **Barri Gòtic,** and increasingly hip clothing stores are located in **El Raval.** Antiques dealers, meanwhile, are largely clustered around the labyrinth of streets near carrer de la Palla, Banys Nous, and Plaça del Pi in the **Barri Gòtic.**

The Maremàgnum mall at the waterfront.

across from La Rambla. It may stick out, but it's convenient for hitting shops like Sephora, FNAC, Camper, and Habitat. *c/ Pelai, 39.* ☎ *93-318-01-08. Metro: Catalunya. Map p 73.*

Maremàgnum WATERFRONT This mall, perched out in the old harbor near L'Aquarium, has plenty for the whole family, from toy stores to high-end fashion. *Moll d'Espanya, 5.* ☎ *93-225-81-00. Metro: Drassanes. Map p 74.*

Designer Home Goods & Furnishings
★ **Ici Et Là** LA RIBERA   A good indication of Barcelona's individualistic, design-crazy personality is this stylish shop. You'll find quirky and limited editions by local artists and designers, as well as interesting "world" pieces, such as African baskets or Indian textiles. *Pl. de Sant Maria, 2.* ☎ *93-268-11-67. MC, V. Metro: Jaume I or Barceloneta. Map p 74.*

★★★ **Vinçón** L'EIXAMPLE   Fernando Amat's temple of good design, Vinçón features more than 10,000 products—everything from household items to the finest Catalan and Spanish contemporary furnishings—housed in the former

home of *modernista* painter Ramón Casas. The singular window displays alone are always a conversation piece. *Pg. de Gràcia, 96.* ☎ *93-215-60-50. AE, MC, V. Metro: Pg. de Gràcia. Map p 73.*

Fashion & Accessories
★★ **Agatha Ruiz de la Prada** L'EIXAMPLE   The playful, brightly colored, almost childlike fashions of this Madrid designer have hit the big time, and she now has shops in Paris, Milan, and New York. *c/ Consell de Cent, 314–316.* ☎ *93-215-52-88. AE, MC, V. Metro: Pg. de Gràcia. Map p 73.*

★★ **Antonio Miró** L'EIXAMPLE Pieces by the Catalan designer Antonio Miró are chic and sleek, with a retro edge; in addition to sophisticated, high-end men's and women's items, you'll find a less-expensive Miró Jeans line. *c/ Consell de Cent, 349.* ☎ *93-487-06-70. AE, MC, V. Metro: Pg. de Gràcia. Map p 73.*

★★ **b huno** RAVAL   An adorable shop with stylish, contemporary dresses, tops, earrings, and bags by

Antonio Miró designs chic clothes for men and women.

a coterie of young Catalan and Spanish designers, some of whose designs are coveted by Spain's fashionable Princess Letizia. *c/ Elisabets, 18. ☎ 93-412-63-05. MC, V. Metro: Liceu. Map p 74.*

★ **Blow by Le Swing** RAVAL Attitude-heavy vintage finds, from sunglasses and bags to boots (including brands like Chanel and Dior) and some provocative fare, too. Hipsters, this is ground zero. Don't miss the retro-fab cafe next door. *c/ Notariat, 3. ☎ 93-301-98-70. MC, V. Metro: Liceu. Map p 74.*

Custo-Barcelona LA RIBERA Custo's emblematic tops and tees, skirts, and pants are emblazoned with wildly colored retro-cool motifs. Seen on Hollywood starlets and in the fashion pages, these now-international pieces aren't cheap, but they are distinctive. There's another location at c/ Ferran, 36. *Pl. de les Olles, 7. ☎ 93-268-78-93. MC, V. Metro: Jaume I. Map p 74.*

★★ **Etxart & Panno** EL BORN Unabashedly sexy fashions for women with style and money to burn, in a cool little shop in the heart of the chic Born district. *Pg. del Born, 14. ☎ 93-310-37-24. MC, V. Metro: Jaume I. Map p 74.*

★★ **Giménez & Zuazo** RAVAL These quirky and cutting-edge creations with audacious prints, interesting fabrics, and contrasting cross-stitches represent Barcelona at its most fashion-conscious. There's another location at c/ Rec, 42. *c/ Elisabets, 20. ☎ 93-412-33-81. AE, MC, V. Metro: Catalunya or Liceu. Map p 74.*

★★ **Jocomomola de Sybilla** EL BORN The brightly colored, informal women's fashions from this Madrileña designer have a retro bent and look as though they might

Custo-Barcelona.

have dressed Amelie, the heroine of the style-conscious French film of a decade or so ago. *c/ Vigatans, 6 (off Princesa). ☎ 93-310-66-66. AE, MC, V. Metro: Jaume I. Map p 74.*

★★★ **Josep Font** L'EIXAMPLE This original Catalan designer, whose gorgeous shop shows off *modernista* details, creates women's clothes that are timeless, sleek, and bold, with a dramatic feel for luxurious materials. *c/ Provença, 304. ☎ 93-487-21-10. MC, V. Metro: Pg. de Gràcia. Map p 73.*

★★★ **Natalie Capell Atelier de Moda** EL BORN Timeless, handmade, oh-so-delicate high-fashion designs for chic and slender women, dramatically lit in an atmospheric boutique that looks like a theater set. *c/ Carassa, 2 (off Princesa). ☎ 93-319-92-19. MC, V. Metro: Jaume I. Map p 74.*

★★ **Nunita** EL BORN Some of the chicest modern women's fashions in the old quarter are found at this pricey, elegant boutique, with a handful of carefully selected designers, most of them Danish. *c/ del Rec, 6. ☎ 93-315-07-70. AE, MC, V. Metro: Arc de Triomf. Map p 74.*

★ **Rafa Teja Atelier** EL BORN Terrific, colorful scarves and shawls from India, Asia, and Spain, as well as embroidered jackets and sumptuous fabrics. c/ Santa María, 18. ☎ 93-310-27-85. MC, V. Metro: Jaume I. Map p 74.

Gifts & Souvenirs

★ **BCN Original Shops** BARRI GOTIC   If you're after particularly Barcelona-themed gifts and souvenirs, this is your place. Art and architecture books, mugs, ceramics, jewelry, T-shirts, notebooks, and more. c/ Citutat, 2. ☎ 93-270-24-29. AE, MC, V. Metro: Jaume I. Map p 74.

★ **Beardsley** BARRI GOTIC   This classic Barcelona shop is seductive-looking, featuring home goods, candles, great glassware, chandeliers and lighting, paper products, and much more. c/ Petritxol, 12. ☎ 93-301-05-76. AE, MC, V. Metro: Liceu. Map p 74.

★ **The Cha Cha Original Shop** LA RIBERA   A funky little pop-art shop, with retro-cool placemats, barware, T-shirts, and more, all with a fun, hipster sensibility. c/ Sant Antoni dels Sombrerers, 7. ☎ 93-319-37-79. MC, V. Metro: Jaume I. Map p 74.

★ **Ivo & Co.** EL BORN   Snag cool kitchen utensils, housewares, journals, candles, and books in this invitingly retro-looking shop. c/ Rec, 20

A mosaic at Escribà.

baixos. ☎ 93-268-33-31. MC, V. Metro: Arc de Triomf. Map p 74.

★★ **Kukuxumusu** LA RIBERA   Don't even try to pronounce the name of this shop, originally from Navarra but now all over Spain. Do pop by for witty, hip T-shirts and accessories. With a fun take on Spanish cultural traditions, they make great souvenirs. c/ L'Argenteria, 69. ☎ 93-310-36-47. AE, MC, V. Metro: Jaume I. Map p 74.

★★ **Vaho Gallery Barcelona** BARRI GOTIC   This funky bag maker uses recycled heavy-duty PVC culture posters (used as cultural advertising by the city and regional governments) to create unique messenger bags and purses (which they call "trashion"). A unique souvenir from Barcelona for eco- and fashion-conscious sorts. There's another location at Bonsuccés, 13. Pl. Sant Josep Oriol, 3. ☎ 93-302-66-57. AE, MC, V. Metro: Liceu. Map p 74.

Gourmet Shopping Tip

For more information on where to buy and eat your favorite gourmet items, check "Gourmet Barcelona," p 46.

Gourmet Food Shops

★★ **Caelum** BARRI GOTIC   Cloistered nuns and religious orders produce everything in this shop, including jams and preserved fruit, biscuits, marzipan, and liquors, all handsomely packaged. In the cafe downstairs are the remains of ancient Jewish baths. c/ de la Palla, 8. ☎ 93-302-69-93. MC, V. Metro: Jaume I. Map p 74.

Demasié LA RIBERA   A gourmet cookie shop with all kinds of treats both sweet and savory, including expected and very unusual cookies (black tea, Roquefort and nuts, mustard, curry). c/ Princesa, 28.

☎ *93-310-42-95. MC, V. Metro: Jaume I. Map p 74.*

★★ Jamonísimo. L'EIXAMPLE This is the place in town to see what the Spanish fascination with fine, cured (and pricey) ham is all about, and you'll be in the company of some of the world's greatest chefs who buy their acorn-fed Bellota, Ibérico, and Serrano *jamones* here. You can sample some thin slices, *croquetas,* or *canellones,* or do a full-on tasting with a glass of wine. *c/ Provença, 85.* ☎ *93-439-08-47. www.jamonisimo.com. MC, V. Metro: Hospital Clínic. Map p 73.*

★ Pastisseria Escribà. LA RAMBLA Talk about eye candy. One of Barcelona's oldest and best-known chocolatiers is this little shop on La Rambla with a shimmering *modernista* exterior (of colorful broken glazed tiles, a la Gaudí) and tea salon within. *La Rambla, 83.* ☎ *93-221-07-29. www.escriba.es. MC, V. Metro: Liceu. Map p 74.*

★★★ Queviures J. Murrià L'EIXAMPLE This food-and-wine emporium has been in the same family since the late 19th century. Its handsome exterior, the work of the *modernista* artist Ramón Casas, is only a prelude to the 200 types of cheese, 300 wines, Iberian *jamón* (ham), and canned goods inside. *c/ Roger de Llúria, 85.* ☎ *93-215-57-89. MC, V. Metro: Pg. de Gràcia. Map p 73.*

Jewelry

★★ Forvm Ferlandina PLAÇA DE CATALUNYA The unique works of several dozen contemporary jewelry designers are on view in this gallery-like shop. *c/ Ferlandina, 31.* ☎ *93-441-80-18. AE, DC, MC, V. Metro: Catalunya. Map p 74.*

★★ Helena Rohner LA RIBERA A very elegant but still edgy collection of silver, porcelain, wood, and leather

Rings on display at Platamundi.

necklaces and big, funky rings for women, men, and even kids, as well as stylish enameled earthenware and lamps for the home. *c/ L'Espaseria, 13.* ☎ *93-319-88-79. MC, V. Metro: Barceloneta. Map p 74.*

Platamundi LA RIBERA This small chain of affordable stores features nicely designed silver pieces by local and international artisans. Another branch is at Portaferrisa, 22. *c/ de Montcada, 11.* ☎ *93-317-13-89. MC, V. Metro: Jaume I. Map p 74.*

Leather Goods

★★ Iriarte Iriarte LA RIBERA Crafters and purveyors of some of the hippest, sexiest handmade leather goods for both men and women, this chic little shop is above all a great spot for men to pick up elegant European-style briefcases that can't be derided as "man purses." *c/ Esquirol, 1.* ☎ *93-319-81-75. AE, DC, MC, V. Metro: Jaume I. Map p 74.*

★★ Loewe L'EIXAMPLE This prestigious Spanish leather-goods and luxury fashion chain occupies the ground floor of a splendid *modernista* building on Passeig de Gràcia. Chic and expensive, this is where the elite shop. *Pg. de Gràcia, 35.* ☎ *93-216-04-00. AE, DC, MC, V. Metro: Pg. de Gràcia. Map p 73.*

★★★ Lupo Barcelona L'EIXAMPLE Hipper and skewing younger than Loewe, Lupo is the

The old-fashioned hat shop Sombrereria Obach.

hottest name in stylish leather goods. Bags and belts mold and fold leather into unexpected shapes and feature vivid colors. *c/ Mallorca, 257 bajos.* ☎ *93-487-80-50. AE, DC, MC, V. Metro: Pg. de Gràcia. Map p 73.*

Music
★★ **Discos Castelló** RAVAL This independent music shop has three locations on one street alone, a corridor replete with music and vinyl outlets. The flagship store at no. 7 is mainly pop rock. Next door, you'll find jazz, Spanish, and world music. *c/ Tallers.* ☎ *93-318-20-41. MC, V. Metro: Catalunya. Map p 74.*

FNAC PLAÇA DE CATALU- NYA The FNAC megastore is full of mainstream choices, with a nice selection of Spanish music and fla- menco. *Pl. de Catalunya, 4.* ☎ *93-344-18-00. AE, DC, MC, V. Metro: Catalunya. Map p 73.*

Old World Emporiums
★★ **Cereria Subira** BARRI GOTIC The oldest continuous shop in Barcelona, this iconic store specializes in candles, from those used at Mass to more creative and colorful numbers. *c/ Baixada de Lli- breteria, 7.* ☎ *93-315-26-06. MC, V. Metro: Jaume I. Map p 74.*

★ **Ganiveteria Roca** BARRI GOTIC An old-school specialty shop dealing exclusively in sharp objects: knives, blades, scissors, and other cutting instruments. *Pl. del Pi, 3.* ☎ *93-302-12-41. AE, MC, V. Metro: Jaume I. Map p 74.*

★★ **Herbolisteria del Rei** RAVAL A purveyor of herbs, natu- ral remedies, cosmetics, and teas since 1823, this atmospheric shop looks the part. *c/ del Vidre, 1.* ☎ *93-318-05-12. MC, V. Metro: Catalunya or Liceu. Map p 74.*

★ **Sombrereria Obach** BARRI GOTIC Proudly old-fashioned, this shop in the old Jewish quarter sells nothing but hats, including classic Spanish berets *(boinas)*. *c/ del Call, 2.* ☎ *93-318-40-94. MC, V. Metro: Jaume I. Map p 74.*

Shoes
★★ **Camper** RAVAL Camper shoes, which originated in Mallorca, are now famous across the globe. You can get the latest models of this hipster shoemaker, in unusual colors and shapes, in Barcelona. Shop inte-

riors are even quirkier than the shoes. *Pl. dels Àngels, 4.* ☎ *93-342- 41-41. AE, DISC, MC, V. Metro: Universitat. Map p 74.*

The classic Camper shoe design.

★ **Casas** BARRI GOTIC Stocking the top Spanish brands of footwear as well as Italian and other imports, this is as close to one-stop shoe shopping as you'll find. *Portal de l'Angel, 40.* ☎ *93-302-11-12. AE, MC, V. Metro: Catalunya. Map p 74.* ●

5 The Great Outdoors

Montjuïc

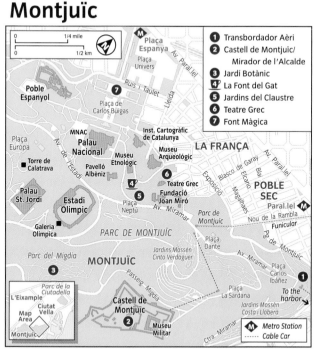

1. Transbordador Aèri
2. Castell de Montjuïc/
   Mirador de l'Alcalde
3. Jardí Botànic
4. La Font del Gat
5. Jardins del Claustre
6. Teatre Grec
7. Font Màgica

The largest green space in Barcelona, this gentle hill overlooking the city and out to the Mediterranean is treasured by families for its serene parkland as well as its museums and cultural attractions. First settled by Iberian Celtic peoples and then used by the Romans for ceremonies, Montjuïc has continued to play a central role in modern celebrations, including the 1929 International Exhibition and the 1992 Olympic Games. For other attractions in Montjuïc, see "The Best in Three Days," p. 18 and "Barcelona with Kids," p. 50.
START: Aerial cable car or funicular to Montjuïc.

1 ★★ kids **Transbordador Aèri del Port.** The best way to get to the green expanse of Montjuïc is to soar over the city in this aerial cable car that travels from the harbor up to the hill—and drops you off near the spectacular cactus **gardens** of **Mossèn Costa i**

Previous page: Bicycles lined up in Parc de la Ciutadella.

Llobera (Ctra. Miramar, 1), the largest of their kind in Europe. *See p 89,* **5**.

2 **Castell de Montjuïc.** Pass the Plaça de la Sardana (marked by a sculpture of the folkloric Catalan group dance) and through the Miramar and Mirador gardens in Parc de Montjuïc. Then head up Carretera Montjuïc to **Mirador de l'Alcalde,**

The fortress (castell) at Montjuïc.

a viewpoint overlooking the sea. Just beyond is a *castell* (fortress) built in the 18th century to defend Barcelona. The courtyard is open to the public, and inside the castle is a modest military museum. The views of the sea, though, are the star attraction. *Ctra. de Montjuïc, 66.* ☎ *93-239-86-13.*

③ ★★ **kids** **Jardí Botànic.** The Botanic Gardens of Barcelona, originally inaugurated in 1930, reopened as a new and improved, and beautifully landscaped, green space in the late '90s. The gardens show off Mediterranean-climate plants from all over the globe, including Africa, Australia, California, the Canary Islands, and Chile. The 71 zones have a cool modern aesthetic and are connected by paths and feature walkways over ponds. *Dr. Font i Quer, 2 (Parc de Montjuïc).* ☎ *93-424-50-53. www. jardibotanic.bcn.es. Oct–Mar daily 10am–5pm; Apr–May, and Sept Mon–Fri 10am–6pm, Sat–Sun 10am–8pm; June–Aug daily 10am–8pm. Admission 3.50€, seniors and students 2.80€, free for ages 15 and under. Free admission the last Sun of every month.*

④ **La Font del Gat.** Down a path from the Fundació Joan Miró (see p 20) is this historic *modernista* cafe, now revived as a cafe and restaurant surrounded by gardens. It's a nice,

open-air spot for a breather and refreshments, which might even be a fixed-price lunch. *Pg. de Santa Madrona, 28.* ☎ *93-289-04-04. $.*

⑤ **Jardins del Claustre.** The Cloister Garden is one of the prettiest spots on Montjuïc, with a tree-lined pond, pergola, and sculpture by the Catalan artist Antoni Alsina for the 1929 International Exposition. *Av. Miramar/Pg. de Santa Madrona.*

⑥ **Teatre Grec.** This replica of a bowl-shaped Greek theater, built for the 1929 World's Fair, continues to host open-air concerts and dance performances. Surrounded by gardens, it's a focal point of the **Festival Grec** music and arts festival held every summer. *Pg. de Santa Madrona, 36.* ☎ *93-413-24-00. www.barcelonafestival.com.*

⑦ ★ **kids** **Font Màgica.** The wondrous waters of the "Magic Fountain" dance to a light and pop-music show at the center of a plaza in front of the Palau Nacional. *See p 53.*

Font Màgica.

Parc de la **Ciutadella**

In a dense city with few green spaces, Barcelona's largest urban oasis is this 30-hectare (74-acre) park between the old city and waterfront. The park makes for an ideal respite from the city, with the Barcelona Zoo, a massive waterfall fountain, lake, sculptures, and monuments, and wide promenades and tree-lined trails for strolling or cycling. The park has a peculiar history: After the end of the Spanish War of Succession in 1714, King Felipe V ordered the neighborhood "of traitors" razed, and he built a citadel, which later functioned as a prison for political opponents, in its place. Local authorities demolished the citadel and in 1872 built a large park, which hosted the 1888 World's Fair. START: **Arc de Triomf.**

1 ★ **Arc de Triomf.** The formal gate to Parc de la Ciutadella is this massive red-brick triumphal arch, built in 1888. The wide avenue Passeig de Lluís Campanys, lined with large palm trees and ornate pale-blue iron lampposts, leads into the park. *Pg. de Lluís Campanys, s/n.*

2 **Museus de Zoologia i Geologia.** The Zoology Museum occupies a Moorish-influenced brick building (popularly called the "Castle of Three Dragons") designed by Domènech i Montaner for the 1888 Universal Exhibition. Next door is the 1878 Geology Museum. *Pg. de*

The Arc de Triomf marks the entrance to Parc de la Ciutadella.

Picasso s/n, Parc de la Ciutadella.
☎ *93-256-22-00.*

**③ kids L'Hivernacle/
L'Umbracle.** The Hivernacle, located between the two museums, is an iron-and-glass greenhouse designed in 1884. Today it occasionally hosts concerts. On the other side of the Geology Museum is the Umbracle, a peaceful spot full of tropical plants and palm trees under its tall nave.

④ Passeig dels Til.lers. The wide "Avenue of Lime Trees" is marked at the southern end by an equestrian statue of General Prim, who ordered the old fortress demolished. Although the original statue was melted down during the Civil War, a replacement was commissioned from the sculptor Frederic Marès in 1940.

⑤ ★ kids Cascada Fountain. This massive ornamental fountain, featuring Aurora's chariot, is the work of Josep Fontserè, although much of its recognition is due to the contributions of his young apprentice, Antoni Gaudí, who was just a student at the time. Gaudí added the decorative lampposts and other details.

⑥ kids El Llac. In the center of the park is this tree-ringed lake, with rowboats for rent, just as they were at the end of the 19th century.

⑦ Parlament de Catalunya. Home to the regional parliament since 1932, this grand building, once the arsenal of the citadel, faces a pond and the 1903 *modernista* sculpture, *El Desconsol* (Grief), by Josep Llimona.

⑧ ★★ kids Parc Zoològic. The Barcelona Zoo, which has been in Ciutadella Park since 1892, features a gardenlike setting that occupies nearly half the park's expanse, with 4,000 animals kept not in cages, but behind moats. *See p 53,* ⑤.

A bear in the Parc Zoològic.

The **Waterfront**

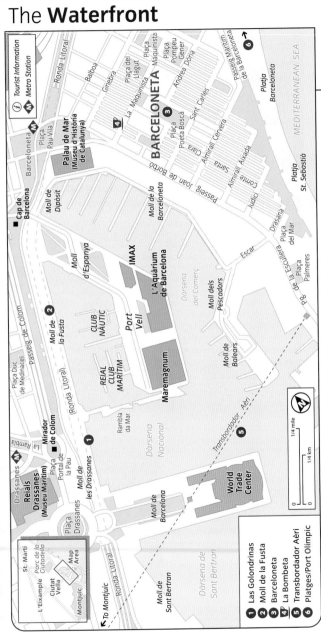

Legend:
- ⓘ *Tourist Information*
- Ⓜ *Metro Station*

1. Las Golondrinas
2. Moll de la Fusta
3. Barceloneta
4. La Bombeta
5. Transbordador Aèri
6. Platges/Port Olímpic

0   ¼ mile
0   ¼ km

For much of the 20th century, Barcelona's Mediterranean waterfront was a polluted, industrial, and marginalized sector. But Barcelona took advantage of the 1992 Olympic Games to completely revamp the old port and beaches and create new areas for leisure. Today it's Barcelona's outdoor playground, an essential part of the city. START: **Metro to Drassanes.**

① kids Las Golondrinas. You'll see these double-decker "swallow boats" lined up across from the Mirador de Colom, boarding passengers for 35- to 90-minute cruises around the old harbor and coast. *Pl. Portal de la Pau, s/n.* ☎ *93-442-31-06. www.lasgolondrinas.com. Mon–Fri 11:45am–7pm; Sat–Sun and holidays 11am–6pm. 6.50€–14€ adults, 2.60€–5€ children ages 4–14.*

② ★ Moll de la Fusta. The tree-lined boardwalk in front of Port Vell (the old port) extends to the Barceloneta district and is extremely popular with locals on weekend strolls. At the eastern end of the promenade are massive pop-art sculptures of a giant crayfish and a head by Roy Lichtenstein.

③ ★ Barceloneta. Barcelona's fishermen and their families inhabited this picturesque beachfront neighborhood for decades before it received a stylistic makeover starting in 1992 (its ongoing renovation continues apace). Although it's gone upscale, a few traditional low-key seafood restaurants called *chiringuitos* have survived.

④ ★ La Bombeta. This authentic tapas joint serves great seafood snacks like mussels and fried calamari. The *bombas* are the house take on *patatas bravas* (fried potatoes with a spicy sauce). *c/ Maquinsta, 3.* ☎ *93-319-94-45. $–$$.*

⑤ ★ kids Transbordador Aèri. The aerial cable car that climbs from the port to Montjuïc starts out in Barceloneta and stops at the World Trade Center before soaring above the harbor. *See p 84,* **①**.

⑥ ★★ kids Platges/Port Olímpic. Barcelona's urban beaches *(platges)* have been wholly transformed, and the water quality is now excellent. Popular with families, topless sunbathers, and surfers, the beaches are lined with public sculptures, bars and restaurants, and paths for biking, in-line skating, and walking. Moving east, they are, in order: Barceloneta, Nova Icària, Bogatell, and Mar Bella (unofficially a nudist beach). Nova Icària is the most popular, the best spot for people-watching and with the most bars and restaurants within easy reach; Bogatell and Mar Bella are even prettier and less populated. The Port Olímpic marina between the first two beaches is full of chic sailboats and trendy restaurants and bars.

The beach at Barceloneta.

Barcelona **by Bike**

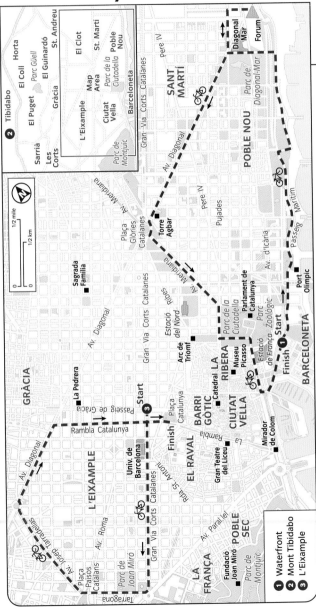

Tibidabo
El Coll   Horta
El Puget   *Parc Güell*   El Guinardó   St. Andreu
Sarrià   Gràcia   El Clot
Les   L'Eixample   **Map**   *Parc de la*   St. Martí
Corts   **Area**   *Ciutadella*   Poble Nou
Ciutat   Barceloneta
Vella
Parc de
Montjuïc

❷ Tibidabo

Diagonal-Mar
Forum

Pere IV

SANT MARTÍ

POBLE NOU

Parc de
Diagonal-Mar

Gran Via Corts Catalanes

Av. Diagonal

Pere IV

Pujades

Passeig Marítim

Av. d'Icària

Port
Olímpic

Plaça
Glòries
Catalanes   **Torre**
Agbar

Av. Meridiana

Sagrada
Família

Av. Diagonal

GRÀCIA

La Pedrera

Gran Via Corts Catalanes

Estació
del Nord

Ribes

Parc de la
Ciutadella

Parlament de
Catalunya

Parc
Zoològic

Estació
de França   **Finish**

Start

BARCELONETA

Arc de
Triomf

Catedral   LA
RIBERA

Museu
Picasso

BARRI
GÒTIC

CIUTAT
VELLA

Mirador
de Colom

Rambla Catalunya

Passeig de Gràcia

Start

Plaça
Catalunya

Finish

Univ. de
Barcelona

L'EIXAMPLE

Gran Via Corts Catalanes

Av. Roma

Av. Diagonal

Rda. St. Antoni

La Rambla

EL RAVAL

Gran Teatre
del Liceu

Av. Josep Tarradellas

Plaça
Països
Catalans

Parc de
Joan Miró

LA
FRANÇA

POBLE
SEC

Av. Paral·lel

Fundació
Joan Miró

Parc de
Montjuïc

Tarragona

½ mile
½ km

❶ Waterfront
❷ Mont Tibidabo
❸ L'Eixample

Barcelona has gone wild for bicycling and you'll see people everywhere using the city's popular community **"bicing"** red-and-white bikes, picking them up in one spot and dropping them off in another. On two wheels you can navigate the narrow streets of the old city and the broad avenues of L'Eixample, but the most relaxed areas for cycling are the designated bike paths of the Waterfront and Tibidabo.

A bike rider on the beach at Barceloneta.

❶ ★★ Waterfront. Starting out at Barceloneta, take Passeig Marítim and head northeast along the beach, to Port Olímpic and Vila Olímpica, where you can ride around the wide avenues of the former Olympic Village. Cycle along the paths lining the beaches; you can continue as far north as Parc del Fòrum. For an easy ride, return to Barceloneta along the same path. Or opt for a more ambitious ride: Travel west along Avinguda Diagonal to Plaça de les Glòries and then head south along Avinguda Meridiana, which leads right to Parc de la Ciutadella. Within the park, you can bike around wide, unpaved avenues. From here, it's a short distance back to Barceloneta.

❷ ★ Mont Tibidabo. Winding across the hillside of Mt. Tibidabo

Carretera de les Aigües, on Mont Tibidabo, is a scenic bike path.

Modernisme by Bike

From the late 19th century until the 1930s, a school of *modernista* architects thrived in Barcelona, building hundreds of private houses and public works, most concentrated in the L'Eixample quarter, a geometric grid that enlarged the city northward from its medieval core. By bike, you'll be able to roam the streets and see dozens more examples of the movement so identified with Barcelona than you could on foot.

is the *Carretera de les Aigües*, a cycling and jogging path that's a favorite of locals on weekends. Part of the Parc de la Collserola, the 8km (5-mile) unpaved path has drinking fountains at regular intervals and splendid views of Barcelona spread out below. The beginning of the route is about 1km (.6 miles) from Avenida del Tibidabo; take the Tramvia Blau (see p 22) there and walk. You'll find a bicycle-rental outfit at the beginning of the path.

❸ **L'Eixample.** Although much of the city is clogged with traffic, there are several major thoroughfares with safe biking lanes. Avinguda Diagonal, Gran Vía de les Corts Catalanes, and Rambla de Catalunya all provide clearly marked lanes on medians. A ride in this neighborhood is a great way to take in the Eixample's dense collection of *modernista* architecture (see p 24 and p 171). ●

Practical Matters: Barcelona by Bike

City bike lanes are indicated on the **CicloBus Barcelona** map, available at the Tourist Information Office (Pl. de Catalunya, 17; underground) or at most bike-rental shops. Bike-rental rates are about 5€ per hour or 15€ to 18€ per day. The ubiquitous red-and-white **bicing** bikes (www.bicing.cat) of the city's massively popular community bicycling program are intended only as alternative transportation for city residents who pay a low annual fee, and are not available to rent for leisure activities.

Un Cotxe Menys ("One Less Car")/**Barcelona by Bike** (c/ Esparteria, 3; ☎ 93-268-21-05; www.bicicletabarcelona.com): Rentals and guided bike tours of the old city and harbor.

Biciclot Marítim (Pg. Marítim de la Barceloneta, 33; ☎ 93-221-97-78; www.biciclot.net): Cruiser, adult tricycle, and tandem bike rentals, as well as organized and self-guided bike tours along nature and cultural routes.

Classic Bikes Barcelona (c/ Tallers, 45; ☎ 93-317-19-70; www.barcelonarentbikes.com): Guided cyclotours and rentals of folding and Dutch bikes.

Barcelonabiking.com (c/ Baixada de Sant Miquel, 6; ☎ 93-656-356-300; http://bicibarcelona.com): Organized bike tours of the city, including routes (and machines) for experienced road cyclists and mountain bikers, as well as rentals for touring on your own.

Terra Diversions (☎ 93-416-08-05; www.terradiversions.com): Organized bike tours that are particularly appealing if you don't want to bike in the city—a family tour of Collserola Nature Reserve and Carretera de les Aigües up on Tibidabo (including transport from downtown), as well as mountain-biking tours in the countryside.

Barcelona Scooter Tour (c/ Enric Morera 3–5; ☎ 93-568-29-98; www.barcelonascootertour.com): If pedaling's not your thing, you could do a neighborhood tour by unmotored scooter; no license is required and the tour is suggested for those 10 and older.

6 The Best Dining

TAPAS del DIA

- Tomàquet amb Tonyina i olivada
- Empedrat de Bacallà amb Vinagreta d'anxoves
- Carxofes del PRAT Fregides
- Calçots amb Romesco
- Porro confitat amb verduretes i olivada
- Arròs amb escamarlans del Dijous — 14
- Bacallà amb Sanfaina — 9
- "Morcilla de BURGOS" amb ceba confitada — 9
- Costelletes de conill arrebossades amb all: oli — 6
- Entraña "amb "CHIMICHURRI" — 9
- D'ànec estrellat amb xanguet

Dining Best Bets

Best Traditional Catalan Dining
★ Agut d'Avignon $$$ *c/ Trinitat, 3 (p 98)*; and ★★ Fonda Gaig $$$ *c/ Provença (p 103)*

Best Upstart Gourmet
★★★ Cinc Sentits $$$ *c/ Aribau, 58 (p 101)*; and ★★★ Dos Palillos $$$ *c/ Elisabets, 9 (p 101)*

Best Worth the Wait
★★ Cal Pep $$ *Pl. des les Olles, 8 (p 100)*; and ★★ Quimet i Quimet $ *c/ Poeta Cabanyes, 25 (p 105)*

Best Desserts (for all courses)
★★ Espai Sucre $$ *c/ de la Princesa, 53 (p 102)*

Best for Foodies, Wine & Design Freaks
★★★ ABaC $$$$ *Av. Tibidabo, 1 (p 98)*; and ★★★ Moo $$$$ *c/ Rosselló, 265 (p 104)*

Best Comfort Food
★ Senyor Parellada $$ *c/ L'Argenteria, 37 (p 105)*

Best Classic Tapas
★★ Alta Taberna Paco Meralgo $$ *c/ Muntaner, 117 (p 99)*; and ★★ Inopia $ *c/ Tamarit, 104 (p 103)*

Best Designer Tapas
★★ Comerç 24 $$$ *c/ Comerç, 24 (p 101)*

Best Mammoth Portions (The Antithesis of Tapas)
★★ 7 Portes $$ *Pg. d'Isabel II, 14 (p 106)*

Best Seaside Dining
★★ Can Majó $$$ *c/ Almirall Aixada, 23 (p 100)*

Best Seafood
★★ Big Fish $$ *Comercial, 9 (p 99)*; and ★★★ Els Pescadors $$$ *Plaça Prim, 1 (p 102)*

Best for a Nice Family Meal
★★ 7 Portes $$ *Pg. d'Isabel II, 14 (p 106)*

Best for Impatient Kids
★ La Paradeta $$ *c/ Comercial, 7 (p 103)*

Best Modernista Digs
★★ Casa Calvet $$$ *c/ Casp, 48 (p 100)*; and Els Quatre Gats $$ *c/ Montsió, 3 (p 102)*

Best Relaxed Beachfront Dining
★ Agua $$ *Ps. Maritim de la Barceloneta, 30 (p 98)*

Best Dining Within a Food Market
★★ El Quim de la Boqueria $$ *La Rambla, 91 (p 102)*; and ★ Els Fogons de la Barceloneta $$ *Pl. de la Font, s/n (p 102)*

Best Lunch Deal
★ Dolso $ *c/ Valencia, 227 (p 101)*; and ★★ Restaurant Embat $$ *c/ Mallorca, 304 (p 105)*

Best Value Foodie Restaurant
★★ Hisop $$ *Pge. Marimón, 9 (p 103)*

Previous page: A menu board at Tapas 24.

L'Eixample Dining

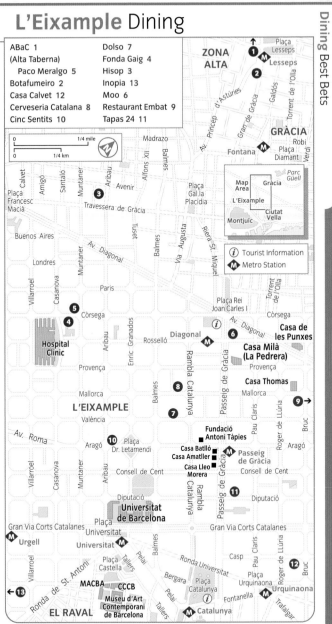

ABaC 1
(Alta Taberna)
  Paco Meralgo 5
Botafumeiro 2
Casa Calvet 12
Cerveseria Catalana 8
Cinc Sentits 10

Dolso 7
Fonda Gaig 4
Hisop 3
Inopia 13
Moo 6
Restaurant Embat 9
Tapas 24 11

0 ──── 1/4 mile
0 ──── 1/4 km

Plaça
Lesseps
ZONA
ALTA
Lesseps

Av. Princep d'Astúries
Gran de Gràcia
Galdós
Torrent de l'Olla

GRÀCIA
Robi
Fontana
Plaça
Diamant
Verdi

Madrazo
Alfons XII
Balmes

Map
Area   Gràcia

L'Eixample

Montjuic   Ciutat
            Vella

Parc
Güell

Plaça
Gal.la
Placidia

Avenir
Aribau
Muntaner

Travessera de Gràcia

Plaça
Francesc
Macià

Calvet
Amigó
Santaló

Buenos Aires

Londres

Av. Diagonal

Paris

Tuset
Balmes
Via Augusta
Riera St. Miquel

(i) Tourist Information
(M) Metro Station

Villarroel
Casanova
Muntaner

Plaça Rei
Joan Carles I

Còrsega

Torrent de l'Olla

Còrsega

Casa de
les Punxes

Diagonal
Av. Diagonal

Rosselló

Enric Granados
Aribau

Hospital
Clinic

Provença

Rambla Catalunya
Passeig de Gràcia

Casa Milà
(La Pedrera)
Provença

Casa Thomas

Mallorca

L'EIXAMPLE

Balmes

Mallorca

Pau Claris
Roger de Llúria
Bruc

València

Av. Roma

Aragó   Plaça
Dr. Letamendi

Villarroel
Casanova
Muntaner
Aribau

Consell de Cent

Diputació
Universitat
de Barcelona

Fundació
Antoni Tàpies

Casa Batlló
Casa Amatller
Casa Lleo
Morera

Passeig
de Gràcia

Aragó

Consell de Cent

Rambla
Catalunya
Passeig de Gràcia

Diputació

Gran Via Corts Catalanes
Plaça
Universitat
Urgell

Universitat

Gran Via Corts Catalanes

Casp

Pau Claris
Roger de Llúria
Bruc

Villarroel

Plaça
Castella

Pelai
Tallers

Ronda Universitat

Plaça
Urquinaona
Urquinaona

MACBA   CCCB
Museu d'Art
Contemporani
de Barcelona

Bergara

Ronda de St. Antoni

EL RAVAL

Plaça
Catalunya

Pelai
Tallers

Fontanella
(i)
Catalunya

Trafalgar

Ciutat Vella & Waterfront Dining

L'Eixample · St. Marti
Parc de la Ciutadella
Ciutat Vella
Map Area
Montjuïc

L'EIXAMPLE

Universitat de Barcelona

Plaça Gran Via Corts Catalanes

Universitat

Ronda Universitat

Plaça Castella

Casa de la Caritat

Museu d'Art Contemporani de Barcelona ❶

Plaça Caramelles

Pintor Fortuny

Carme

Antic Hospital de la Sta. Creu

Hospital

Plaça Sant Agustí

EL RAVAL

Gran Teatre del Liceu

Marquès de Barberà

Nou de la Rambla

Palau Güell

Arc del Teatre

Centre d'Art Sta. Monica

Portal Sta. Madrona

Reials Drassanes (Museu Marítim)

Plaça Drassanes

Plaça Portal de la Pau

Moll de les Drassanes

Moll de Barcelona

World Trade Center

Universitat

Pelai

Balmes

Tallers

Bergara

Plaça Catalunya

Rambla Catalunya

Pg. de Gràcia

Casp

Plaça Urquinaona

Urquinaona

Fontanella

Catalunya

Santa Anna

Canuda

Comtal

Montsió

Betlem

Palau de la Virreina

Palau Moja

Mercat de la Boqueria

St. Felip Neri

Sta. Maria del Pi ❹

Liceu

Boqueria

Ferran

Generalitat

Plaça St. Jaume

Cal

Lleona

Plaça Reial

Escudellers

Palau March

La Mercè

Cap de Barcelona

Passeig de Colom (Ronda Litoral)

Mirador de Colom

Golondrinas

Moll de la Fusta

Moll d'Espanya

Port Vell

IMAX

L'Aquàrium de Barcelona

Maremàgnum

Moll dels Pescadors

Moll de la Barceloneta

Moll de Balears

Transbordador Aeri

Rambla da Mar

CIUTAT VELLA

Ataülf

Avinyó

Còdols

Gignàs Ample

Mercè

Plaça Antonio López

Portaferrissa

Palau de la Música Catalana

St. Pere Més Alt

LA RIBERA

St. Pere Més Baix

Av. Catedral Antoni Maura

Av. Francesc Cambó

Mercat Santa Caterina

Plaça Allada Vermell

Bòria

Catedral

BARRI GÒTIC

Jaume I

Via Laietana

Princesa

Museu Picasso

Rec

Comerç

Banys Vells

Montcada

Pg. del Born

Santa Maria del Mar ❶❺ ❶❻

Llotja de Mar ❶❹

Plaça del Palau

Marquesa

Barceloneta

Plaça Pau Vila

Moll de Dipòsit

Palau de Mar (Museu d'Història de Catalunya)

Ginebra

La Maquinista

BARCELONETA

Plaça Poeta Boscà

Passeig Joan de Borbó

Comte Sta. Clara

Almirall Cervera

Almirall Aixada

Sant Carles

Judici

Escar

Pg. de la Escullera Drassana

Plaça del Mar

Plaça Palmeres

Platja St. Sebastià

ⓘ Tourist Information

Ⓜ Metro Station

❶ ❷ ❸ ❹ ❺ ❻ ❼ ❽ ❾ ❿ ⓫ ⓬ ⓭ ⓮ ⓯ ⓰ ⓱ ⓲ ⓳

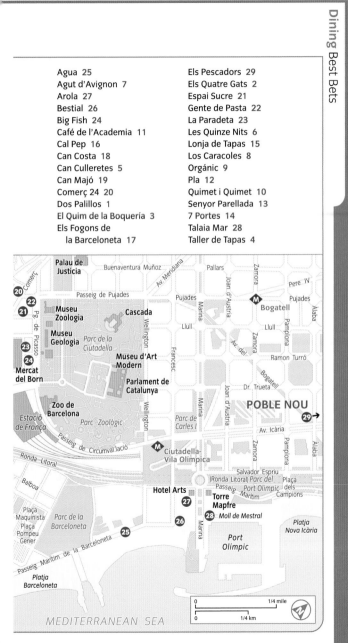

Barcelona Restaurants A to Z

Dining Hours Tip

Catalans generally have lunch between 2 and 4pm and dinner (sometimes well) after 9pm. Most kitchens stay open until 11:30pm if not later.

★★★ **ABaC** ZONA ALTA *CATALAN/ INTERNATIONAL* A longtime favorite with in-the-know foodies, ABaC is now part of a designer boutique hotel in new uptown digs, but the quiet confidence and creativity that garnered two Michelin stars continue—even if original chef Xavier Pellicer is now departed. The (pricey) menu is innovative to the point of being experimental. *Av. Tibidabo, 1.* ☎ *93-319-66-00. www. abacbarcelona.com. Entrees 38€– 56€; tasting menus 125€–145€. AE, DC, MC, V. Lunch and dinner Tues– Sat, dinner only Mon. Closed Aug. Map p 95.*

★ **kids Agua** WATERFRONT (VILA OLIMPICA) *MEDITERRANEAN* A casually cool spot with great beach views, Agua is popular for simply prepared fresh fish, rice dishes, and vegetarian items. It's a great spot for families with boisterous and picky young ones. *Pg. Maritim, 30.* ☎ *93-225-12-72. www.aguadeltrag aluz.com. Entrees 9€–21€. AE, DC, MC, V. Lunch and dinner daily. Metro: Ciutadella. Map p 96.*

★ **Agut d'Avignon** BARRI GOTIC *CATALAN* A classic revered among locals for its consistently fine, traditional Catalan cooking, this rustic spot is one of my favorite places in the city to sample the down-to-earth ingredients of *cuina catalana* such as duck with figs and *langostino* (prawn) *alioli. c/ Trinitat, 3 (alley off Avinyó, 8).* ☎ *93-317-36-93. Entrees 19€–44€. MC, V. Lunch and dinner daily. Closed last 3 weeks in Aug. Metro: Jaume I or Liceu. Map p 96.*

Bestial's waterfront location is ideal for alfresco dining.

Arola, in the Hotel Arts.

★★ Alta Taberna Paco Meralgo L'EIXAMPLE *TAPAS*

A casual, boisterous spot, popular with locals in the know, this amiable neighborhood restaurant is serious about its classic tapas; graze at the bar or grab a tall seat in one of the two dining rooms to taste through a long list of tapas and original *montaditos* (gourmet sandwiches). Be prepared to wait if you don't have a reservation. The name, by the way, is a play on words, meaning roughly "to grab a bite." *c/ Muntaner, 117.* ☎ *93-430-90-27. www.pacomeralgo. com. Tapas 6€–15€. DC, MC, V. Lunch and dinner daily. Metro: Hospital Clínic. Map p 95.*

★★ Arola WATERFRONT (VILA OLIMPICA) *CATALAN/SPANISH*

Amid colorful, pop-art decor, chef Sergi Arola does a modern take on *pica-pica* ("nibbles") and adds bursts of flavor to Mediterranean standards such as steamed mussels with citrus juice and saffron. The sleek, dark **Enoteca** within the hotel is another superb option. *c/ Marina, 19–21 (Hotel Arts).* ☎ *93-221-10-00. www.arola-arts.com. Entrees 12€– 38€; tasting menu 60€. AE, DC, MC, V. Lunch and dinner Wed–Sun. Closed Jan. Metro: Ciutadella–Vila Olímpica. Map p 96.*

kids Bestial WATERFRONT (VILA OLIMPICA) *MEDITERRANEAN/ITALIAN*

This hip but relaxed spot has large picture windows framing a very attractive outdoor space and magnificent views of the beach. The Mediterranean menu has an Italian bent, offering pastas, risottos, and individual pizzas with fresh ingredients, and there's a good-value midday menu. *c/ Ramón Trias Fargas, 2–4.* ☎ *93-224-04-07. www.grupotragaluz.com. Entrees 10€–24€. AE, DC, MC, V. Lunch and dinner daily. Metro: Ciutadella–Vila Olímpica. Map p 96.*

★★ Big Fish LA RIBERA *SEAFOOD*

A romantic place with high ceilings, funky chandeliers, and boho-chic style to burn, this new restaurant, opened by a fifth-generation fishmonger, is very serious about market-fresh fish, with classic Mediterranean preparations and fun takes on sushi. *c/ Comercial, 9.* ☎ *93-268-17-28. www.bigfish.cat. Entrees 12€–28€. MC, V. Lunch and dinner daily. Metro: Arc de Triomf or Barceloneta. Map p 96.*

★★★ Botafumeiro GRACIA *SEAFOOD*

Among seafood restaurants, none has more pedigree than this perennial favorite, which has entertained Barcelona's elite as well as the king of Spain for years. Much of the incredibly fresh seafood is flown in daily from Galicia (meaning: it's not cheap). The long seafood bar has repeatedly been named the best in Spain. *Gran de Gràcia, 81.* ☎ *93-218-42-30. www.botafumeiro.es. Entrees 24€–65€. AE, DC, MC, V. Lunch and dinner daily. Closed last 3 weeks in Aug. Metro: Fontana or Diagonal. Map p 95.*

★ Café de L'Academia BARRI GOTIC *CATALAN*

This dark, ancient-looking little restaurant sits

on a lovely medieval square, is a local favorite, and it is usually packed for lunch, when it offers a superb fixed-price menu. In warm weather, tables are set out on the terrace, a perfect place to drink in this quintessential Barri Gòtic corner. c/ Lledó, 1. ☎ 93-319-82-53. Entrees 10€– 18€. AE, MC, V. Lunch and dinner Mon–Fri. Closed 3 weeks in Aug. Metro: Jaume I. Map p 96.

★★ **Cal Pep** LA RIBERA/WATERFRONT SEAFOOD This tiny place used to be a secret, but local foodies and those from abroad now know that it serves some of the most succulent seafood in town. Cal Pep doesn't take reservations (except for groups of four or more), so you wait until a seat at the counter opens up. There's no menu, either, but Pep and his boys will set you up with the works. Pl. des les Olles, 8. ☎ 93-310-79-61. www.calpep.com. Entrees 15€–27€. AE, DC, MC, V. Dinner Mon; lunch and dinner Tues–Fri; lunch only Sat. Closed Aug. Metro: Barceloneta or Jaume I. Map p 96.

An innovative dish at Cinc Sentits.

★ **Can Costa** WATERFRONT (BARCELONETA) SEAFOOD Since the 1930s this has been one of the most dependable restaurants in Barcelona. Although there's no harbor view, the freshly prepared seafood makes up for it. Longtime admirers claim the sautéed baby squid is unequalled. I love the fideuà de peix, similar to shellfish paella but made with thin, dark noodles rather than rice. Pg. de Joan de Borbón, 70. ☎ 93-221-59-03. www.cancosta.com. Entrees

16€–41€. AE, DC, MC, V. Lunch and dinner Mon–Tues and Thurs–Sat; lunch only Sun. Closed Wed. Metro: Barceloneta. Map p 96.

★ **Can Culleretes** BARRI GOTIC CATALAN Barcelona's oldest restaurant has been serving traditional Catalan cooking since 1786. It's down-home and old-school, a good place to try standards like espinacas a la catalana (spinach with pine nuts and raisins) and butifarra (white sausage). c/ Quintana, 5. ☎ 93-317-64-85. www.culleretes. com. Entrees 8€–20€. MC, V. Lunch and dinner Tues–Sat; lunch only Sun. Closed late July to early Aug. Metro: Liceu. Map p 96.

★★ **Can Majó** WATERFRONT (PORT VELL) SEAFOOD Insiders know that this tavern-style, harborfront restaurant is one of the top places in Barcelona for super-fresh seafood. Try the excellent sopa de pescado y marisco (fish and shellfish soup), sautéed squid, or paellas. c/ Almirall Aixada, 23. ☎ 93-221-54-55. www.canmajo.es. Entrees 14€–30€. AE, DC, MC, V. Lunch and dinner Tues–Sat; lunch only Sun. Metro: Barceloneta. Map p 96.

★★ **Casa Calvet** L'EIXAMPLE CATALAN/MEDITERRANEAN Casa Calvet is housed within one of Antoni Gaudí's first modernista apartment buildings, with a gorgeous white-brick and stained-glass decor. The contemporary Catalan cuisine doesn't take a back seat to the surroundings. c/ Casp, 48. ☎ 93-412-40-12. www.casacalvet.es. Entrees 23€–31€; tasting menus 49€–75€. AE, DC, MC, V. Lunch and dinner Mon–Sat. Closed last 2 weeks in Aug. Metro: Pg. de Gràcia. Map p 95.

★ Cerveseria Catalana

L'EIXAMPLE *TAPAS/CATALAN* It certainly doesn't sound ("Catalan beer tavern") or look like much: primarily a beer tavern with finger foods, but Barcelonans know that some of the best tapas in town are served at this bustling institution. Knock back the *montaditos* (little sandwiches) and classic plates of shrimp and Spanish ham with one of the many international beers on hand. But be prepared to wait; this mainstay is as enduringly popular as they come. *c/ Mallorca, 236.* ☎ *93-216-03-68. Tapas 6€–15€. AE, DC, MC, V. Breakfast, lunch, and dinner daily. Metro: Pg. de Gràcia. Map p 95.*

★★★ Cinc Sentits

L'EIXAMPLE *MEDITERRANEAN* Haute cuisine, but also family-run—this relative newcomer is a unique synthesis of the Barcelona dining scene. The innovative fusion cuisine of Chef Jordi Artal, Catalan by way of Canada, is best sampled on the "Gourmet" tasting menu. Prepare yourself for monkfish sprinkled with bacon "dust" or a soft poached egg with tomato jam. *c/ Aribau, 58.* ☎ *93-323-94-90. www.cincsentits.com. Entrees 18€–36€; tasting menu 45€–65€. AE, DC, MC, V. Lunch Mon; lunch and dinner Tues–Sat. Closed Easter week and last 2 weeks in Aug. Metro: Pg. de Gràcia. Map p 95.*

★★ Comerç 24

LA RIBERA (EL BORN) *CATALAN/INTERNATIONAL* The small plates of celebrity chef Carles Abellán are so creative that it's a disservice to call them tapas. The theatrical dishes offer a visionary take on Catalan classics. *c/ Comerç, 24.* ☎ *93-319-21-02. www.projectes24.com. Entrees 12€–28€; tasting menus 62€–84€. AE, DC, MC, V. Lunch and dinner Tues–Sat. Closed Christmas week and last 3 weeks in Aug. Metro: Jaume I. Map p 96.*

★ Dolso

L'EIXAMPLE *MEDITERRANEAN* Although best known for its heavenly desserts, this smart, slender cafe is a real find for a smoking lunch *menú* deal (just 11€) and creative tasting menus at night—with Asian touches and of course spectacular sweet endings. *c/ València, 227.* ☎ *93-487-59-64. Tasting menu 25€–50€. AE, DC, MC, V. Lunch and dinner Mon–Sat. Metro: Pg. de Gràcia. Map p 95.*

★★★ Dos Palillos

RAVAL *CATALAN/ASIAN FUSION* The "in" spot in Barcelona, launched by a former chef de cuisine at famed El Bulli, is both playful and deadly serious about fusing Catalan, Japanese, and Chinese ingredients and techniques. The creativity and execution are stunning—and a relative steal for this level of forward-looking dining. A sensual feast, in a wickedly cool sushi restaurant–like space reached through an amusing neighborhood bar. *c/ Elisabets, 9.* ☎ *93-304-05-13. www.dospalillos.com. Tasting menus 50€–65€. AE, DC, MC, V. Lunch and dinner Thurs–Sat; dinner only Tues–Wed. Closed last week in Dec, 1st week in Jan, and last 3 weeks in Aug. Metro: Catalunya or Universitat. Map p 96.*

The minimalist design at Comerç 24.

★★ **El Quim de la Boquería** LA RAMBLA *CATALAN* Tucked within the sumptuous La Boqueria food market, this unsung kiosk with a tiny kitchen and a handful of stools around a bar is a gourmet secret, serving up spectacular Catalan comfort food and fresh seafood sourced from just a few feet away, and specialties like scrambled eggs with *llanguetas* (tiny whitefish) or baby squid. *La Rambla, 91.* ☎ *93-301-98-10. www.elquimdelaboqueria.com. Entrees 8€–18€. AE, DC, MC, V. Breakfast and lunch Tues–Sat. Metro: Liceu. Map p 96.*

★ kids **Els Fogons de la Barceloneta** WATERFRONT (BARCELONETA) *TAPAS/CATALAN* In a hip industrial spot tucked into the Barceloneta food market, with bright orange chairs on the new square outdoors, this is a great stop near the waterfront for tapas and fresh seafood listed on a chalkboard. The chef, Àngel Pascual, earned a Michelin star at his other restaurant, Lluçanès, in the same *mercat*. *Pl. de la Font, s/n (Mercat de la Barceloneta).* ☎ *93-224-26-26. www. restaurantllucanes.com/fogons. Tapas 4€–15€; tasting menu 32€. MC, V. Breakfast, lunch, and dinner Tues–Sat; lunch Sun. Metro: Barceloneta. Map p 96.*

★★★ kids **Els Pescadors** WATERFRONT (POBLE NOU) *SEAFOOD* Family-run, "the Fishermen" focuses, naturally, on providing superb fresh seafood, with just a hint of new-school preparations. The dining rooms comprise an atmospheric, old-world tavern with marble tables and ceiling beams and a more modern room; in warm weather, though, you can't beat the outdoor terrace on the classic Barcelona square dominated by an ombú tree. The kids' menu is a nice find at such an exalted fish house. *Pl. Prim, 1.* ☎ *93-225-20-18. www.*

A dish at Dos Palillos (p 101).

elspescadors.com. Entrees 15€– 38€. AE, DC, MC, V. Lunch and dinner daily. Closed Easter week. Metro: Poble Nou. Map p 96.

kids **Els Quatre Gats** BARRI GOTIC *CATALAN* This legendary cafe was the turn-of-the-20th century hangout of Picasso and other bohemian intellectuals. The "Four Cats" today is on the *modernista* tourist circuit, but it's a surprisingly good spot for simple, homey Catalan fare using fresh market ingredients. *c/ Montsió, 3.* ☎ *93-302-41-40. www.4gats.com. Entrees 14€–24€. AE, DC, MC, V. Breakfast, lunch, and dinner daily. Metro: Catalunya. Map p 96.*

★★ **Espai Sucre** LA RIBERA *DESSERT* Were Willy Wonka a restaurateur, this might be his temple. Yes, this tiny, minimalist restaurant ("Sugar Space") exclusively serves dessert, but the tasting menus of dessert courses actually work as (more or less) balanced dinner menus. For those fearful of sugar overload, you can add a savory dish, such as magret of duck or ginger couscous. *c/ de la Princesa, 53.* ☎ *93-268-16-30. www.espaisucre. com. Entrees 10€–15€; tasting menus 28€–48€. MC, V. Dinner Tues–Sat. Closed mid-Aug and Christmas week. Metro: Arc de Triomf. Map p 96.*

★★ **Fonda Gaig** L'EIXAMPLE *CAT-ALAN* Carles Gaig is one of the best-known chefs in town, but his signature restaurant, Gaig, is prohibitively expensive for most; this new, more value-driven venture goes back to his traditional Catalan roots, in a large and modern space that's popular with a sophisticated local crowd. *c/ Còrsega, 200.* 93-453-20-20. *www.fondagaig.com. Entrees 18€–38€. AE, DC, MC, V. Lunch and dinner Tues–Sat; lunch only Sun. Metro: Pg. de Gràcia. Map p 95.*

kids Gente de Pasta LA RIBERA *ITALIAN* This clean, loftlike space isn't your typical *trattoria*, but it's a good place for families, with kid-friendly dishes like risottos, basic pastas, and salads. *Pg. de Picasso, 10.* 93-268-70-17. *www.gentede pasta.com. Entrees 7€–21€. AE, MC, V. Lunch and dinner daily. Metro: Jaume 1 or Barceloneta. Map p 96.*

★★ **Hisop** GRACIA *CONTEMPO-RARY CATALAN* Less intimidating than some of Barcelona's super-chic restaurants featuring *cocina de autor* (Catalan haute cuisine), Hisop is small, inviting, and dynamic. Although difficult to find on a tiny side street edging toward Gràcia, it's worth the hunt for subtly complex dishes, such as scallops with figs and Jabugo ham. *Pg. Marimón, 9.* 93-241-32-33. *www.hisop.com. Entrees 22€–24€; tasting menu 48€. AE, DC, MC, V. Lunch and dinner Tues–Sat. Closed last 2 weeks in Aug. Metro: Hospital Clínic. Map p 95.*

★★ **Inopia** L'EIXAMPLE (ESQUERRA) *TAPAS* People hear that this tapas joint is run by the brother of the legendary chef Ferran Adrià (of El Bulli fame) and expect all kinds of funky foams. But it's a classic tapas bar serving up superb Spanish and Catalan tapas. The standards, such as

patatas bravas (spicy fried potatoes) and *croquetas de jamón ibérico* (croquettes stuffed with Spanish ham), are rarely this tasty elsewhere. *c/ Tamarit, 104.* 93-424-52-31. *www.barinopia.com. Tapas 4€–15€. MC, V. Dinner Tues–Fri; lunch and dinner Sat. Closed in Aug. Metro: Poble Sec. Map p 95.*

★ **kids La Paradeta** LA RIBERA *SEAFOOD* You can pick your own seafood and *mariscos* (shellfish) from large plastic tubs; it's then weighed and served on a platter. Kids should love it, and parents can accompany dinner with a nice selection of wines. *c/ Comercial, 7.* 93-268-19-39. *www.laparadeta.com. Entrees (cost is per kilo) 12€–26€. No credit cards. Dinner Tues–Sat; lunch Sat–Sun. Closed Dec 22–Jan 22. Metro: Arc de Triomf. Map p 96.*

kids Les Quinze Nits LA RAMBLA/BARRI GOTIC *MEDITERRANEAN* This smart, bargain-priced restaurant under the arches on Plaça Reial draws long lines of people looking for a solid meal and great deal.

Els Fogons de la Barceloneta.

A lively scene at Inopia (p 103).

Dishes are simple and straightforward, but surprisingly well prepared, and the lunch *menú* is a steal. *Pl. Reial, 6.* ☎ *93-317-30-75. www.lesquinzenits.com. Entrees 5€–16€. MC, V. Lunch and dinner daily. Metro: Liceu. Map p 96.*

kids Lonja de Tapas WATERFRONT/ LA RIBERA *TAPAS* A bright and casual tapas restaurant, in a good-looking space with high ceilings, this place is solid, especially if you're just in the mood for grazing or don't quite know what you want. Tapas cover the Spanish standards, from Iberian ham and steamed cockles to paellas and monkfish with wild mushrooms. There's another location on carrer Montcada. *Pl. del Palau, 7.* ☎ *93-268-72-58. www.lonjadetapas.com. Tapas 4€–20€; tasting menu 30€. AE, DC, MC, V. Lunch and dinner daily. Metro: Barceloneta. Map p 96.*

Los Caracoles BARRI GOTIC *CATALAN* Popular with tourists, this old-school restaurant is one of those only-in-Spain places. You're first greeted by an open spit roasting chickens; inside is an ancient, atmospheric labyrinth of cluttered dining rooms. "The Snails" is all about Catalan comfort food, such as *arroz negre* (rice cooked in squid ink), grilled squid, and roast chicken. *c/ Escudellers, 14.* ☎ *93-302-31-85.*

www.los-caracoles.es. Entrees 10€– 28€; tapas tasting menu 49€. AE, DC, MC, V. Lunch and dinner daily. Metro: Liceu. Map p 96.

★★★ **Moo** L'EIXAMPLE *MODERN MEDITERRANEAN* You can't get much more mod than Hotel Omm, home to this exquisite restaurant by three Catalan brothers (with a stellar restaurant in Girona). Unusually, all the dishes are available in half-size portions, so you can design your own *menú de desgustación*. Or just saddle up for the "Joan Roca" tasting menu: five gourmet dishes served with well-chosen wines. *c/ Rosselló, 265.* ☎ *93-445-40-00. www.hotelomm.es. Entrees 18€– 32€; midday menu 37€; tasting menu 75€–100€. AE, DC, MC, V. Lunch and dinner Mon–Sat. Metro: Diagonal. Map p 95.*

★ **Orgánic** RAVAL *VEGETARIAN* It's taken a while for vegetarian restaurants to catch on, but this cool, laid-back place with large communal tables really fills a void. There's a help-yourself soup and salad bar, and organic-focused main courses that include vegetarian pizza, pasta, and stir-fries. *c/ Junta de Comerç, 11.* ☎ *93-301-09-02. www.antonia organickitchen.com. Main courses 6€–15€. AE, DC, MC, V. Lunch and dinner daily. Metro: Liceu. Map p 96.*

★ **kids** **Pla** BARRI GOTIC *MEDITER-RANEAN* Popular with locals and visitors alike for its well-prepared dishes at exceedingly fair prices, this attractive restaurant serves excellent carpaccios, tasty salads, and gently exotic main courses, such as Thai curry or Moroccan couscous. *c/ Bellafila, 5.* ☎ *93-412-65-52. www.pla-repla.com. Entrees 15€–22€. DC, MC, V. Dinner daily. Closed Dec 25–27. Metro: Jaume I. Map p 96.*

★★ **Quimet i Quimet** POBLE SEC *TAPAS* In the Poble Sec neighborhood, this incredible hole in the wall—the walls lined to the ceiling with liquor bottles and canned foods—is always jam-packed with hungry patrons and drinkers in the know, who come for the stunningly creative and delicious *montaditos* (little gourmet sand-wiches). *c/ Poeta Cabanyes, 25.* ☎ *93-442-31-42. Tapas 3€–12€. MC, V. Lunch and dinner Mon–Fri; lunch Sat. Metro: Paral.lel. Map p 96.*

★★ **Restaurant Embat** L'EIXAMPLE *CONTEMPORARY CATA-LAN* This smart little restaurant, part of the "Bistronomic" wave in Barcelona, does clever Catalan cuisine at an extremely reasonable price. The dining room is relaxed,

The very mod Moo.

rustic chic, with rough-hewn tables and brown linens. Lunch is one of the best deals in the city. *c/ Mallorca, 304.* ☎ *93/458-08-55. www.restaurantembat.es. Entrees 18€–22€. AE, DC, MC, V. Lunch Tues–Fri; dinner Thurs–Sat. Metro: Pg. de Gràcia. Map p 95.*

★ **Senyor Parellada** LA RIBERA *CATALAN/MEDITERRANEAN* One of the best values in Barcelona is this cheery, stylish restaurant carved out of a 19th-century man-sion. The colorfully staged dining rooms are merely a prelude to dependably executed, fresh prepa-rations of authentic Catalan fare like

7 Portes.

baked monkfish with mustard and garlic sauce, at welcome bargain prices. *c/ L'Argenteria, 37.* ☎ *93-310-50-94. www.senyorparellada.com. Entrees 8€–21€. AE, DC, MC, V. Lunch and dinner daily. Metro: Jaume I. Map p 96.*

★★ kids **7 Portes** WATERFRONT *CATALAN* A favorite of large dining parties since 1836, this elegant but unassuming place really does have seven doors under porticoes (hence the name). It's famous for its rice dishes, such as black rice with squid in its own ink; portions are enormous and reasonably priced. *Pg. d'Isabel II, 14.* ☎ *93-319-30-33. www.7portes.com. Entrees 15€–35€. AE, DC, MC, V. Lunch and dinner daily. Metro: Barceloneta or Drassanes. Map p 96.*

★ **Talaia Mar** WATERFRONT (PORT OLIMPIC) *MEDITERRANEAN* The Olympic Port teems with restaurants, but none of them is as good as this one. The innovative chef has created a seafood-dominated menu, featuring grilled fresh fish and more audacious dishes that tempt the senses, including barnacles with a seawater sorbet. *Marina, 16.* ☎ *93-221-90-90. www.barcelona-comercio.com/talaia. Entrees*

18€–32€; *fixed-price menu 51€. AE, DC, MC, V. Lunch and dinner Tues–Sun. Metro: Ciutadella–Vila Olímpica. Map p 96.*

kids **Taller de Tapas** BARRI GOTIC *TAPAS* This pleasant "Tapas Workshop" simplifies the ordering of tapas. Though not innovative, the small dishes from across Spain—such as marinated anchovies, prawns with scrambled eggs, and sizzling *chorizo* cooked in cider—are prepared fresh in an open kitchen. There's another location at c/ L'Argentaria, 51. *Pl. Sant Josep Oriol, 9 (Pl. del Pi).* ☎ *93-301-80-20. www.tallerdetapas.com. Tapas 5€–26€. AE, DC, MC, V. Lunch and dinner daily. Metro: Liceu. Map p 96.*

★★ **Tapas 24** L'EIXAMPLE *CREATIVE TAPAS* Ultra-cool Comerç 24 does designer tapas, while this below-street-level bar is the more informal offshoot. But it shares an interest in fresh ingredients and just the right touch of creativity, and this actually may be the more enjoyable of the two. *c/ Diputació, 269.* ☎ *93-488-09-77. www.projectes24.com. Tapas 4€–18€. MC, V. Lunch and dinner Mon–Sat. Metro: Pg. de Gràcia. Map p 95.* ●

For innovative Spanish tapas, try Tapas 24.

Nightlife Best Bets

Previous page: Dancing after dark in Barcelona. This page: Absinthe at Marsella.

L'Eixample Nightlife

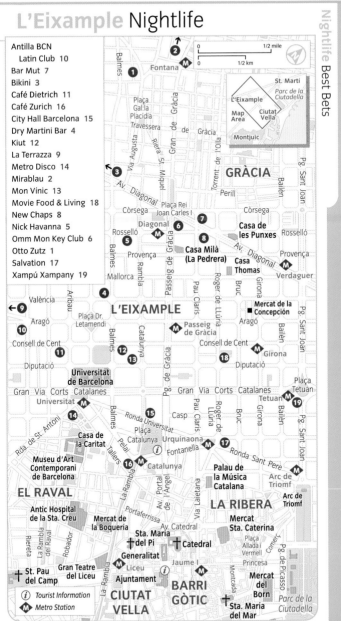

Antilla BCN
  Latin Club 10
Bar Mut 7
Bikini 3
Café Dietrich 11
Café Zurich 16
City Hall Barcelona 15
Dry Martini Bar 4
Kiut 12
La Terrazza 9
Metro Disco 14
Mirablau 2
Mon Vinic 13
Movie Food & Living 18
New Chaps 8
Nick Havanna 5
Omm Mon Key Club 6
Otto Zutz 1
Salvation 17
Xampú Xampany 19

Ciutat Vella & Waterfront Nightlife

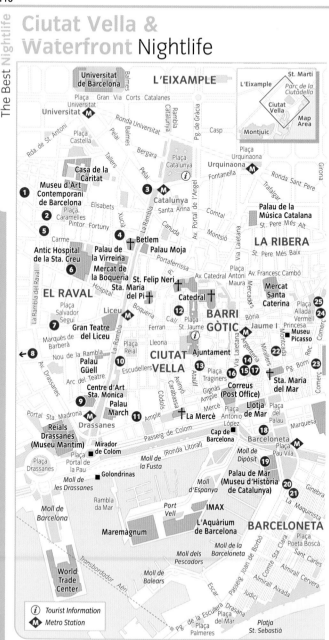

- Universitat de Barcelona
- L'EIXAMPLE
- Plaça Gran Via Corts Catalanes
- Universitat M
- Rda. de St. Antoni
- Balmes
- Rambla Catalunya
- Pg. de Gràcia
- Casp
- Ronda Universitat
- Plaça Castella
- Pelai
- Bergara
- Balmes
- Plaça Catalunya (i)
- Plaça Urquinaona
- Urquinaona M
- Ronda Sant Pere
- Trafalgar
- Girona
- St. Marti
- Parc de la Ciutadella
- Map Area
- L'Eixample
- Ciutat Vella
- Montjuic
- Tallers
- Pelai
- Fontanella
- Casa de la Caritat
- **1** Museu d'Art Contemporani de Barcelona
- Elisabets
- Nuclà
- **3** M Catalunya
- Santa Anna
- Canuda
- Av. Portal de l'Angel
- Comtal
- Montsió
- Pl. de Catalunya
- Plaça Urquinaona
- Palau de la Música Catalana
- St. Pere Més Alt
- **2** Caramelles
- Pintor Fortuny
- Carme
- **5**
- **4** † Betlem
- Palau Moja
- St. Pere Més Baix
- LA RIBERA
- Antic Hospital de la Sta. Creu
- **6** Palau de la Virreina
- Portaferrissa
- Av. Catedral
- Antoni Maura
- Av. Francesc Cambó
- Mercat de la Boqueria
- Sta. Maria del Pi
- St. Felip Neri †
- Plaça
- Mercat Santa Caterina
- EL RAVAL
- Hospital
- **12**
- Catedral †
- BARRI
- Mercadé
- Plaça Allada Vermell
- **25**
- **24**
- Plaça Salvador Seguí
- Liceu M
- Boqueria
- Cal/ Plaça St. Jaume
- GÒTIC
- Bòria
- Princesa
- Museu Picasso
- **7** Gran Teatre del Liceu
- Ferran
- (i)
- Jaume I M
- **22**
- Marquès de Barberà
- Lleona
- CIUTAT
- Ajuntament
- Via Laietana
- Argenteria
- Miralles
- Montcada
- Rec
- Comerç
- **8** Nou de la Rambla
- Plaça Reial
- VELLA
- **13** Plaça Traginers
- **14**
- Pg. Born
- **23**
- Palau Güell
- Escudellers
- **10**
- Avinyó
- Carabassa
- Còdols
- **16** **15** **17**
- Sta. Maria del Mar
- Arc del Teatre
- Centre d'Art Sta. Monica
- Gignàs
- Ample
- Correus (Post Office)
- **9**
- Palau March
- **11** Ample
- † La Mercè
- Mercè
- Plaça Antonio López
- Llotja de Mar
- Plaça del Palau
- Portal Sta. Madrona
- M Drassanes
- **18**
- Marquesa
- Reials Drassanes (Museu Marítim)
- Mirador de Colom
- Passeig de Colom
- Cap de Barcelona
- Barceloneta M
- Plaça Pau Vila
- Plaça Drassanes
- Plaça Portal de la Pau
- Moll de (Ronda Litoral)
- la Fusta
- Moll del Dipòsit
- **19**
- Golondrinas
- Moll de les Drassanes
- Moll d'Espanya
- Palau de Mar (Museu d'Història de Catalunya)
- **20**
- **21**
- La Maquinista
- Ginebra
- Moll de Barcelona
- Rambla da Mar
- Port Vell
- IMAX
- BARCELONETA
- Plaça Poeta Boscà
- World Trade Center
- Maremàgnum
- L'Aquàrium de Barcelona
- Moll de la Barceloneta
- Comte Sta. Clara
- Sant Carles
- Almirall Cervera
- Transbordador Aeri
- Moll de Balears
- Moll dels Pescadors
- Passeig Joan de Borbó
- Almirall Aixada
- Escar
- Pg. de la Escullera
- Drassana
- Plaça del Mar
- Platja St. Sebastià
- Judici
- Plaça Palmeres

(i) Tourist Information
M Metro Station

Barcelona Nightlife A to Z

Bars & Pubs

★★ **Almirall** RAVAL   An old-school, dimly lit place with a bohemian bent and massive Art Nouveau mirror behind the bar. *c/ Joaquin Costa, 33.* ☎ *93-412-15-35. Metro: Sant Antoni or Universitat. Map p 110.*

★★ **Bar Lobo** RAVAL   A chic, high-ceilinged tapas and cocktail joint, sleek, modern, and cool with graffiti art and theater posters, and boasting a lovely outdoor terrace that's ideal for people-watching. *c/ Pinto Fortuny, 3.* ☎ *93-481-53-46. Metro: Sant Antoni or Universitat. Map p 110.*

★★ **Bar Mut** L'EIXAMPLE   A smart, classic old Barcelona tapas joint and watering hole—its name is a play on the local pronunciation of vermouth—it has great snacks, all written on a chalkboard, and plentiful wines tucked behind glass. *c/ Pau Claris, 192.* ☎ *93-217-43-38. Metro: Diagonal. Map p 109.*

The Black Horse LA RIBERA
With a host of British beers on tap, dartboards, and several TVs tuned to sports, this English free house with a worn pub feel is where expats come to watch soccer and put back a few pints. *c/ Allada Vermell, 16.* ☎ *93-268-33-38. Metro: Jaume I. Map p 110.*

★★ **Boadas** LA RAMBLA   A classic cocktail bar from the 1930s, Boadas is lined with old photos and has an intellectual, pre-revolutionary Havana vibe. A good place for a pre-dinner drink, like a classic daiquiri. *c/ Tallers, 1.* ☎ *93-318-88-26. Metro: Catalunya. Map p 110.*

★ **Dry Martini Bar** L'EIXAMPLE
In this sober, narrow bar, popular with cocktail connoisseurs of a certain age, the mixologist Javier de las Muelas serves up the classics, in the stylish, dark-wood-and-banquettes ambience they deserve. *c/ Aribau, 162.* ☎ *93-217-50-72. Metro: Diagonal. Map p 109.*

El Bosc de las Fades BARRI GOTIC
A freaky, and kitschy, plunge into a fairy-tale forest, complete with gnomes, fairies, mermaids, waterfalls, and trees with faces. It's fanciful and trying hard to be cinematic. *Pg. de la Banca, 7.* ☎ *93-317-26-49. Metro: Drassanes. Map p 110.*

★ **El Jardí** RAVAL   Tucked into the Gothic courtyard of a historic hospital, this secretive little garden terrace is a terrific place to escape the Rambla crowds and grab a glass of wine or a cocktail and some tapas. Occasionally a jazz or bossa nova combo will be on hand. *c/ de L'Hospital, 56.* ☎ *93-201-53-06. Metro: Liceu. Map p 110.*

The Fastnet Bar WATERFRONT
This Irish pub with good grub has an outdoor terrace and location near the marina. Soccer and rugby fans gather around the large-screen TV. *Pg. Juan de Borbón, 22.* ☎ *93-295-30-05. Metro: Barceloneta. Map p 110.*

A sign for Boadas cocktail bar.

A bartender pours a drink at Gimlet.

★★★ **Gimlet** LA RIBERA   People who know their cocktails frequent this sophisticated, retro-styled bar, where excellent bartenders and cool jazz on the stereo complete the scene. Perfect for pre-dinner drinks, especially mojitos and fruity versions of Collins. *c/ Rec, 24.* ☎ *93-310-10-27. Metro: Arc de Triomf. Map p 110.*

★★ **Ginger** BARRI GOTIC   A small, retro-styled cocktail bar on a lovely little Gothic Quarter square. Its comfortable sofas and good selection of tapas make it a place to linger. One entrance leads to a wine bar, the other to a cocktail bar. *Palma de Sant Just, 1 (at c/ Lledó).* ☎ *93-310-53-09. Metro: Jaume I. Map p 110.*

★ **La Fianna** LA RIBERA   This bar/restaurant's ramshackle, vaguely North African ambience appeals to late-nighters and international sorts, who kick back on the cozy, cushion-topped platforms. All that's missing are hookah pipes. *c/ Banys Vells, 15.* ☎ *93-315-18-10. Metro: Jaume I. Map p 110.*

★★★ **L'Ascensor** BARRI GOTIC   Named for its fantastic old-world elevator that serves as an entrance, this delightfully romantic spot on a tiny street has been around for 3 decades and is renowned for its rum-based *caipirinhas* and mojitos. One of my go-to late-night spots. *c/ Bellafila, 3.* ☎ *93-318-53-47. Metro: Jaume I. Map p 110.*

★★ **Marmalade** RAVAL   In a gorgeous, dimly lit space that was once a cafe on the wrong side of the tracks, this sexy place has a terrific roster of well-priced cocktails, some tasty tapas to go with them, and one swanky pool table. *c/ Riera Alta, 4–6.* ☎ *93-442-39-66. Metro: Liceu. Map p 110.*

★★★ **Marsella** RAVAL   This dusty joint—around since 1820—is *the* place to try absinthe *(absenta)*, the wickedly strong anise-flavored liqueur distilled from wormwood, said to be hallucinogenic and still banned in some countries. Picasso, Dalí, and Hemingway were said to be regulars here. *c/ Sant Pau, 65.* ☎ *93-442-72-63. Metro: Liceu. Map p 110.*

★ **Mirablau** TIBIDABO   The bar itself isn't anything special, really, but the view is stunning. Have an early evening cocktail and gaze from a picture window over all of Barcelona, laid out spectacularly beneath

Picasso and Hemingway were regulars at Marsella.

your feet. The bar is next to the funicular near the top of Mt. Tibidabo. *Pl. Doctor Andreu, 2 (top of Av. Tibidabo).* ☎ *93-418-58-79. Tramvia Blau from Metro: Tibidabo. Map p 109.*

★★★ **Pastís** LA RAMBLA/RAVAL This darkly romantic, midcentury spot, a shrine to Edith Piaf, reeks of an old seaside bar. The house special is pastis, the French anise-flavored elixir. The place isn't for everyone, but those with a sense of camp or an ascot will be in heaven here. *c/ Santa Mònica, 4.* ☎ *93-318-79-80. Metro: Drassanes. Map p 110.*

Casino

Casino Barcelona WATERFRONT Hugely popular, this casino also contains a disco, a restaurant, and all the gaming opportunities you could want. Don't forget to take your passport. *c/ Marina, 19–21.* ☎ *93-225-78-78. www.casino-barcelona.com. Admission 4.50€. Metro: Citutadella–Vila Olímpica. Map p 110.*

Dance Clubs

★★★ **Antilla BCN Latin Club** L'EIXAMPLE A fixture among Barcelona's large Latin American and Caribbean community, this

Check out the fantastic views from Mirablau.

happening *salsateca* is a great place to shake it if you know what you're doing (and if you don't, check out the club's dance school, Mon and Wed–Fri 9–11:30pm, free on Tues with cover). It also gets some big-name Latino performers. *c/ Aragó, 141.* ☎ *93-451-21-51. Cover 10€. Metro: Urgell. Map p 109.*

★★ **Apolo** POBLE SEC On Fridays and Saturdays this wildly diverse nightclub, in a venerable turn-of-the-20th-century theater/ballroom, is a dance club called Nitsa. On other nights, it plays host to movies, funk music, and rock shows; Sunday it's transformed into a very popular gay club. *c/ Nou de la Rambla, 113.* ☎ *93-441-40-01. www.sala-apolo.com. Cover 10€–20€. Metro: Poble Sec. Map p 110.*

★★ **Bikini** DIAGONAL/SANTS This cool, sprawling bar hosts live rock music but is also a great dance club. You'll find thumping Latin tunes in one salon, alternative rock in another. *c/ Deu i Mata, 105.* ☎ *93-322-00-05. www.bikinibcn.com. Cover 15€. Metro: Maria Cristina/Hospital Clinic. Map p 109.*

★ **City Hall Barcelona** L'EIXAMPLE A popular, two-level club that draws lots of rambunctious clubbers and their tourist counterparts, who come to party to techno and house music. The garden out back provides a nice respite from all the action. *Rambla de Catalunya, 2–4.* ☎ *93-238-07-22. www.ottozutz.com. Cover 12€. Metro: Catalunya. Map p 109.*

★★★ **La Paloma** RAVAL A lavish ballroom more than a century old, this theater—with its red-velvet entry, murals, and glimmering chandeliers—is an extraordinary place to dance. In the early evening, that means fox trot, tango, and bolero, accompanied by live orchestras. Late night Thursday to Sunday, it

A DJ spins records late into the Barcelona night.

morphs into a much younger and hipper nightclub. *c/ Tigre, 27.* ☎ *93-301-68-97. Cover 5€–15€. Metro: Universitat. Map p 110.*

★ **La Terrazza** MONTJUIC This summer-only, open-air dance club is tucked inside Poble Espanyol, the faux Spanish village built for the 1929 World's Fair. La Terrazza rocks until dawn. An indoor dance option, Discotheque, is available by separate entrance and cover fee. *Poble Espanyol, Av. Marquès de Comillas, s/n.* ☎ *93-508-63-30. Metro: Espanya. Map p 109.*

★ **Le KasBah** WATERFRONT With a Moroccan feel near the Olympic port—in the Palau del Mar building that houses the Museu de Catalunya—

this bar's dance floor heats up as the evening wears on. Nice outdoor terrace. *Pl. Pau Vila, 1.* ☎ *93-238-07-02. Metro: Barceloneta. Map p 110.*

★ **New York** BARRI GOTIC It still looks the part of erstwhile strip club and cathouse, and the young hipsters who hang out here make very late nights of it, dancing to indie, R&B, and vintage disco. *c/ Escudellers, 5.* ☎ *93-318-87-30. Cover (after 2am) 10€. Metro: Drassanes. Map p 110.*

★★★ **Otto Zutz** GRACIA The granddaddy of clubs in Barcelona, this multilevel favorite still draws trendsetters, the rich, the famous, and the wannabes. With eight bars and four main dance areas, spanning a variety of musical genres, you're bound to find something—or someone—you like. *c/ Lincoln, 15.* ☎ *93-238-07-22. www.ottozutz.com. Cover 15€–20€. Metro: Gràcia. Map p 109.*

★★★ **Razzmatazz** WATERFRONT (POBLE NOU) This five-in-one club, a monster multilevel warehouse, offers something for everyone, as long as you're young and overflowing with energy and hormones. From techno to Goth, pop to punk and metal, a single admission to all five spaces can leave you dizzy. It's also a great live-music venue. *c/ Almogàvers, 122.* ☎ *93-272-09-10. Cover (except*

Head to La Paloma for dancing of all kinds.

for special concerts) 12€–15€.
Metro: Bogatell. Map p 110.

Gay & Lesbian Bars/Clubs

★★ Café Dietrich L'EIXAMPLE
For a great drag show, you can't
beat this glam cafe, one of the city's
most enduring popular gay hang-
outs. The bartenders wear little and
seem to enjoy the attentions of their
patrons. *c/ Consell de Cent, 255.*
☎ 93-451-77-07. Metro: Gràcia or
Universitat. Map p 109.

Kiut L'EIXAMPLE   With few clubs
catering to lesbians in Barcelona, this
stylish spot—pronounced "cute"—
with a mirrored dance floor draws a
fashionable crowd of women (as well
as a mix of straights on Thurs nights).
c/ Consell de Cent, 280. ☎ 93-487-83-
42. Metro: Pg. de Gràcia. Map p 109.

★ Metro Disco LA RAMBLA/
RAVAL   Cruisy, with two dance
floors, Metro remains one of the
most popular gay discos in Barcelona. The crowd ranges from pretty
fashionistas to handlebar-mous-
tache, macho types. One dance floor
even spins traditional Spanish music
and Spanish pop. The backroom
isn't for the meek. *c/ Sepulveda,
185.* ☎ 93-323-52-27. Cover 10€.
Metro: Universitat. Map p 109.

New Chaps L'EIXAMPLE   This bar
is the place to find gay cowboys and
bears. The downstairs darkroom is
where the action is in the wee hours.

Even the sign is glamorous at Café Dietrich.

*A glass of cava is sure to make your eve-
ning more bubbly.*

Av. Diagonal, 365. ☎ 93-215-53-65.
Metro: Diagonal. Map p 109.

Salvation L'EIXAMPLE   A young
crowd frequents this flashy dance
club with two *salones,* one featuring
house and DJs, the other commercial pop. *Ronda de Sant Pere, 19–21.*
☎ 93-318-06-86. Metro: Urquinaona. Map p 109.

Lounges & Beach Hangouts

★ CDLC Barcelona WATERFRONT
This trendy place is all attitude and
gente bella (beautiful people). If you
want to see and be seen, it's appro-
priately swanky, and right on the
edge of the beach. To chill on the
luxe white beds, you'll have to pony
up for a pricey bottle of whiskey. I'm
partial to the outdoor terrace. Make
sure you wear your best duds. *Pg.
Marítim, 32.* ☎ 93-224-04-70. Metro:
Ciutadella–Vila Olímpica. Map p 110.

★ Luz de Gas Port Vell WATER-
FRONT   A summer-only lounge bar
on a boat in the marina, this sister
bar of the very cool nightspot Luz
de Gas is ideal in warm weather for
evening cocktails. Candlelit tables
and a dance floor overlook the pier.
Moll del Dipòsit, s/n (in front of Palau

de Mar). ☎ 93-484-23-26. Metro: Drassanes or Barceloneta. Map p 110.

★ **MIX** LA RIBERA Scenesters gather at this fashionable hangout in the trendy Born district to imbibe colorful cocktails and groove to nightly DJs spinning jazz, soul, funk, and freestyle mixes Tuesday through Saturday nights. The cocktail for four called an orgy might get things rolling. *Comerç, 21.* ☎ 93-319-46-96. Metro: Ciutadella–Vila Olímpica. Map p 110.

★★ **Movie Living & Food** L'EIXAMPLE An unusual restaurant and lounge, Movie says it's a "visual music club," and that means screens with concert videos and films, comfortable maroon sofas, and theater-style seats. It's the kind of high-tech place where a DJ doubles as a VJ. *c/ Roger de Llúria, 50.* ☎ 93-467-54-81. Metro: Pg. de Gràcia. Map p 109.

★ **Nick Havanna** L'EIXAMPLE Barcelona's original design bar began life in the 1980s. As other bars have caught the bug, Nick Havanna now revels in its retro glory. Its bathrooms are still conversation-worthy. *c/ Rosselló, 208.* ☎ 93-215-65-91. Metro: Diagonal. Map p 109.

★★ **Omm Lobby Lounge/Mon Key Club** L'EIXAMPLE Oozing mod style, this swanky lounge in the ultra-cool Hotel Omm is a favorite of design types, models, and others with beauty and euros to spare. After 1am, head to the dramatically lit, and oh-so-chic, sofa-laden night club. *c/ Rosselló, 265.* ☎ 93-445-40-00. Metro: Diagonal. Map p 109.

Shôko WATERFRONT A beachside lounge bar that's also an Asian-themed restaurant, this self-conscious place draws plenty of pretty and pouty fashionable sorts who don't have a problem with the cheesy decor, an odd backdrop for the amped-up weekend *fiestas* set to house, trance, and hip-hop. *Pg.*

Marítim, 36. ☎ 93-225-92-00. Metro: Ciutadella–Vila Olímpica. Map p 110.

Wine (& *Cava*) Bars

★★ **Can Paixano** WATERFRONT Usually jampacked, this landmark bar with no sign out front serves the cheapest *cava* in Barcelona, as well as an interminable list of sandwiches. In the evening, the rustic standing-room-only space gets pretty crazed (and you've got to fight for a bottle of *cava,* which will only set you back about 5€). *c/ Reina Cristina, 7.* ☎ 93-310-08-39. Metro: Barceloneta. Map p 110.

★★★ **El Xampanyet** LA RIBERA A revered institution, as comfortable as an old tweed jacket, this is one place I pop into every time I'm wandering through La Ribera, for a fizzy *copa de cava* and some excellent snacks. Family-owned since the 1930s, it is as authentic as they come, with colored tiles, marble

Luz de Gas Port Vell is ideal for evening cocktails in the summertime.

On a cava crawl? A required stop is El Xampanyet.

tables, an old zinc bar, and wine barrels. *c/ de la Montcada, 22.* ☎ *93-319-70-03. Closed Aug. Metro: Jaume I. Map p 110.*

★ **La Vinateria del Call** BARRI GOTIC   A dark and romantic wine haunt, right in the midst of the ancient Jewish Quarter, this is a good, non-touristy spot to sip *vino* with locals. *c/ de Sant Domènec del Call, 9.* ☎ *93-302-60-92. Metro: Jaume I. Map p 110.*

★★ **La Vinya del Senyor** LA RIBERA   Across from Santa Maria del Mar, this tiny wine bar with an enviable terrace draws hordes of tourists and local wine connoisseurs for its spectacular list of Spanish wines and *cavas* and yummy selection of tapas. *Pl. Santa Maria, 5.* ☎ *93-310-33-79. Metro: Barceloneta or Jaume I. Map p 110.*

★★ **Mon Vínic** L'EIXAMPLE   A sleek and sophisticated, even futuristic, design-and-wine temple, with a digital list 4,000 bottles strong, 30

wines by the glass (different each day), and a reference library for true wine geeks. Closed weekends. *c/ Diputació, 249.* ☎ *93-272-61-87. Metro: Pg. de Gràcia. Map p 109.*

★ **Va de Vi** BARRI GOTIC   This wine bar, owned by an artist and wine aficionado, inhabits a cinematic, stone-walled medieval house with Gothic arches. It has an extraordinary wine list, including some very coveted bottles such as L'Ermita from Priorat. *c/ Banys Vells, 16.* ☎ *93-319-29-00. Metro: Jaume I. Map p 110.*

★ **Xampú Xampany** L'EIXAMPLE   Although the name may look impossible to pronounce for foreigners, this longtime *xampanyeria* (*cava* bar) is anything but intimidating. It serves up lots of excellent tapas alongside its house *cava* and wines, and makes a good first stop. The tables outside are the place to be. *Gran Via de les Corts Catalanes, 702 (corner Bailén).* ☎ *93-265-04-83. Metro: Girona. Map p 109.* ●

Arts & Entertainment Best Bets

Best **Concert Acoustics**
★ L'Auditori, *c/ Lepant, 150 (p 124)*

Best **Jazz Club**
★★★ Harlem Jazz Club, *Comtessa de Sobradiel, 8 (p 127)*

Best **Flamenco, Flashy Dresses & All**
★★ Tablao Flamenco Cordobés, *La Rambla, 35 (p 127)*

Best **Opera House**
★★★ Gran Teatre del Liceu, *La Rambla, 51–59 (p 124)*

Best **Summer Arts Festival**
★★ Grec, *Montjuïc (p 129)*

Best **Sporting Event**
★★ Fútbol Club Barcelona, *Av. del Papa Joan XXIII (p 130)*

Best **Theater Performances**
★★★ Teatre Mercat de Les Flors, *c/ Lleida, 59 (p 130)*

Best **Impression Made by a Concert Hall**
★★★ El Palau de la Música Catalana, *c/ Sant Francesc de Paula, 2 (p 124)*

Best **All-Around Live Music Venue**
★★★ Luz de Gas, *c/ Muntaner, 246 (p 128)*

Best **Hipster Live Music Shows**
★★ Sala Razzmatazz, *c/ dels Almogavers, 122 (p 129)*

Best **Unexpected Theater/ Music**
★ La Casa dels Músics, *c/ Encarnació, 25 (p 125)*

Best **Hangout for Electronic Music Freaks**
Sonar, El Raval, and other venues *(p 129)*

Best **Movie House for V.O. (Subtitles)**
★★★ Verdi, *c/ Verdi, 32 (p 126)*

Best **Alternative Rock Festival**
Primavera Sound, *Parc del Fòrum (p 129)*

Most **Unusual Venue for Opera Arias**
★ Espai Barroc, *c/ de la Montcada, 20 (p 127)*

Previous page: A scene from a Tchaikovsky opera at Gran Teatre del Liceu.
This page: A performance at El Palau de la Música Catalana.

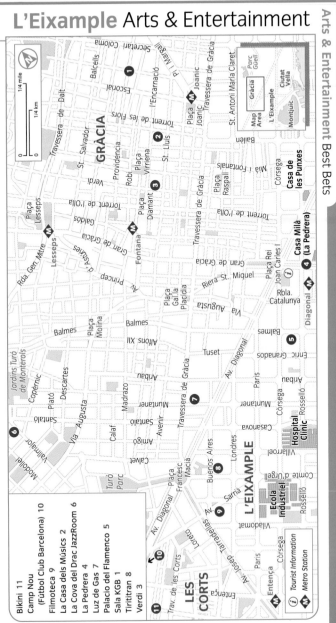

Bikini 11
Camp Nou
(Fútbol Club Barcelona) 10
Filmoteca 9
La Casa dels Músics 2
La Cova del Drac JazzRoom 6
La Pedrera 4
Luz de Gas 7
Palacio del Flamenco 5
Sala KGB 1
Tirititran 8
Verdi 3

ⓘ Tourist Information
Ⓜ Metro Station

Ciutat Vella & Waterfront

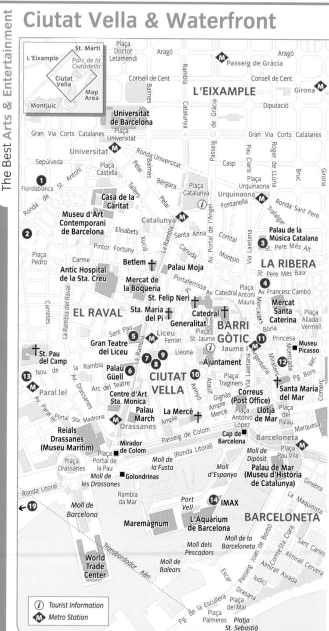

St. Martí

L'Eixample

Parc de la Ciutadella

Ciutat Vella

Map Area

Montjuic

Plaça Doctor Letamendi

Aragó

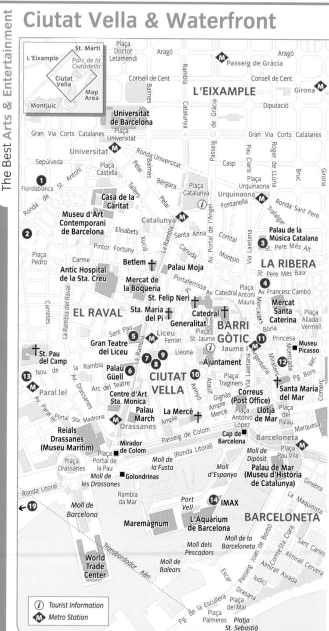 Passeig de Gràcia

Aragó

Consell de Cent

Balmes

Rambla

Consell de Cent

Girona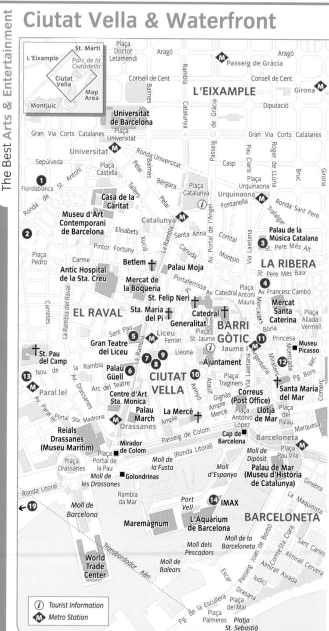

L'EIXAMPLE

Diputació

Universitat de Barcelona

Gran Via Corts Catalanes

Plaça Universitat

Passeig de Gràcia

Pau Claris

Roger de Llúria

Bruc

Girona

Gran Via Corts Catalanes

Sepúlveda

Universitat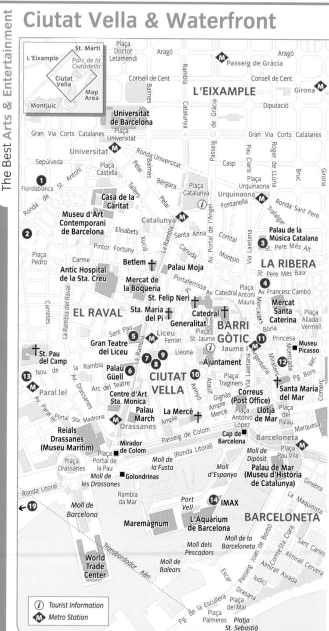

Ronda Universitat

Pelai

Balmes

Bergara

Plaça Castella

Talless

Caspe

Plaça Urquinaona

Floridablanca

Ronda de

St. Antoni

Pelai

Plaça Catalunya (i)

Urquinaona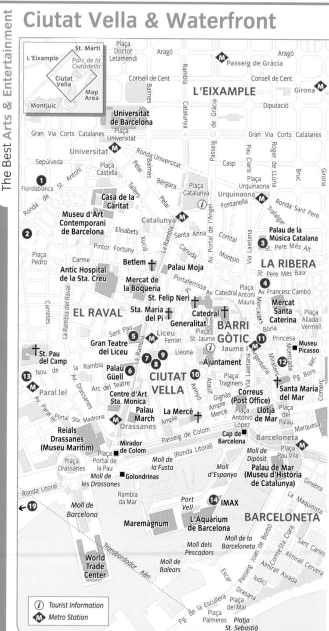

Fontanella

Ronda Sant Pere

Trafalgar

1

Casa de la Caritat

Catalunya

Elisabets

Santa Anna

Av. Portal de l'Angel

Comtal

Via Laietana

Palau de la Música Catalana

3 St. Pere Més Alt

Museu d'Art Contemporani de Barcelona

Pintor Fortuny

Xucla

La Rambla

Canuda

Montsió

LA RIBERA

St. Pere Més Baix

2

Plaça Pedro

Carme

Betlem †

Palau Moja

Portaferrissa

Plaça Antoni Maura

Av. Francesc Cambó

4

Antic Hospital de la Sta. Creu

Mercat de la Boqueria

Av. Catedral

Mercat Santa Caterina

Plaça Allada i Vermell

Carretes

Sant Pau

St. Felip Neri

EL RAVAL

Sta. Maria del Pi

Catedral †

Mercadés

Bòria

Princesa

11

Plaça

La Rambla del Raval

5 Liceu

Generalitat

Plaça St. Jaume

BARRI GÒTIC

Jaume I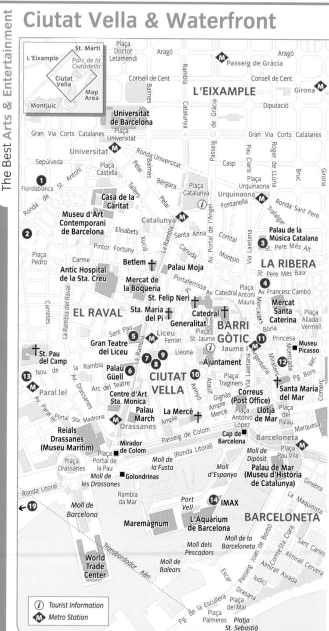

Montcada

Museu Picasso

† St. Pau del Camp

Gran Teatre del Liceu

Ferran

Lleona

(i)

Argenteria

12

Nou de la Rambla

7 **9**

8

Ajuntament

Santa Maria del Mar

Pg. Born

Rec

Comerç

13

Palau Güell **6**

Arc del Teatre

CIUTAT VELLA

Avinyó

10

Plaça Traginers

Gignàs

Correus (Post Office)

Plaça del Palau

Paral.lel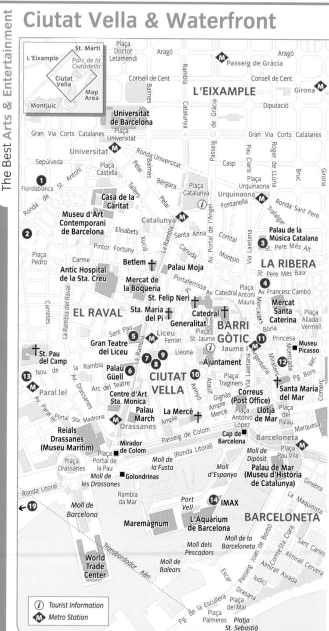

Centre d'Art Sta. Monica

Palau March

La Mercè

Ample

Ample

Plaça Antonio López

Llotja de Mar

Marquesa

Av. Paral.lel

Portal Sta. Madrona

Drassanes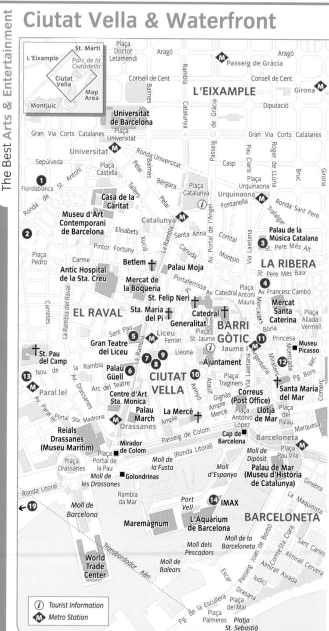

Mercè

Barceloneta

Reials Drassanes (Museu Marítim)

Mirador de Colom

Passeig de Colom

Cap de Barcelona ■

Plaça Pau Vila

Barceloneta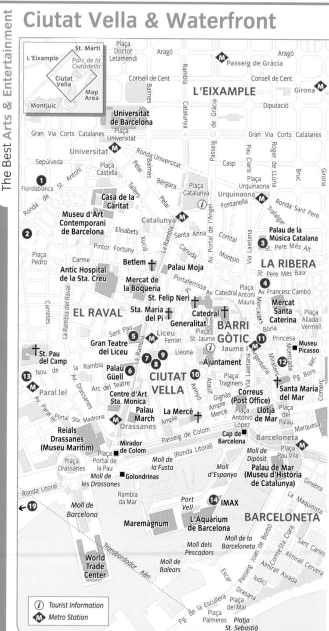

Plaça Drassanes

Portal de la Pau

Moll de (Ronda Litoral) la Fusta

Moll de Dipòsit

Palau de Mar (Museu d'Història de Catalunya)

Ginebra

Moll de les Drassanes

■ Golondrinas

Moll d'Espanya

La Maquinista

Ronda Litoral

19 ←

Moll de Barcelona

Rambla da Mar

Port Vell

14 IMAX

BARCELONETA

Comte.Sta. Clara

Sant Carles

World Trade Center

Transbordador Aeri

Maremàgnum

L'Aquàrium de Barcelona

Moll de la Barceloneta

Passeig Joan de Borbó

Almirall Cervera

Moll dels Pescadors

Moll de Balears

Escar

Pg. de la Escullera

Judici

Drasana

Almirall Aixada

Plaça del Mar

Plaça Palmeres

Platja St. Sebastià

(i) *Tourist Information*

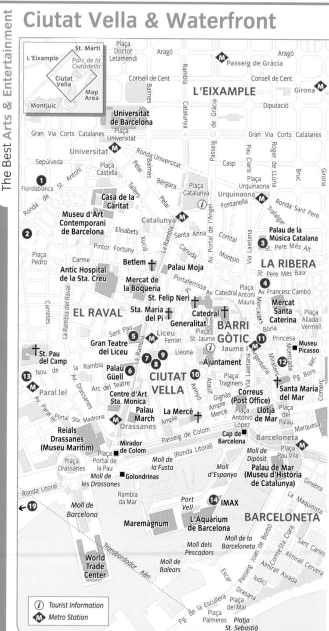 *Metro Station*

Arts & Entertainment

El Palau de la Música Catalana 3
El Tablao del Carmen 19
Espai Barroc 12
Gran Teatre del Liceu 5
Harlem Jazz Club 10
Icária 18
IMAX Port Vell 14
Jamboree 7
Jazz Sí Club (Taller de Músics) 2
L'Antic Teatre 4
L'Auditori 15
Los Tarantos 8
Palau Sant Jordi 19

PocketClub 19
Renoir Floridablanca 1
Restaurante Nervión Flamenco 11
Sala Apolo 13
Sala Razzmatazz 17
Sidecar Factory Club 9
Tablao Flamenco Cordobés 6
Teatre Mercat de les Flors 19
Teatre Nacional de Catalunya 16

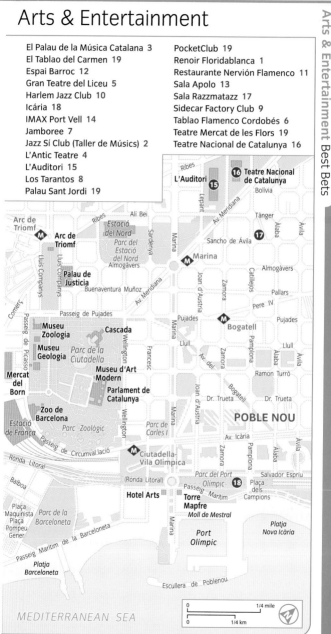

Barcelona Arts & Entertainment A to Z

The lobby of the Gran Teatre del Liceu.

Classical Music & Concert Venues

★★★ El Palau de la Música Catalana

LA RIBERA This 1908 concert hall, designed by Domènech i Montaner, is a *modernista* masterpiece. Concerts are primarily classical, though the administration has sought to widen exposure to the hall by adding jazz, world, and alternative rock. For daily guided tours of the building, see p 15. A recent extension called Petit Palau includes a luxury restaurant and rehearsal space, and occasionally hosts "Opera and Flamenco" programs (also held at Teatre Poliorama on La Rambla). *c/ Sant Francesc de Paula, 2.* ☎ *902-44-28-82. Tickets 20€– 70€. www.palaumusica.org. Metro: Urquinaona. Map p 122.*

★★★ Gran Teatre del Liceu

LA RAMBLA Barcelona's great opera house, founded in 1874, is one of the grandest in the world. Though it was gutted by fire in 1994, it was quickly rebuilt with donations, preserving the look and feel of the original. The Liceu has long been the home turf of the international opera stars José Carreras and Montserrat Caballé, both from Barcelona. In addition to opera, you'll find concerts, as well as recitals and chamber music, in the smaller **El Petit Liceu.** *La Rambla, 51–59.* ☎ *93-485-99-00. Tickets 20€– 95€. www.liceubarcelona.com. Metro: Liceu. Map p 122.*

★ L'Auditori

POBLE NOU A modern concert hall for classical music designed by the preeminent Spanish architect Rafael Moneo, this is the permanent home for the Orfeó Catala choral society and the OBC (Barcelona's Symphony Orchestra). It also plays host to renowned international musicians. Acoustics are superb. *c/ Lepant, 150.* ☎ *93-247-93-00. Tickets 15€–60€. www.auditori.org. Metro: Glòries. Map p 122.*

★ **La Casa dels Músics** GRACIA Claiming to be the smallest opera house in the world, this tiny, atmospheric stage, in the 19th-century home of the pianist Luís de Arquer, offers a unique opportunity for music lovers. Singers in the small-scale opera productions and *bel canto* are so close that you can see or even feel them sweat. Call ahead for reservations. *c/ Encarnació, 25.* ☎ *93-284-99-20. Tickets 20€–25€. www.lacasadelsmusics.com. Metro: Fontana. Map p 121.*

★ **Palau Sant Jordi** MONTJUIC This sleek indoor sports stadium, built for the '92 Olympics by the Japanese architect Arota Isozaki, hosts major rock and pop concerts by artists of the stature of Bruce Springsteen and the Cure. *Av. de L'Estadi, s/n.* ☎ *93-247-93-00. Tickets 20€–75€. Metro: Glòries. Map p 122.*

An orchestra plays at L'Auditori.

Film

★★ **Filmoteca** L'EIXAMPLE An art-house cinema funded by the Catalan government and a favorite of local and international *cineastes*. It shows classics and puts on festivals like "Italian Neorealism." *Cinema Aquitania, Av. Sarria, 31–33.* ☎ *93-410-75-90. www20.gencat.cat. Tickets 2.70€. Metro: Hospital Clínic. Map p 121.*

★ **Icária** WATERFRONT (VILA OLIMPICA) This multiplex of 15 screens is in a large mall in the Port Olimpic zone. Most films are mainstream releases, although a surprising number are small independent and European movies. Online booking all the time (general admission); numbered seats on weekends only. *Salvador Espriu, 61 (Vila Olimpica).* ☎ *93-221-75-85. www.yelmocineplex.es. Tickets 7.40€ (5.70€ Mon). Metro: Ciutadella–Vila Olimpica. Map p 122.*

★★ **IMAX Port Vell** WATERFRONT Barcelona's terrific IMAX theater shows all the latest large-format releases on three different types of projection systems (IMAX, OMNIMAX, and 3-D). *Moll de Espanya, s/n.* ☎ *93-225-11-11. www.imaxportvell.com. Tickets 9€. Metro: Drassanes. Map p 122.*

★ **Renoir Floridablanca** L'EIXAMPLE A multitude of mainstream international releases (in their original language) show on seven screens (as many as 10 different films in a single day). A sister cinema, the **Renoir Les Corts,** has six screens with some overlap. *Floridablanca, 135.* ☎ *93-426-33-37. Tickets: 6.80€ (4.80€ Mon). www.cinesrenoir.com. Metro: Universitat or Sant Antoni. Renoir Les Corts: c/ Eugenie d'Ors, 12.* ☎ *93-490-55-10. Metro: Les Corts. Map p 122.*

★★★ **Verdi** GRACIA A legendary movie house for true film fans, and the first in Barcelona to show original-version movies, Verdi's five screens are usually devoted to the most artistic and challenging films. A nearby annex, Verdi Park, has four additional screens. *Verdi: c/ Verdi, 32; Verdi Park, c/ Torrijos 49 (Gràcia).* ☎ *93-238-79-90. www. cines-verdi.com. Tickets: 7.50€ (5€ Mon). Late shows Fri and Sat. Metro: Fontana. Map p 121.*

Flamenco

El Tablao de Carmen MONTJUIC Within Poble Espanyol is this tourist favorite, presenting a pretty reliable flamenco show. Tuesday to Sunday 8pm to 1am. First show 9:30pm, second 11:30pm (midnight Fri–Sat). *Poble Espanyol de Montjuïc.* ☎ *93-325-68-95. www.tablaodecarmen. com. Dinner and show 45€ (tapas), 69€ (dinner); drink and show 35€. Metro: Espanya. Map p 122.*

★★ **Los Tarantos** BARRI GOTIC The oldest flamenco club in Barcelona (1963) has hosted the likes of Antonio Gades and Rosario, and respected Andalusian flamenco artists regularly make the pilgrimage here. An attractive theater space is excellent for both dance performances and music concerts. *Pl. Reial, 17.* ☎ *93-319-17-89. www.masimas. com/tarantos. Cover (includes 1 drink) 20€. Metro: Liceu. Map p 122.*

★★ **Palacio del Flamenco** L'EIXAMPLE Barcelona's newest flamenco dinner show inhabits a handsome old theater, with a very nice ambience. Two shows Monday to Saturday with dinner: 7 and 8:30pm. *Balmes, 139.* ☎ *93-218-72-37. www.palaciodelflamenco.com. Dinner and show 65€–75€; 1 drink and show 32€. Discounted (5€ cheaper) tickets available at bcnshop.barcelonaturisme.com. Metro: Provença. Map p 121.*

Restaurante Nervión Flamenco LA RIBERA This small space near the Picasso Museum stages a more informal, and cheaper, version of the flamenco shows in town. It's intimate and the restaurant serves all kinds of inexpensive tapas and paellas. Shows Friday 10pm. *Princesa, 2.* ☎ *93-315-21-03. www. restaurantenervion.com. Dinner and show 35€; drink and show 12€. Metro: Jaume I. Map p 122.*

Flamenco dancers and a singer at El Tablao de Carmen.

★★ **Tablao Flamenco Cordobés** LA RAMBLA   Near the waterfront, this Andalusian-style club has been around since 1970. The upstairs room hosts traditional *cuadro flamenco,* performances by singers, dancers, and a guitarist. Shows, though they don't approach the passionate displays seen in the deep south, are perhaps the most authentic in Barcelona. Three shows nightly with dinner: 7, 8:30, and 10pm. *La Rambla, 35.* ☎ *93-317-57-11. www.tablaocordobes.com. Dinner and show 60€–68€; 1 drink and show 37€. Metro: Drassanes. Map p 122.*

★ **Tirititran** L'EIXAMPLE   This *colmao flamenco*—a neighborhood restaurant-bar with live flamenco performances near Avenida La Diagonal—is a good option for those uninterested in slick, costumed productions aimed primarily at tourists. Downstairs is a small stage for concerts, which are often informal. *c/ Buenos Aires, 28.* ☎ *93-405-38-71. Metro: Urgell. Map p 121.*

Jazz & Cabaret

★ **Espai Barroc** LA RIBERA   This place is proudly over-the-top. Rooms in a medieval mansion, overflowing with objets d'art, busts, and Baroque-framed art, make a grand spot for a drink. But on Thursday nights, singers perform arias from opera's greatest hits. *c/ de la Montcada, 20.* ☎ *93-310-06-73. Cover varies. Metro: Jaume I. Map p 122.*

★★★ **Harlem Jazz Club** BARRI GOTIC   One of Barcelona's oldest and finest jazz clubs was remodeled, but the tiny spot remains intimate and the music wide-ranging, covering bebop, blues, bossa nova, and more. *Comtessa de Sobradiel, 8.* ☎ *93-310-07-55. www.harlemjazz club.es. Free admission Mon–Thurs; 4€–10€ Fri–Sat, 1-drink min. Closed Aug. Metro: Jaume I. Map p 122.*

The Harlem Jazz Club.

★ **Jamboree** BARRI GOTIC   Tucked into a basement of Plaça Reial, this longtime standard-bearer for live blues and jazz—going strong for more than 5 decades—occasionally draws big names (back in the day, Chet Baker, Ella Fitzgerald, and Elvin Jones played here), though often the headlining acts are talented up-and-comers. Late in the evening, it gets rowdier and the space becomes a nightclub for a younger crowd, with hip-hop downstairs and world music upstairs. *Pl. Reial, 17.* ☎ *93-301-75-64. www. masimas.com/jamboree. Shows 5€–10€. Metro: Liceu. Map p 122.*

Jazz Sí Club (Taller de Músics)

RAVAL   A free-flowing program of live music nightly is the *raison d'etre* of this intimate music school, auditorium, and bar. Miguel Poveda and Enrique Morente, two current stars of flamenco, have played for students, teachers, and an enthusiastic public. Every night features a different musical genre, and programs go late. *c/ Requesens, 2.* ☎ *93-329-00-20. www.tallerde musics.com. Admission 5€–8€. Metro: Sant Antoni. Map p 122.*

★★ La Cova del Drac Jazz-Room

ZONA ALTA   This sleek, modern, and posh new jazz club in the upper Barcelona neighborhood of Sant Gervasi—the uptown sister of Jamboree—offers live jazz from top international acts and DJ/dance music, but the tiny spot remains intimate and the music wide-ranging, covering bebop, blues, bossa nova, and more. *Vallmajor, 33 (Pl. Adrià).* ☎ *93-319-17-89. www.masimas. com/la-cova-del-drac. Free admission Mon–Thurs; 4€–10€ Fri–Sat, 1-drink min. Closed Aug. Metro: Jaume I. Map p 121.*

★ La Pedrera

L'EIXAMPLE   Concerts are no longer staged up on the rooftop of Gaudí's emblematic *modernista* apartment building, though Caixa de Catalunya still offers occasional jazz (and classical) performances in the auditorium. *Pg. de Gràcia, 92 (at Provença).* ☎ *902-40-09-73 or 93-484-59-00. http://obra social.caixacatalunya.es. Admission 3€–10€. Schedule varies. Metro: Diagonal or Provença. Map p 121.*

★★★ Luz de Gas

L'EIXAMPLE   For years, this glamorous turn-of-the-century music hall has reigned supreme in Barcelona for its stylish looks (chandeliers and thick red curtains) and programming of live music, which is very often Latin jazz; past artists include Charlie Haden and Danilo Pérez. Several performance areas each have their own bars. The lineup covers jazz, pop, folk, R&B, and salsa. Sala B is another space next door with a more modern, industrial look. *c/ Muntaner, 246.* ☎ *93-209-77-11. www.luzdegas. com. Cover (includes 1 drink) 20€– 25€. Metro: Diagonal. Map p 121.*

Pop & Rock

★ Bikini

SANTS   An out-of-the-way rock club near the L'illa shopping center, this space has a great dance floor and three separate areas. It has hosted some pretty big names in pop and rock, including Thievery Corporation and Marianne Faithful. The club stays open late Wednesday through Sunday, after shows, spinning funk and hip-hop. *c/ Déu i Mata, 105 (off Av. Diagonal), Les Corts.* ☎ *93-322-08-00. www.bikinibcn. com. Admission 7€–15€. Metro: Les Corts or Maria Cristina. Map p 121.*

Advance Tickets & Listings

For the latest concert, theater, and event listings, pick up a copy of the weekly **Guía del Ocio** (www.guiadelociobcn.com), a guide to all entertainment in Barcelona. It's available at newsstands and written in Spanish, but it's pretty comprehensible even to non-Spanish speakers, with a small section in English at the back. Also worth a look are **Barcelona Metropolitan** (www.barcelona-metropolitan.com), **Go-Mag** (www.go-mag.com), and **What's On Barcelona** (www.whatsonbcn.com).

Other helpful services are **Tel-Entrada** (☎ 902-10-12-12; www.telentrada.com), **ServiCaixa** (☎ 902-33-22-11; www.servicaixa.com), and **Tick Tack Ticket** (☎ 902-15-00-25; www.ticktackticket.com [from abroad, ☎ 34/93-445-06-60]).

Barcelona Music Festivals

A summer tradition in Barcelona is ★★ Grec (☎ 93-301-77-75; www.barcelonafestival.com), an annual festival of international theater, music, and dance. From the last week of June to the end of the first week in August, Grec showcases big names (such as Van Morrison) and everything from blues to Brazilian bossa nova and avant-garde dance at the Teatre Grec on Montjuïc and other venues. **Primavera Sound** (www.primaverasound.com), an alternative-rock festival held at the Parc del Forum in late May and early June, attracts major bands like Sonic Youth, Wilco, and Drive-By Truckers. **Sonar** (www.sonar.es), one of the biggest electronic-music festivals in the world (held in mid-June), showcases avant-garde dance music and multimedia art from across Europe. But its sheer size—on multiple stages both day and night—and headlining artists like Björk and Massive Attack mean this is no marginal, niche festival. In Barcelona, it's pretty much mainstream.

★★ **PocketClub** MONTJUIC Part of Teatre Mercat de les Flors, this cool little club schedules infrequent performances (just two Thurs a month), but they're the kind of alternative-rock shows that draw hipsters, such as Iron and Wine, Destroyer, the Clientele, and other indie bands. *c/ Lleida, 59 (Mercat de les Flors).* ☎ *93-285-26-26. www.pocketbcn.com. Admission 10€–25€. Metro: Espanya. Map p 122.*

★★ **Sala Apolo** POBLE SEC This 1940s dance hall covers the bases: besides "Nasty Mondays" and "Crappy Tuesdays," it programs alternative cinema, Latin music, funk nights, and gay nights, and on Fridays and Saturdays it becomes a happening dance club, Nitsa, with occasional big-name DJs. And they fit in rock and jazz shows, too. *c/ Nou de la Rambla, 113 (Poble Sec).* ☎ *93-441-40-01. www.sala-apolo.com. Admission varies. Metro: Poble Sec. Map p 122.*

★ **Sala KGB** GRACIA Not exactly secretive, but a little out of the way, this club, a longtime hangout of young underground and garage rockers, programs independent rock, metal, and reggae bands, as well as electronic house and dance music. *c/ Alegre de Dalt, 55.* ☎ *93-210-59-06. www.salakgb.net. Cover 10€. Metro: Lesseps. Map p 121.*

★★ **Sala Razzmatazz** PORT OLIMPIC/POBLE NOU This sprawling, young-skewing club—with five separate music ambiences within—is also a rocking concert venue. Its "Pop Club" hosts Spanish and celebrated international pop, alternative, hip-hop, and rock acts, such as Arctic Monkeys, LCD Soundsystem, and Sonic Youth. *c/ dels Almogavers, 122 (at Pamplona).* ☎ *93-320-82-00. www.salarazzmatazz.com. Cover varies. Metro: Bogatell or Marina. Map p 122.*

★ **Sidecar Factory Club** BARRI GOTIC Check out Barcelona's indigenous indie-rock scene at this basement club, which occasionally scores bands with international followings, such as Portastatic. *Pl. Reial, 7.* ☎ *93-302-15-86. www.side carfactoryclub.com. Shows 5€–20€. Metro: Liceu. Map p 122.*

The Best Arts & Entertainment

Spectator Sports

★★ Fútbol Club Barcelona

SANTS   Barcelona's immensely popular football, or soccer, team—perennially one of the best in Europe—plays at Camp Nou, a 120,000-seat stadium. To see "Barça" (*bar-sa*), as the locals affectionately refer to the team, take on one of its chief rivals, such as Real Madrid, is a treat that transcends sport and approaches social anthropology. Although many games are sold out long in advance, individual tickets are frequently available. How popular is the team? The **Museu del Fútbol Club Barcelona (Soccer Museum)** is one of the most-visited museums in Spain. *Av. del Papa Joan XXIII; ticket office c/ Aristides Maillol, 12–18.* ☎ *93-496-36-00. Tickets start at 30€. www.fcbarcelona.com. Museum: c/ Aristides Maillol, 7–9.* ☎ *93-496-36-08. Admission 14€–17€. Metro: María Cristina, Palau Reial, or Collblanc. Map p 121.*

Teatre Mercat de Les Flors.

Theater

★ L'Antic Teatre LA RIBERA

This small, 18th-century theater is just steps from El Palau de la Música Catalana. It programs innovative and risky performances, which are likely to be all over the cultural map: dance, theater, multimedia, circus, music, and more, from both local and touring companies. The resident company is Semolina Tomic, headed by a Croatian residing in Barcelona. Tickets are inexpensive, so it's a good place for those looking for something new. *c/ Verdaguer i Callis, 12.* ☎ *93-315-23-54. Tickets 6€–15€. www.lanticteatre.com. Metro: Urquinaona. Map p 122.*

★★★ Teatre Mercat de Les Flors

MONTJUIC   Although the structure dates to the 1929 World's Fair, this Catalan theater's first performance was *Carmen* in 1983. The theater plays host to respected companies of drama, dance, and music, and schedules occasional avant-garde art festivals. There's a restaurant overlooking the city's rooftops. *c/ Lleida, 59.* ☎ *93-426-18-75. www.mercatflors.org. Ticket prices vary. Metro: Pl. Espanya. Map p 122.*

★★ Teatre Nacional de Catalunya

POBLE NOU   A swanky, pseudo-Roman modern theater, the work of the architect Ricardo Bofill, is home to a major Catalan company that puts on both classic and contemporary plays, including those of writers such as Tom Stoppard, Oscar Wilde, and Harold Pinter, as well as modern dance. Productions are in Catalan except in rare instances. *Pl. de les Arts, 1.* ☎ *93-306-57-00. www.tnc.cat. Tickets 5€–35€. Metro: Glòries. Map p 122.* ●

Lodging **Best Bets**

Best **Old-City Location**
★★ Hotel Neri $$$ c/ Sant Sever, 5
(p 142)

Best **In-House Restaurants**
★★★ ABaC $$$$ Av. Tibidabo, 1
(p 136); and ★★★ Hotel Omm $$$$
c/ Rosselló, 265 (p 142)

Best **for Would-Be Aristocrats**
★★ El Palace Barcelona $$$$
Gran Via de les Corts Catalanes, 668
(p 137)

Best **Affordable Design**
★★ Praktik Rambla $$ Rambla de
Catalunya, 67 (p 143); and ★★★
The 5 Rooms $$ c/ Pau Claris, 72
(p 144)

Best **Cutting-Edge Design**
★★★ Hotel Omm $$$$ c/ Rosselló,
265 (p 142)

Best **Antidote to Minimalism**
★ Hostal L'Antic Espai $$ Gran Via
de les Cortes Catalanes, 660 (p 139)

Best **Business Hotel**
★★★ Hotel Arts $$$$ c/ de la
Marina, 19–21 (p 139)

Best **In-House Museum**
★★★ Hotel Claris $$$$ c/ Pau
Claris, 150 (p 140)

Best **Service**
★★★ Mandarin Oriental Barcelona
$$$$ Pg. de Gràcia, 28–30 (p 142)

Best **Gay Hotel**
★ Hotel Axel $$$ c/ Aribau, 33
(p 140)

Best **Boutique Hotels**
★★★ ABaC $$$$ Av. Tibidabo, 1
(p 136); and ★★ Duquesa de Car-
dona $$$ Pg. Colom, 12 (p 137)

Best **City Views**
★★★ Gran Hotel La Florida $$$$
Ctra. de Vallvidrera, 83–93 (p 138)

Best **Sea Views**
★★★ Hotel Arts $$$$ c/ de la
Marina, 19–21 (p 139); and ★ W
Barcelona $$$ Pl. de la Rosa dels
Vents, 1 (p 144)

Best **for Families**
★ Hispanos Siete Suiza $$
c/ Sicilia, 255 (p 138)

Best **Chic Bed & Breakfast**
★★★ The 5 Rooms $$ c/ Pau Claris,
72 (p 144)

Best **Swimming Pools**
★★ Grand Hotel Central $$$ Via
Laietana, 30 (p 138); and ★★ Hotel
1898 $$$ La Rambla, 109 (p 141)

Best **Luxurious Hideaways**
★★★ ABaC $$$$ Av. Tibidabo, 1
(p 136); and ★★★ Gran Hotel La
Florida $$$$ Ctra. de Vallvidrera,
83–93 (p 138)

Best **Steps Up from a Hostel**
★ Gat Xino $ c/ Hospital, 155
(p 138); and ★ Hostemplo $
c/ Sicilia, 276 (p 139)

Best **Historic (Modernista)
Hotel**
★★★ Hotel Casa Fuster $$$$
Pg. de Gràcia, 132 (p 140)

Best **Hipster Hotels**
★ Casa Camper $$$ c/ Elisabets, 11
(p 136); and ★★ Chic & Basic Born
$$ c/ de la Princesa, 50 (p 136)

Best **Spa Pampering**
★★★ Hotel Arts $$$$ c/ de la
Marina, 19–21 (p 139); and ★★★
Gran Hotel La Florida $$$$ Ctra. de
Vallvidrera, 83–93 (p 138)

Previous page: A room at the Hotel 1898.

L'Eixample Lodging

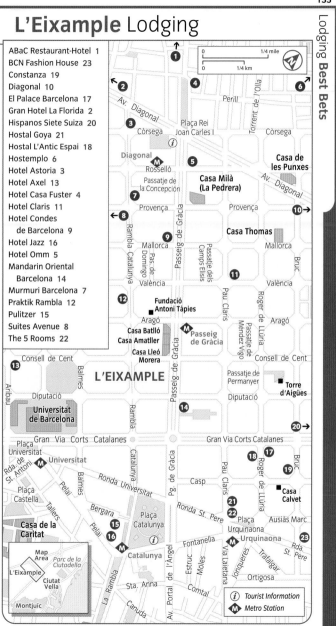

ABaC Restaurant-Hotel 1
BCN Fashion House 23
Constanza 19
Diagonal 10
El Palace Barcelona 17
Gran Hotel La Florida 2
Hispanos Siete Suiza 20
Hostal Goya 21
Hostal L'Antic Espai 18
Hostemplo 6
Hotel Astoria 3
Hotel Axel 13
Hotel Casa Fuster 4
Hotel Claris 11
Hotel Condes
  de Barcelona 9
Hotel Jazz 16
Hotel Omm 5
Mandarin Oriental
  Barcelona 14
Murmuri Barcelona 7
Praktik Rambla 12
Pulitzer 15
Suites Avenue 8
The 5 Rooms 22

Ciutat Vella & Waterfront Lodging

Tourist Information
Metro Station

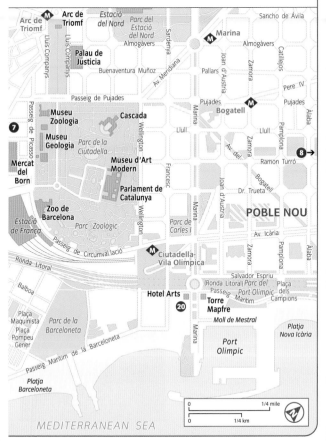

Barcelona Hotels A to Z

★★★ **kids** **ABaC** ZONA ALTA
This new concept—gastrohotel—is a delight for sybarites and ideal for this design- and gastronomy-crazed city. A small, luxurious boutique hotel in a 19th-century villa on one of Barcelona's swankiest streets, it is built around a Michelin two-star restaurant that was formerly a centerpiece of the old quarter. This new, high-design place, which also offers seductive modern rooms and a small spa, is the perfect place for guests who come to take in the best of Barcelona with all their senses. *Av. Tibidabo, 1.* ☎ *93-319-66-00. www.abacbarcelona.com. 15 units. Doubles 320€–700€. AE, DC, MC, V. Metro: Pl. Kennedy. Map p 133.*

kids **BCN Fashion House**
L'EIXAMPLE One of few bed-and-breakfasts in Barcelona, this comfortable spot, in a nicely restored 19th-century town house with a leafy communal terrace, is a good-value, homey place to stay. Each pair of bedrooms shares one bathroom. Families should check out the suite, a self-catering apartment. *c/ Bruc, 13.* ☎ *93-790-40-44. www.bcn-fashion house.com. 35 units. Doubles 55€–125€, including breakfast. MC, V. Metro: Urquinaona. Map p 133.*

★ **Casa Camper** RAVAL If you're a fan of funky Camper shoes, this idiosyncratic, design-trippy place, where all rooms have sitting rooms, is probably for you. The hotel's aesthetics are as playful as the company's shoe stores, though it's a little pricey for the transitional neighborhood and the young, design-obsessed crowd it courts. *c/ Elisabets, 11.* ☎ *93-342-62-80. www.camper.com/ web/en/casacamper.asp. 25 units. Doubles 215€–293€. AE, DC, MC, V. Metro: Catalunya. Map p 134.*

★★ **kids** **Chic & Basic Born** LA RIBERA The concept is simple: IKEA-design, Euro-minimalist rooms that attract the hordes of young and hip travelers, in neighborhoods where they'll be partying as well as sleeping (more of the former). Rooms in the 100-year-old building are white-on-white and playfully urbane, with colored "light curtains." Rooms are M, L, and XL—some are quite compact, others very generous in size, with quiet balconies. Also offers apartments. *c/ de la Princesa, 50.* ☎ *93-295-46-52. www.chicandbasic.com. 78 units. Doubles 120€–195€. AE, DC, MC, V. Metro: Jaume I. Map p 134.*

★ **Ciutat Barcelona Hotel** LA RIBERA A bargain hotel that offers a lot of cool design and comfort, this addition to the hip neighborhood,

Quirky touches can be found throughout Casa Camper.

A room at Duquesa de Cardona.

just steps from the Picasso Museum, is a winner. Rooms are crisply contemporary and clean, and there's a nice little rooftop pool and deck. *c/ de la Princesa, 35.* ☎ *93-269-74-75. www.ciutatbarcelona.com. 78 units. Doubles 150€–170€. AE, DC, MC, V. Metro: Arc de Triomf or Jaume I. Map p 134.*

★★ **Constanza** L'EIXAMPLE Travelers looking for affordable Barcelona style will be pleased with this small boutique hotel. Although rooms aren't large, they are modern and comfortable, and the hotel's very well located, within walking distance of Plaça de Catalunya. A room with its own private terrace is a real bargain. *c/ Bruc, 33.* ☎ *93-270-19-10. www.hotelconstanza.com. 20 units. Doubles 140€–160€. AE, MC, V. Metro: Urquinaona. Map p 133.*

★★ **Diagonal** L'EIXAMPLE/GRACIA Upping the ante of cutting-edge architecture is this massive Silken hotel. Mod and flashy, it may look playful, but the hotel is dead serious about hip design. Next to Torre Agbar, some rooms have straight-shot views of La Sagrada Família. *Av. Diagonal, 205.* ☎ *93-489-53-00. www.hoteles-silken. com. 240 units. Doubles 130€–240€. AE, DC, MC, V. Metro: Catalunya or Liceu. Map p 133.*

★★ **Duquesa de Cardona** WATERFRONT A sedate boutique hotel across the street from the marina, this restored 19th-century palace is elegant and intimate. It also has something unique: a large rooftop solarium terrace with a pool and great views of the port. *Pg. Colom, 12.* ☎ *93-268-90-90. www.hduquesa decardona.com. 44 units. Doubles 185€–285€. AE, DC, MC, V. Metro: Jaume I or Drassanes. Map p 134.*

El Jardí Hotel BARRI GOTIC Simple and easygoing, this small budget hotel has an extraordinary location, overlooking two of the prettiest plazas in the heart of Ciutat Vella. Rooms are somewhat austere, with bright lighting, but five have private terraces. *Pl. Sant Josep Oriol, 1.* ☎ *93-301-59-00. www.hoteljardi-barcelona.com. 40 units. Doubles 60€–120€. MC, V. Metro: Liceu. Map p 134.*

★★ **El Palace Barcelona** L'EIXAMPLE Though this 1919 Art Deco hotel has changed names, many still refer to it as the Ritz, and the grace and old-money elegance remain. It's white-glove treatment all the way here. Public rooms are grand and aristocratic; guest rooms are large and formal. Currently undergoing a massive renovation, which has reduced the size of the

The luxurious lobby at El Palace Barcelona.

hotel. *Gran Vía de les Corts Cat-alanes, 668.* ☎ *93-510-11-30. www.hotelpalacebarcelona.com. 122 units. Doubles 195€–585€. AE, DC, MC, V. Metro: Pg. de Gràcia. Map p 133.*

★ **kids** **Gat Xino** RAVAL   Just because you don't want to spend a lot of money doesn't mean you don't want some style. A major step up from hostels, this groovy place is popular with hipsters, design sorts, young families, and travelers with more style than cash. Rooms are small and spare, with a bright green, white, and black aesthetic, and there's a cool rooftop terrace. A sister hotel, Gat Raval (c/ Joaquín Costa, 4; ☎ 93-481-66-70), in the same 'hood, is similar in style, but cheaper and a tad plainer (not all have en-suite bathrooms). *c/ Hospi-tal, 149–155.* ☎ *93-324-88-33. www.gataccommodation.com. 35 units. Doubles 78€–110€, including break-fast. MC, V. Metro: Liceu. Map p 134.*

★★ **Grand Hotel Central** LA RIBERA   In a palatial 1926 mansion owned by an old Catalan family, this property has been beautifully con-verted to a contemporary luxury hotel. Rooms are warmly decorated in rich creams and chocolates. The spectacular rooftop infinity pool, surrounded by wood decking and views of the Gothic Quarter and the sea, is a bonus and privilege. *Vía Laietana, 30.* ☎ *93-295-79-00. www.grandhotelcentral.com. 147 units. Doubles 140€–275€. AE, DC, MC, V. Metro: Jaume I. Map p 134.*

★★★ **kids** **Gran Hotel La Flor-ida** MT. TIBIDABO/ENVIRONS   High above Barcelona, this palatial hotel is a magnificent refuge if pampering, luxury, and relaxation are your pri-mary concerns. While the views across Barcelona to the sea are astounding, the hotel's not conve-nient if you're set on seeing and doing lots of things. Yet the hotel, originally from the 1920s, certainly earns the *gran* (great) in its name, with plush, soothing designer rooms, a spa, and an infinity pool. *Ctra. Vall-vidrera (al Tibidabo), 83–93 (7km/4.3 miles from Barcelona).* ☎ *93-259-30-00. www.hotellaflorida.com. 74 units. Doubles 230€–610€. AE, DC, MC, V. Map p 133.*

★ **kids** **Hispanos Siete Suiza** L'EIXAMPLE   An aparthotel with the comforts of a top-flight hotel, the Suiza—with a lobby of vintage auto-mobiles—is perfect for families and long-term stays. Apartments in the historic house are two-bedroom, two-bath, with a living room and kitchen, and guests have free access to a sports center with pool and yoga. But best of all, some of the hotel's profits go toward a cancer foundation established by the original owner of the house. *c/ Sicilia, 255.* ☎ *93-208-20-51. www.hispanos7suiza.com. 19 units. Doubles (2-bedroom apt) 220€–240€, including breakfast. AE, DC, MC, V. Metro: Sagrada Família. Map p 133.*

★ **Hostal Goya** L'EIXAMPLE A refreshingly smart, centrally located *hostal* and very good value, this small inn is clean and friendly. The best and quietest rooms are in the recently renovated Principal wing; others are small and dark. Most who stay here are young people in Barcelona to have a good time. *c/ Pau Claris, 74.* ☎ *93-302-25-65. www. hostalgoya.com. 19 units. Doubles 90€–105€. MC, V. Metro: Urquinaona. Map p 133.*

★ **Hostal L'Antic Espai** L'EIXAMPLE If you've had it with generic contemporary minimalism, this is your place, a guesthouse stuffed to the gills with antiques of the (faux) Louis XV variety. Run by a Brazilian and a Cuban, it's also an antidote to impersonal and overpriced hotels. *c/ Gran Via de les Cortes Catalanes, 660.* ☎ *93-304-19-45. www.anticespai.com. 10 units. Doubles 65€–135€. MC, V. Metro: Urquinaona. Map p 133.*

★ **Hostemplo** L'EIXAMPLE Just above Avinguda Diagonal, just a couple blocks from Gaudí's Sagrada Família, this agreeable small hotel, inaugurated in 2009 in a *modernista* building, is clean and simple, and a very good value, even if rooms are a little tight. *c/ Sicilia, 276.* ☎ *93-476-55-75. www.hostemplo.com. 10 units. Doubles 110€–155€. MC, V. Metro: Sagrada Família. Map p 133.*

★★★ **Hotel Arts** WATERFRONT One of only three skyscrapers in Barcelona, this sleek, high-tech luxury hotel is on the beach and enjoys sweeping beach views. Service is personable and efficient, as you'd expect from a Ritz-Carlton property, making this a favorite of business travelers and celebs. The outdoor pool, swanky new spa overlooking the marina, and restaurant by star chef Sergi Arola only add to the allure. *c/ de la Marina, 19–21.* ☎ *800/241-3333 or 93-221-10-00. www.ritz carlton.com/hotels/barcelona. 482 units. Doubles 350€–800€. AE, DC, MC, V. Metro: Ciutadella–Vila Olimpica. Map p 134.*

★ kids **Hotel Astoria** L'EIXAMPLE A renovated 1950s hotel with enduring style, this winning member of the Derby chain (which owns the Claris) is elegant but relaxed. Its warmly decorated accommodations and rooftop pool and sauna make it a very good value, even if you'll have to walk a few blocks to restaurants and attractions near Passeig de Gràcia. *c/ París, 203.* ☎ *93-209-83-11. www.derbyhotels.com. 114 units. Doubles 140€–250€. AE, DC, MC, V. Metro: Diagonal. Map p 133.*

The Hotel Arts offers spectacular water views.

The Hotel Banys Orientals.

★ **Hotel Axel** L'EIXAMPLE   Filling a niche in Barcelona, this recently refurbished midsize hotel serves an international gay population and is confident enough to decorate rooms with erotic art (but declare itself "heterofriendly"). Rooms are stylish, with top-quality bedding, and the hip cocktail bar, rooftop pool, and sun deck are prized. *c/ Aribau, 33.* ☎ *93-323-93-93. www. hotelaxel.com. 105 units. Doubles 150€–220€. AE, DC, MC, V. Metro: Universitat. Map p 133.*

★ **Hotel Banys Orientals** LA RIBERA   A pioneer leading the way for stylish but inexpensive boutique hotels, this cool place is immensely popular, as much for its bargain rates and hip style as its terrific location near El Born. Rooms are small but chic, though noise-sensitive guests should seek one at the back; the area is full of late-night revelers. *c/ L'Argenteria, 37.* ☎ *93-268-84-60. www.hotelbanysorientals.com. 43 units. Doubles 100€–130€. AE, DC, MC, V. Metro: Jaume I. Map p 134.*

★ **kids Hotel Barcelona Cate-dral** BARRI GOTIC   Right across from the Cathedral, this stylishly modern midsize hotel features unexpected bonuses, including a pool, terrace, cooking lessons, wine tastings, and guided tours around

the old city. *c/ Capellans, 4.* ☎ *93-304-22-55. www.barcelonacatedral. com. 80 units. Doubles 185€–225€. AE, DC, MC, V. Metro: Jaume I. Map p 134.*

★★★ **Hotel Casa Fuster** GRA-CIA   Occupying a lovely *modernista* building, Casa Fuster is one of the most emblematic places to stay in the city. It has a feel of period indulgence, with every modern amenity, including pool, restaurant, bar, lounges, illuminated night terrace, and cool jazz club. Rooms are very luxe, with splashes of color and texture. *Pg. de Gràcia, 132.* ☎ *902-20-23-45 or 93-255-30-00. www. hotelcasafuster.com. 105 units. Doubles 175€–475€. AE, DC, MC, V. Metro: Diagonal. Map p 133.*

★★★ **Hotel Claris** L'EIXAMPLE   Long one of my favorite luxury hotels in Barcelona, where modern design commingles with a landmark 19th-century palace facade and a for-guests-only museum of Egyptian art. Rooms, many of which are split-level and even two-story, are a mix of cool chic and warm sophistication. On the top-floor terrace are a small pool and lovely views of the surrounding Eixample neighborhood. *c/ Pau Claris, 150.* ☎ *90-099-00-11 or 93-487-62-62. www. derbyhotels.com. 120 units.*

Doubles 190€–645€. AE, DC, MC, V. Metro: Pg. de Gràcia. Map p 133.

★ Hotel Condes de Barcelona

L'EIXAMPLE   With a prestigious corner location on Passeig de Gràcia, this late-19th-century mansion is elegant and sophisticated, though an annex across the street doesn't have quite the same style. The recent arrival of one of the Basque Country's most celebrated chefs, Martín Berasategui, and his restaurant, Lasarte, have given the hotel a new verve. *Pg. de Gràcia, 73–75.* ☎ *93-445-00-00. www.condesde barcelona.com. 183 units. Doubles 145€–325€. AE, DC, MC, V. Metro: Pg. de Gràcia. Map p 133.*

★ kids Hotel Curious EL RAVAL

In tune with the funky style of this emerging, artsy neighborhood, this value-oriented boutique hotel has a fun name and fun with its interiors, which have splashes of color and large-format, black-and-white landscape photographs above the beds. A good choice if you're looking for something different. *c/ Carme, 25.* ☎ *93-301-44-84. www.hotelcurious.*

com. 25 units. Doubles 80€–105€. MC, V. Metro: Liceu. Map p 134.

★★ kids Hotel 1898 LA RAMBLA

This large hotel, opened in 2002, occupies a late-19th-century building that was once the Philippine Tobacco Co. headquarters. It has been strikingly converted, with bold artwork, stripes, and colors; most spectacular is the underground pool beneath brick arches (although the rooftop bar and pool are a close second). *La Rambla, 109 (entrance on c/ Pintor Fortuny).* ☎ *93-552-95-52. www.hotel1898.com. 169 units. Doubles 165€–370€. AE, DC, MC, V. Metro: Catalunya. Map p 134.*

★ Hotel Jazz L'EIXAMPLE

Around the corner from La Rambla, Hotel Jazz aims, by name and middle-of-the-road contemporary design, for a wide international clientele (many of whom appear to be young people on group junkets). The impressive lobby has plenty of glass and bleached-wood floors; soundproof rooms are attractive if a bit generic. But the star of the show is the rooftop pool and wood-deck terrace. *c/*

The underground pool at the Hotel 1898.

Pelai, 3. ☎ *93-552-96-96. www. nnhotels.es. 180 units. Doubles 165€–205€. AE, DC, MC, V. Metro: Catalunya or Universitat. Map p 133.*

★ **kids** **Hotel Miramar Barcelona** MONTJUIC   Tucked into the hillside, next to the Montjuïc Park gardens and with majestic views over the city and the Mediterranean, this 1920s palace was restored and converted into a hotel. A bold, modern new addition by Oscar Tusquets envelops the original mansion. The result is a chic mix of period details and modern decor. Gardens and indoor and outdoor pools make this a relaxing option for families. *Pl. Carlos Ibáñez, 3.* ☎ *93-281-16-00. www. hotelmiramarbarcelona.com. 75 units. Doubles 170€–320€. AE, DC, MC, V. Metro: Paral.lel. Map p 134.*

★★ **Hotel Neri** BARRI GOTIC   A sumptuous Gothic palace discreetly tucked away on charming Plaça Felip Neri, this small, upscale hotel is romance incarnate, all velvet drapes and soft-lit rooms. Rooms are luxurious and intimate, with fine linens, and the restaurant and cafe on the square are unexpected bonuses. A true find in the Old City, it's unlike any other hotel. *c/ Sant Sever, 5.* ☎ *93-304-06-55. www. hotelneri.com. 22 units. Doubles 265€–280€. AE, DC, MC, V. Metro: Jaume I. Map p 134.*

The Hotel Neri is well located on the delightful Plaça Felip Neri.

★★★ **Hotel Omm** L'EIXAMPLE
The hotel with perhaps the most positive buzz in Barcelona is this sleek temple of hip, Zen-like design and an even cooler clientele. Its restaurant, Moo (p 104), is one of the city's best, and the lounges attract Barcelona's most stylish scenemakers. Design freaks will be in heaven; the place was created for them. The rooftop lap pool and deck have views of La Pedrera. *c/ Rosselló, 265.* ☎ *93-445-40-00. www.hotelomm.es. 59 units. Doubles 230€–330€. AE, DC, MC, V. Metro: Diagonal. Map p 133.*

H10 Racó Del Pi BARRI GOTIC   A member of a small, Barcelona-based hotel chain, this attractive, small hotel is intimate and perfectly located, in a historic building on one of the most atmospheric streets in the Gothic Quarter. Rooms aren't huge, but they do feature a clean, stylish aesthetic. *Plaça del Pi, 7.* ☎ *93-342-61-90. www.hotelraco delpi.com. 37 units. Doubles 160€– 195€. AE, DC, MC, V. Metro: Jaume I or Liceu. Map p 134.*

★★★ **Mandarin Oriental Barcelona** L'EIXAMPLE   In former bank headquarters and a superb Passeig de Gràcia location, the new Mandarin has created a splash with its ultrastylish, Zen-like rooms (light-filled, starkly modern, and largely white), stunning spa (in the old bank vault), jaw-dropping rooftop lap pool, and restaurant by a star female chef with five Michelin stars. It has quickly become Barcelona's most prestigious hotel address and *the* place to be seen. *Pg. de Gràcia, 28–30.* ☎ *93-151-88-88. www.mandarin oriental.com/barcelona. 98 units. Doubles 325€–525€. AE, DC, MC, V. Metro: Pg. de Gràcia. Map p 133.*

kids **Marina Folch** WATERFRONT
If you're looking for beachside accommodations without busting your budget, this small and friendly

The hip lobby of Hotel Omm.

guesthouse in Barceloneta is a good bet. Rooms—some of which have balconies and port views—are very no-nonsense but clean and comfortable, and worth every euro. *c/ del Mar, 16.* ☎ *93-310-37-09. 10 units. Doubles 60€–75€. AE, DC, MC, V. Metro: Barceloneta. Map p 134.*

★★ Murmuri Barcelona

L'EIXAMPLE   Barcelona's penchant for great design and the reinvigoration of classic buildings continues unabated, and this is one of the newest and best examples. Noted British designer Kelly Hoppen's touch (most evident in public spaces) is warmer and more romantic, with a bit more classic elegance than most of the new crop of hotels. *Rambla de Catalunya, 104.* ☎ *93-492-22-44. www.murmuri.com. 43 units. Doubles 179€–509€. AE, DC, MC, V. Metro: Diagonal. Map p 133.*

★ Park Hotel LA RIBERA   This

sleek, recently updated hotel at the edge of El Born is a handsome example of midcentury architecture, notable for its spiral staircase and the lobby's mosaic-tiled bar. The crisply modern rooms are not huge, but they are a pretty fair value, and in a good location for someone who wants to be near, but not on top of, El Born. *Av. Marquès de l'Argentera, 11.* ☎ *93-319-60-00. www.park hotelbarcelona.com. 91 units. Doubles*

169€–179€. *AE, DC, MC, V. Metro: Barceloneta or Jaume I. Map p 134.*

Petit Palace Opera Garden LA

RAMBLA   A member of a successful Spanish chain, this midsize hotel is near, but not on, La Rambla, and just seconds from La Boquería food market. Rooms have laptop computers with free Wi-Fi connections. *c/ La Boquería, 10.* ☎ *93-302-00-92. www. hthoteles.com. 69 units. Doubles 190€–220€. Metro: Liceu. Map p 134.*

★★ Praktik Rambla L'EIXAMPLE

In a smartly converted, gorgeous 19th-century apartment building (by the original architect of La Sagrada Família!), on the quieter of the Ramblas, this midsize boutique hotel delivers chic design on a budget. It's the perfect blend of old and new Barcelona, and has a coveted outdoor terrace. Its nearby sister property, Praktik, is cheaper but not nearly as stylish. *Rambla de Catalunya, 67.* ☎ *93-343-66-90. www. hotelpraktikrambla.com. 43 units. Doubles 120€–180€. AE, DC, MC, V. Metro: Catalunya. Map p 133.*

★ Pulitzer L'EIXAMPLE   Sleek and

trendy, but pretty affordable for a hotel of its design and amenities, this relative newcomer to the scene has a stylish cocktail bar and alluring candlelit rooftop terrace—and is understandably popular. *c/ Bergara, 8.*

A room at The 5 Rooms.

☎ 93-481-67-67. www.hotelpulitzer.
es. 91 units. Doubles 170€–220€. AE,
DC, MC, V. Metro: Catalunya. Map
p 133.

★★★ kids Suites Avenue

L'EIXAMPLE   Behind a curvy stain-
less steel facade by noted Japanese
architect Toyo Ito, these swank luxury apartments with full kitchens
ooze sleek style. Great for longer
stays, business trips, or the style-
conscious family. Some apartments
overlooking Passeig de Gràcia have
privileged direct views of Gaudí's La
Pedrera. Pg. de Gràcia, 83. ☎ 93-487-
41-59. www.derbyhotels.com/Suites-
Avenue-Barcelona. 43 units. Doubles
175€–400€. AE, DC, MC, V. Metro: Pl.
Provença. Map p 133.

★★★ kids The 5 Rooms

L'EIXAMPLE   Much more like staying in a friend's cool Eixample apartment than anything resembling a
hotel, this intimate and urbane, well-
decorated B&B on two floors is great
for both Bs, and perfectly located,
within walking distance of the old
quarter and major modernista sights.
Despite the name, there are actually
12 rooms, as well as a handful of
apartments, great for families.
c/ Pau Claris, 72. ☎ 93-342-78-80.
www.thefiverooms.com. 7 units. Doubles 135€–185€. DC, MC, V. Metro:
Urquinaona. Map p 133.

★ Vincci Marítimo Hotel

WATERFRONT (POBLE NOU)   In a
recently developed waterfront district near Mar Bella beach, this forward-looking hotel pushes the
envelope of sleek design, with miles
of glass, warm wood, and brushed
steel. Perfect if you're mostly inter-
ested in hanging out at less-popu-
lated beaches, and a fair deal, too.
c/ Llull, 340. ☎ 93-356-26-00. www.
vinccihoteles.com. 144 units. Doubles 95€–190€. AE, DC, MC, V.
Metro: Poble Nou. Map p 134.

★ W Barcelona WATERFRONT

(BARCELONETA)   One of Barcelona's newest hotels, this huge, gleaming, sail-shaped building rising high
over the old port is not without con-
troversy. But it was designed by
Ricardo Bofill, a Barcelona native,
and has stunning panoramic sea
views from rooms, the sleek bar, and
the terrace pool. Rooms are crisp
and modern, in that chic, contemporary W style, and there's a Bliss
spa—but it's way out past Barceloneta, requiring taxis or a lot of walking. Pl. de la Rosa dels Vents, 1 (Pg.
Joan de Borbó). ☎ 93-295-28-00.
www.w-barcelona.com. 473 units.
Doubles 295€–620€. AE, DC, MC, V.
Metro: Barceloneta. Map p 134. ●

10 The Best Day Trips & Excursions

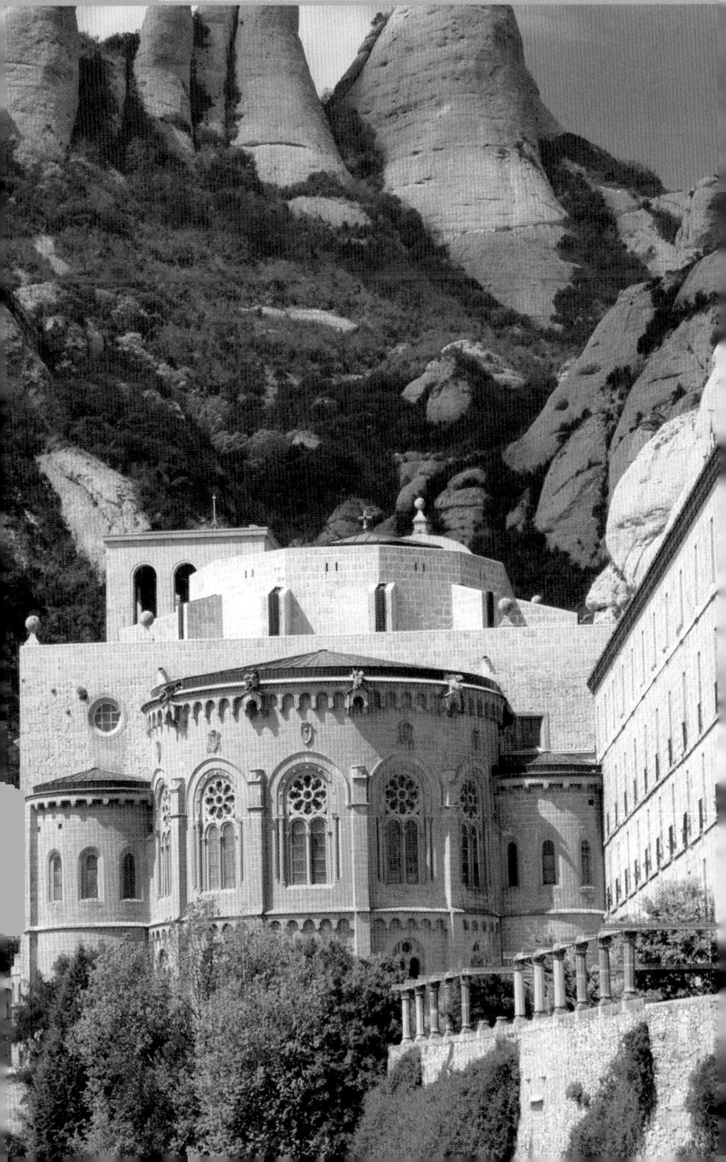

Montserrat

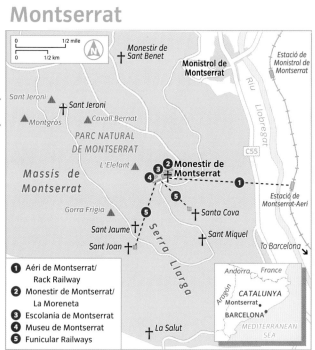

- **1** Aéri de Montserrat/
  Rack Railway
- **2** Monestir de Montserrat/
  La Moreneta
- **3** Escolania de Montserrat
- **4** Museu de Montserrat
- **5** Funicular Railways

A very popular half-day inland trip, this spectacularly jagged peak (the "saw-tooth mountain"), 50km (31 miles) northwest of Barcelona, is home to a Benedictine monastery founded in A.D. 1025 and La Moreneta (the Black Madonna), the patron saint of Catalunya. A sacred place of pilgrimage, Montserrat is overrun on the holy days April 27 and September 8. It's also a popular place for hiking and hard-core cycling.

1 ★★ **Aéri de Montserrat/ Rack Railway.** The most scenic way to Montserrat is by 1930 cable car. The FGC train leaves from Barcelona and connects to it both ways. However, the more comfortable, panoramic **Montserrat rack railway** is also a spectacular way to get there, and it leaves you right in the middle of the monastery. ☎ *93-205-15-15.* *www.aeridemontserrat.com or www. fgc.net/eng/bitllets_oci_turisme.asp.*

Previous page: Montserrat Monastery.

The cable car to Montserrat.

The Montserrat monastery nestled into the mountain.

Cable car 8.50€ round-trip; rack railway 7.20€.

❷ ★ Monestir de Montserrat/ La Moreneta. The Benedictine monastery, tucked into the 1,219m (4,000-ft.) ridges of Montserrat, holds a shrine to the famous Black Madonna icon, which according to legend was discovered in the 12th century (and said to have been carved by St. Luke in A.D. 50). The library holds some 300,000 volumes, though many were lost during raids by Napoleon's forces in 1811 (they also razed the 16th-c. Basilica). About 100 Benedictine monks continue in residence at Montserrat. ☎ 93-877-77-66. www.montserrat visita.com. Free admission. Daily 7:30am–8pm.

❸ ★★ Escolania de Montserrat. One of the oldest boys' choirs in Europe (dating to the 14th c.) performs Monday to Friday at 1pm (Salve) and Monday to Thursday at 6:45pm (Vespers). On Sundays and holidays, you can hear them at 11am and again at 6:45pm. ☎ 93-877-77-67. For more information about the choir (including an amusing FAQ) and the current calendar, visit www.escolania.cat.

❹ ★ Museu de Montserrat. The museum next door to the Basilica contains minor paintings by such artists as Caravaggio, Degas, Monet, and El Greco, as well as early works by Picasso, Miró, and Dalí. Pl. de Santa María, s/n. ☎ 93-877-77-77. www.abadiamontserrat.net. Admission 6.50€. Mon–Fri 10am–6:45pm.

❺ ★★ Funicular Railways. A funicular climbs to the peak of **Sant Joan,** where there's a small hermitage and panoramic views, but the only way up to the **Sant Jeroni** hermitage and summit beyond is by foot (about a 45-min. walk). A separate funicular goes to **Santa Cova,** a 17th-century chapel built in the shape of a cross, where La Moreneta was allegedly discovered. www.cremallerademontserrat.cat. Combined funicular ticket 8.10€ round-trip; included in Tot Montserrat and TransMontserrat tickets.

Practical Matters: Montserrat

The convenient **Tot Montserrat** ticket (39€) includes the Barcelona Metro, a round-trip train to Montserrat, entry into the museum, funiculars, and lunch at the Montserrat restaurant; the **TransMontserrat** ticket (23€), is for the Metro, train, and funiculars only. Trains depart from Barcelona's Plaça d'Espanya station (☎ 93-205-15-15; www.fgc.net/eng/bitllets_oci_turisme.asp; Metro: Espanya). By car, take the A-2 out of Barcelona toward Tarragona and Martorell, or the Barcelona–Terrassa highway via the Túneles de Vallvidrera. The **Tourist Information Office** is on Plaça de la Creu, s/n; ☎ 93-877-77-77. Additional information on Montserrat and transport, including funiculars and hiking in the area, can be found at www.cremallerademontserrat.cat or by calling ☎ 902-31-20-20.

Sitges

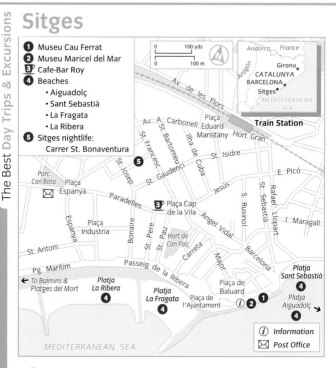

1. Museu Cau Ferrat
2. Museu Maricel del Mar
3. Cafe-Bar Roy
4. Beaches
   • Aiguadolç
   • Sant Sebastià
   • La Fragata
   • La Ribera
5. Sitges nightlife:
   Carrer St. Bonaventura

ⓘ Information
✉ Post Office

An excellent day or overnight trip is to the pretty beach town of Sitges, 37km (23 miles) southwest of Barcelona along the Costa Daurada (Golden Coast). Long a cultural and intellectual center, with a wealth of *modernista* architecture, Sitges was a favorite of the painters Santiago Rusiñol and Salvador Dalí, as well as the poet Federico García Lorca. Often this is no quiet beach town, though; it's one of Spain's most prominent gay resorts (especially during Carnaval).

① ★★ **Museu Cau Ferrat.** The former home of Rusiñol is packed to the rafters with *modernista*-period paintings; artwork by El Greco, Ramón Casas, Ignacio Zuloaga, and others; ceramics and wrought iron; and a collection of the artist's personal effects. The house served as a bohemian refuge from the end of the 19th century until Rusiñol's death in 1936. The edifice of the home is worth the visit alone. *c/ del Fonollar, s/n.* ☎ *93-894-03-64. www.mnac.cat/museus/mus_ferrat.jsp?lan=001. Admission 3€. Tues–Sat 9:30am–2pm and 4–7pm; Sun 10am–3pm.*

② ★ **Museu Maricel del Mar.** This early-20th-century mansion, the one-time residence of the painter Ramon Casas and the American Charles Deering, houses a collection of Gothic and Romantic artworks, as well as modern Catalan sculpture, ceramics, and drawings. *c/ del Fonollar, s/n.* ☎ *93-894-03-64.*

Practical Matters: Sitges

Trains (40 min.; ☎ 902-32-03-20; www.renfe.es) make departures (every 15–30 min.) from Barcelona's Sants station. By car, take C-246 or toll highway A-7 (40km/25 miles south of Barcelona; allow 45 min. to an hour). The **Tourist Information Office** (☎ 93-810-93-40; www.sitgestour.cat) is at c/ Sínia Morera, 1 (the website has good hotel links). A simple round-trip is 4.50€. Gay travelers should consult www.gaysitgesguide.com for information on Carnaval and gay-friendly hotels, restaurants, and bars.

Lodging: El Xalet, c/ Isla de Cuba, 33–35 (☎ 93-811-00-70; www. elxalet.com; doubles 60€–100€), is a quirky *modernista* house within walking distance of the beach; **Estela Barcelona Hotel del Arte** (Av. Port d'Aiguadolç, 8; ☎ 93-811-45-45; www.hotelestela.com; doubles 193€–235€ but big discounts online) is an art-filled place overlooking the marina and beach, with a full spa and good restaurant.

Dining: The finest restaurant in Sitges is the sleek, elegant **Fragata** ($$$; Pg. de la Ribera, 1; ☎ 93/894-10-86), serving innovative Mediterranean fare and seafood. With its terrace facing the sea, it's a place to splurge. Less exalted but still very dependable restaurants on Passeig de la Ribera include **El Velero de Sitges** at no. 38 ($$; ☎ 93-894-20-51) and **Mare Nostrum** at no. 60 ($$; ☎ 93-894-33-93).

The hall at Cau Ferrat.

Admission 3€. Tues–Sat 9:30am–2pm and 4–7pm; Sun 10am–3pm.

3 Cafe-Bar Roy. A good stop for a coffee or a glass of *cava* and snacks, this classic, old-fashioned coffeehouse has marble tables, hand-painted tiles, and Art Nouveau touches (and free Wi-Fi). *c/ de les Parellades, 9.* ☎ 938-11-00-52. $.

4 ★★ Beaches. Sitges's biggest draw is its 17 beaches. Those in the town center and along the eastern end are the most laid-back. The most popular are **Aiguadolç** and **Balmins. Sant Sebastià** and **La Fragata** are known as family beaches, something that would probably not be said for those to the west. A young crowd heads to **La Ribera,** and farthest west are the beaches, such as **Platges del Mort,** that are the haunts of the least inhibited beachgoers, including nudists and large groups of gays.

5 ★ Nightlife. In the town center, **Carrer Sant Bonaventura,** a 5-minute walk from the beach, teems with gay bars and party spots. **Mediterráneo,** c/ Sant Bonaventura, 6 (no phone), is the largest gay disco. One of Spain's most flamboyant parties is **Carnaval** in Sitges, celebrated the week before Lent.

Girona

1. El Call
2. Banys Àrabs
3. Catedral
4. Roman Walls
5. Museu d'Art
6. Monestir de
   St. Pere de Galligants
   (city archaeology
   museum)
7. Lola Café
8. Cases de l'Onyar/
   Pont de Ferro
9. Museu del Cinema

An hour north of Barcelona is Girona, one of Spain's most historic cities. Its pristine Old Quarter is among the most beautiful in Spain. Built on an old Roman settlement and steeped in the layered histories of the Romans, Moors, and Jews, the town center is a compact jumble of narrow stone streets, dark alleyways, and the medieval arches of El Call—the ancient Jewish neighborhood. Bustling by day, the cobblestone streets of the Old Quarter turn quiet as night falls. Though one of Spain's wealthiest cities, Girona has a reputation as a provincial and emphatically Catalan city.

1 ★★★ **El Call.** Girona was home to a prosperous Jewish community for more than 6 centuries, until its members were expelled in 1492. The Jewish district ("El Call" in Catalan) is a tangle of narrow, dark, atmospheric streets tucked within the Old Quarter and said to be the best-preserved ghetto in western Europe. Carrer de la Força is the principal street, where buildings date from the 13th to 15th centuries. The **Museu d'Historia dels Jueus** is a well-designed history center that documents the Jewish population of Girona; the last known synagogue in the city, built in the 15th century, is part of the center. *c/ de la Força, 8.* ☎ *972-21-67-61. www.girona.cat/call. Admission to*

A street in Girona's El Call neighborhood.

the best preserved in Spain. *c/ Ferran el Católic, s/n.* ☎ *972-21-32-62.* *www.banysarabs.org.* Admission 1.60€ adults, .80€ seniors and students. Apr–Sept Mon–Sat 10am–7pm and Sun 10am–2pm; Oct–Mar Mon–Sat 10am–2pm.

③ ★ Catedral. Steep Baroque stairs climb to Girona's imposing cathedral overlooking the city. The cloister and tower are the only surviving elements of the original, early-11th-century Romanesque building. The single nave is the widest Gothic nave in the world (and the second-widest of any style, after St. Peter's in the Vatican). In the treasury is a magnificent collection of religious art. Perhaps the most important piece is the 11th– or 12th–century *Tapestry of the Creation,* an embroidered depiction of humans and animals in the Garden of Eden. *Pl. de la Catedral.* ☎ *972-21-44-26. www. catedraldegirona.org.* Admission (nave, cloister, and treasury) 5€ adults, 3€ seniors and students (audio guide included); free admission on Sun. Apr–Oct daily 10am–8pm; Nov–Mar daily 10am–7pm.

museum 2€, 1.50€ students and seniors (audio guide including admission 4€). July–Aug Mon–Sat 10am–8pm, Sun 10am–2pm; Sept–June Mon 10am–2pm, Tues–Sat 10am–6pm, and Sun 10am–2pm.

② ★ Banys Àrabs. The 12th-century Arab baths are one of the few reminders of Girona's Moorish community. Restored in the 1920s, the Romanesque baths are among

④ ★ Roman Walls. For great views of the old town, walk along a 5km (3.1-mile) portion of the original

Banys Àrabs.

Roman wall, which dates to the 1st century A.D. Afterward, don't miss the pretty, serene gardens tucked behind the cathedral and just below the city wall: Jardins de la Francesa (French Woman's Gardens) and Jardins de les Alemans (German Gardens).

⑤ ★★ Museu d'Art. Girona's Art Museum, in a former Episcopal palace, covers almost 1,000 years of history and art. It features excellent Catalan Romanesque and Gothic paintings, as well as a significant collection of contemporary art. Among the highlights is a 15th-century altarpiece, Sant Miquel de Cruïlles, one of the finest works of Catalan Gothic art anywhere. The museum also boasts its altarstone of Sant Pere de Roda, from the 10th and 11th centuries; this work in wood and stone, depicting figures and legends, was once embossed in silver. *Pujada de la Catedral, 12.* ☎ *972-20-38-34. www.museuart.com. Admission 2€ adults, 1.50€ students and seniors, free for children 15 and under. Mar–Sept Mon–Sat 10am–7pm, Sun 10am–2pm; Oct–Feb Mon–Sat 10am–6pm and Sun 10am–2pm.*

⑥ ★ Monestir de Sant Pere de Galligants. This 12th-century Catalan Gothic Benedictine monastery

The Tapestry of the Creation *in the Girona cathedral (p 151).*

houses the city archaeology museum, with several items culled from the Roman ruins at nearby Empúries. *Pl. de Santa Llúcia, s/n.* ☎ *972-20-26-32. www.mac.cat. Admission 2.30€ adults, free for seniors and children 15 and under. Oct–May Tues–Sat 10am–2pm and 4–6pm; June–Sept Tues–Sat 10:30am–1:30pm and 4–7pm; Sun 10am–2:30pm.*

⑦ Lola Café. On the most atmospheric street in the old Jewish Quarter, this hip, dark cafe frequently features live music on weekend nights. *c/ de la Força, 7.* ☎ *972-22-88-24. $$.*

Houses on the Onyar River.

Practical Matters: Girona

By car from Barcelona, take the ronda (beltway) in the direction of France and then the A-7 to Girona; the trip is 97km (60 miles). Frequent (90-min.) trains leave from Barcelona's Estació Sants and arrive at Girona's Plaça de Espanya (☎ 902-24-02-02; www.renfe.es); if you're only traveling to Girona (city), the train is the way to go. The main **Oficina de Turisme** is on the pedestrian-only main drag, Rambla de la Llibertat, 1 (☎ 972-22-65-75; www.girona.cat/turisme). A trip to Girona can (and really should, if you have the time) easily be combined with visits to L'Empordà and the Costa Brava (see p 154).

Lodging: The swankest hotel in town is **AC Palau de Bellavista,** just outside the Old Quarter and near Plaça de Catalunya, with a glass-box exterior and elegant rooms (Pujada Polvorins, 1; ☎ 872-08-06-70; www.hotelacpalaudebellavista.com; doubles 95€–194€). **Hotel Citutat de Girona** (c/ Nord, 2; ☎ 972-48-30-38; www.hotel-ciutatde girona.com; doubles 150€–202€) is a stylishly modern midsize hotel at the edge of the Old Quarter. **Bellmirall** is a charming guesthouse in the heart of the Old Quarter, with just seven rooms in a restored 14th-century stone mansion (c/ Bellmirall, 3; ☎ 972-20-40-09; www.grn.es/bellmirall; doubles 70€–80€; no credit cards; closed Jan–Feb).

Dining: **Le Bistrot** ($), a terrific little place that spills out onto the steep steps of an Old Quarter alleyway with candlelit tables, is a great place for gourmet pizzas, salads, and crepes (Pujada Sant Domènec, 4; ☎ 972-21-88-03). **Blanc** ($), connected to the Hotel Ciutat de Girona, is a chic, excellent-value restaurant that serves Catalan and Mediterranean dishes (c/ Nord, 2; ☎ 972-41-56-37). **El Celler de Can Roca** ($$$$), in sleek new surroundings, is one of the top upscale restaurants in Catalunya, if not in all of Spain—by itself it may be worth a trip to Girona (Can Sunyer, 48, in Taialà, northeast of Girona; ☎ 972-22-21-57; www.cellercanroca.com).

8 ★ **Cases de l'Onyar.** The picturesque, multicolored houses (cases) along the Onyar River shimmer in the water's reflection, with drying laundry fluttering in the breeze. Many of the houses date to the Middle Ages, when they were outside the original walls of the Old City. Leading to the modern city is the **Pont de Ferro,** an iron bridge built by the Eiffel Company in 1877, 12 years before the Eiffel Tower.

9 ★ **Museu del Cinema.** Spain's only cinema museum is the extensive private collection of one man, Tomàs Mallol. The museum houses his collection of some 25,000 cinema artifacts, including photographs, posters, engravings, and interactive exhibits, as well as the original camera of the Luimière brothers. *c/ Sèquia, 1. ☎ 972-41-27-77. www.museudelcinema.org. Admission 5€ adults, 2.50€ students and seniors. May–Sept Tues–Sun 10am–8pm; Oct–Apr Tues–Fri 10am–6pm, Sat 10am–8pm, Sun 11am–3pm.*

L'Empordà & Costa Brava

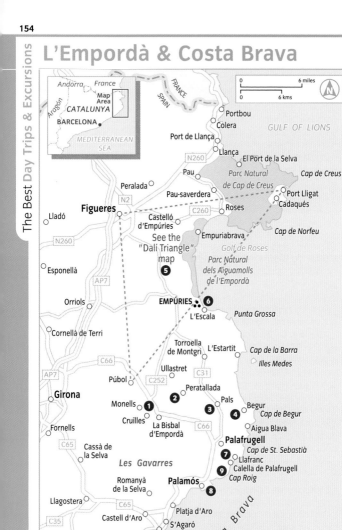

1 Cruïlles & Monells
2 Peratallada
3 Pals
4 Begur
5 Dalí Triangle
6 Empúries
7 Palafrugell beach coves
8 Palamós
9 Cap Roig
10 Sant Feliu de Guixols

L'Empordà, the plains and rolling green hills surrounding Girona, is Spain's Tuscany. Inland from the coast are small and mostly unassuming medieval villages, clusters of ancient stone houses—many converted into weekend and summer homes by affluent Barcelonans. The Costa Brava, the "untamed coast," is a stretch of rocky coves and sandy beaches, with deep cobalt-blue Mediterranean waters, pine trees, and whitewashed fishing villages. Sadly, the natural beauty of the coastline's southern end, nearest Barcelona, has been marred by sand-and-sun mass-market tourism.

❶ ★★ Cruïlles & Monells.
These two quiet villages are attractive enclaves of medieval stonework. Monells's main claim to fame is a magnificent porticoed main square, while at the center of Cruïlles, once enclosed by walls, is a Romanesque 11th-century monastery.

❷ ★★★ Peratallada.
Less slick than Pals (see below), this picturesque town grew up around an unusual castle. You'll also find a 14th-century palace, a porticoed main square, and houses rich with Gothic details, several of which house inns and antiques shops.

❸ ★★★ Pals.
Almost too pretty and perfect, this medieval town rising above the plains is hugely popular with tourists. Pals's alleyways and stone walls look as though they might be part of a movie set.

❹ ★★ Begur.
This attractive hilltop town is topped by the ruins of a 13th-century castle, with commanding 360-degree views of the whole of L'Empordà and the Costa Brava, all the way up the coast to Cadaqués. Many houses below are colonial in style, built by returning locals who set out for Cuba in the early 19th century. On the outskirts of Begur are excellent beaches, including Aiguablava, Sa Riera, and Sa Tuna.

❺ ★★★ Dalí Triangle.
The Empordà region is marked by the trail of Spain's famous oddball, the surrealist painter Salvador Dalí, who hailed from northern Catalunya and lived much of his life on the Costa Brava. Three points, including a museum and two curious homes, form the Dalí Triangle. Together they are a must-see for anyone with an appreciation for Dalí and the absurd.

Pals, a picturesque town.

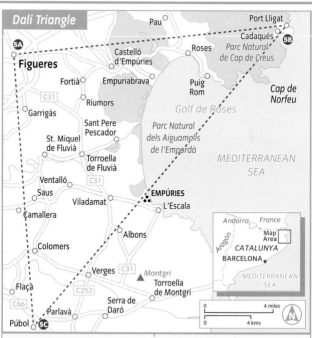

Dali Triangle

Pau • Port Lligat • Cadaqués **5B** • Roses • Figueres **5A** • Castelló d'Empúries • Parc Natural de Cap de Creus • Cap de Norfeu • Fortià • Empuriabrava • Puig Rom • Golf de Roses • C31 • Riumors • Garrigàs • Sant Pere Pescador • Parc Natural dels Aiguamolls de l'Empordà • St. Miquel de Fluvià • MEDITERRANEAN SEA • Torroella de Fluvià • C31 • Ventalló • Saus • Viladamat • EMPÚRIES • L'Escala • Camallera • Albons • Andorra • France • Aragon • Map Area • CATALUNYA • BARCELONA • MEDITERRANEAN SEA • Colomers • Verges • C31 • Montgri • Torroella de Montgri • Flaçà • C252 • Serra de Daró • C66 • Parlavà • Púbol **5C** • 0 4 miles • 0 4 kms

5A ★★★ Figueres: Teatre Museu Dalí.

Dalí's Museum-Theater, which he designed as his legacy in his birthplace of Figueres, is part theater, part amusement park— fittingly idiosyncratic and witty. The red building is topped by giant white eggs and decorated with glazed ceramic loaves of bread; inside is a salon with furniture re-creating Mae West's face and a long black Cadillac with sprinklers inside. Dalí is buried in a crypt here. *Pl. de Gala–Salvador Dalí, 5.* ☎ *972-67-75-00.* www. salvador-dali.org.

5B ★★ Cadaqués/Port Lligat: Casa-Museu Salvador Dalí.

Next to the seaside village of Cada-qués, Dalí built his first home with Gala, his eccentric Russian-born wife.

They cobbled together several fish-ers' residences and decorated them in Daliesque fashion: with stuffed swans, a lip sofa, and Dalí-designed chimneys. ☎ *972-25-10-15.* www. salvador-dali.org.

5C ★ Púbol: Casa-Museu Cas-tell Gala Dalí.

Dalí bought a medi-eval castle in an isolated L'Empordà village for his beloved princess in the late 1960s, but Gala allowed Dalí to visit only when she invited him. Even into her late 60s, she entertained a coterie of much younger men here. There are odd Daliesque touches throughout, though the castle is less nutty than the other two points in the Triangle. ☎ *972-48-86-55.* www. salvador-dali.org.

The bizarre meets the absurd at the Dalí Museum in Figueres.

6 ★★ **Empúries.** The extensive ruins of a Greco-Roman city, one of the most fascinating archaeological finds in Spain, are on view at the **Museu d'Empúries.** Three different civilizations settled on the coast here between the 7th and 3rd centuries B.C.: Empúries is the only place in Spain with incarnations as a Greek village, an Iberian settlement, and a Roman town. ☎ *972-77-02-08. www. mac.es. Admission 2.50€ adults, 2€ seniors and students 16–18, free for children 15 and under. June–Sept daily 10am–8pm; Oct–May daily 10am–6pm.*

7 ★★ **Palafrugell Beach coves.** Several of the most beautiful coves and sandy beach spots along the Costa Brava are near Palafrugell. Calella de Palafrugell, Llafranc, and Tamariu are gentle, protected spots with good swimming and walking paths through pine-forested hills.

8 **Palamós.** The tensions of a Costa Brava town caught between tradition and modern development focused on tourism are apparent in this old fishing village.

9 ★ **Cap Roig.** On a cliff-top peninsula is a magnificent estate that once belonged to a Russian army general and is now home to beautiful Mediterranean botanical gardens (Jardí Botànic) with extraordinary

Calella de Palafrugell.

Practical Matters: L'Empordà & Costa Brava

Car is by far the best way to travel around the region. Figueres is 150km (93 miles) north of Barcelona on A-7 and 50km (31 miles) north of Girona. To get to Cadaqués, take C-260 from Figueres and then a long, twisting, maddening road (GI-614). Púbol is 40km (25 miles) south of Figueres along highway C-252 or 16km (10 miles) east of Girona along C-255. From Girona, **trains** travel to the Costa Brava towns of Llançà, Blanes, and Colera, as well as Figueres. For additional information, see **www.cbrava.es**.

Lodging & Dining: The following hotels all have very good, and in some cases, superb, restaurants: **El Far Hotel-Restaurant** is a cliff-top property formed by a 17th-century hermitage and a 15th-century lighthouse, with drop-dead views of the bay and Mediterranean and nine elegant, cheery rooms (Platja de Llafranc, near Palafrugell; ☎ 972-30-16-39; www.elfar.net; doubles 185€–320€, suites 230€–390€). In L'Empordà, near the coast, is **Castell de'Empordà,** a 700-year-old castle converted to an outstanding luxurious small hotel. It's 3km (2 miles) from La Bisbal (☎ 972-64-62-54; www.castelldemporda.com; doubles 135€–240€; closed Nov–Mar). **La Plaça de Madremanya,** in a small Catalan village halfway between Girona and the coast, is a gorgeous country hotel, with one of the region's finest restaurants, and a comparatively great value (c/ Sant Esteve 17, Madremanya; ☎ 972-49-04-87; www.laplacamadremanya.com; doubles 107€–166€, suites 174€–338€). In Begur, **AiguaClara Hotel-Restaurant** is an exquisite, excellent-value boutique hotel in a small colonial-style palace, with charmingly shabby-chic decor (Sant Miquel, 2; ☎ 972-62-29-05; www.aiguaclara.com; doubles 85€–155€, suites 125€–175€). A terrific little restaurant in Begur is **Can Climent i Sa Cuina** ($$), with an elegantly rustic dining room like the kitchen of an old farmhouse and fresh and creative market Catalan cuisine by a young chef; the set menu at lunch is a steal (Av. Onze de Setembre; ☎ 972-62-20-31).

views of the coast. In summer months, the **Festival Jardins de Cap Roig** features live jazz, rock, flamenco, world music, theater, and opera (including big names like Bob Dylan). ☎ *972-61-45-82. www. caproig.cat. Free admission. The gardens are open daily, Apr–Sept 9am–8pm and Oct–Mar 9am–6pm.*

On concert days (July–Aug), they close at 2pm.

⓾ Sant Feliu de Guixols. The beginning of the "good" Costa Brava after miles of overdevelopment, this easygoing town has a 10th-century church and chapel, Sant Martí, high on a hill overlooking the coastline. ●

The
Savvy Traveler

Before You Go

Government Tourist Offices

In the U.S.: 666 Fifth Ave., Fifth Floor, New York, NY 10103 (☎ 212/265-8822); 8383 Wilshire Blvd., Ste. 956, Beverly Hills, CA 90211 (☎ 323/658-7188); 845 N. Michigan Ave., Ste. 915E, Chicago, IL 60611 (☎ 312/642-1992); and 1221 Brickell Ave., Ste. 1850, Miami, FL 33131 (☎ 305/358-1992). **In Canada:** 102 Bloor St. W., Ste. 3402, Toronto, Ontario M5S 1M9, Canada (☎ 416/961-3131). **In the U.K.:** 79 New Cavendish St., 2nd Floor; W1W 6XB, London (☎ 207/317-2010; www. spain.info/uk/TourSpain). A full list of Spanish tourist offices worldwide can be found at www.spain.info.

The Best Times to Go

March to May and **September to late October** are perhaps the best times to visit Barcelona, with fewer crowds than in summer. Weather-wise, however, almost any time of year is the right time to go. Barcelona is not nearly as dreadfully hot in summer as Madrid and the south. In **August**, much of the city shuts down as residents head for the beaches. August is the major vacation month in Europe, and traffic from England, France, the Netherlands, and Germany to Spain becomes a stampede. **November** to **February** can be pleasantly temperate, crowds are nonexistent, and prices drop for hotels and airfares. But some coastal resorts, especially on the Costa Brava, shut down during this slow season. The **Christmas** season in Barcelona, beginning in early **December** and extending through the first week of **January,** is especially festive.

Barcelona is officially Spain's most popular destination, and

tourism is now year-round; it is also a major international trade fair and conference destination throughout the year, so mid- to high-range hotels should be booked well in advance.

Festivals & Special Events

SPRING. One of the high points is **Semana Santa (Holy Week).** On Palm Sunday, palm leaves are blessed in La Sagrada Família, while in the city cathedral's cloister, the curious *L'ou com balla*—a hollowed-out egg shell—is placed on top of a fountain to bob around and "dance." **La Diada de St. Jordi,** on April 23, is the colorful celebration of Saint George (St. Jordi in Catalan), the patron saint of Catalunya; the tradition is for men to give a single red rose to the significant women in their lives (mother, girlfriend, sister, and so on), and for women to give a book in return (though many forward-thinking men now also give women books). Rose-sellers are everywhere, and bookshops set up open-air stalls along Passeig de Gràcia. May 1 is **May Day,** or Labor Day, and the streets are full of marching trade-union members. During **Corpus Christi,** which falls in either May or June, the streets of Sitges are carpeted in flowers.

SUMMER. During the **Verbena de Sant Joan** (June 23), Catalunya celebrates the Twelfth Night with fireworks ablaze in streets and squares, bonfires lit along the beach, and liters of *cava* consumed. It's traditional to have the first dip of the year in the sea at dawn (officially the first day of summer). **El Grec,** at the beginning of July, is a culture festival that brings marquee names in all genres of music and theater to perform in various open-air venues. **Festa Major de**

Previous page: The Liceu Metro stop.

Useful Websites

- **www.okspain.org**: The Tourist Office of Spain's official U.S. site; it has detailed "Before You Go" information (including U.S. air departures).
- **www.tourspain.es**: Turespaña's website, with helpful primers on leisure travel, adventure travel, and business travel, as well as a feature of Spanish news from around the world.
- **www.spaininfo.com**: Loads of practical advice and tips on driving, destinations, travel routes, recipes, and wines; bringing in pets; and even learning Spanish.
- **www.renfe.es**: The official site of Spanish rail, for routes, schedules, and booking.
- **www.barcelonaturisme.com**: The city's official tourism site, with excellent information in English as well as Catalan and Spanish.
- **www.barcelona.com**: For one-stop tour, hotel, and activity booking.
- **www.cbrava.es**: Information about Costa Brava, the city of Girona, and other parts of Catalunya, including L'Empordà.

Gràcia (early to mid-Aug) is a week-long *festa* held in the Gràcia neighborhood, which is elaborately decorated; by day, long tables are set up for communal lunches and board games, and at night, thousands invade the narrow streets for outdoor concerts and revelry.

FALL. **La Diada de Catalunya** (Sept 11), the National Day of Catalunya, is the most politically and historically significant holiday in the region, celebrating the region's autonomy and the date the city was besieged by Spanish and French troops in 1714 during the War of Succession. Demonstrations calling for independence are everywhere, and the *senyera,* the flag of Catalunya, is hung from balconies. **La Mercè** (Sept 24) honors Our Lady of Mercy, the city's patron saint (who according to legend rid Barcelona of a plague of locusts). Free concerts are held in squares, and folkloric figures such as the *gigants* (giants) and

cap grosses (big heads) take to the streets. People come out to perform the *sardana* (traditional Catalan dance) and to watch the forming of *castellers* (human towers). Fireworks displays light up the night, and the hair-raising *correfocs,* parades of fireworks-brandishing "devils" and dragons, are the grand finale. One of the best times to be in Barcelona, especially for children.

WINTER. **All Saints' Day** (Nov 1), a public holiday, is reverently celebrated: relatives and friends lay flowers on the graves (or *nichos*—in Spain, people are often buried one on top of another in tiny compartments) of the dead. The night before, some of the bars in the city hold Halloween parties. The weeks leading to **Nadal,** or Christmas, are marked by *Fira de Santa Llucia,* a huge open-air market near the cathedral selling handicrafts, Christmas decorations, trees, and figurines (including *caganers;* see p 62) for their *pessebres* (nativity dioramas).

A life-size nativity is constructed in Plaça Sant Jaume. **Día de los Reyes** (Three Kings Day), January 6, remains the traditional Catholic celebration of Christmas gift-giving (even though Santa Claus has made inroads and many families now exchange gifts on Dec 25). The evening prior, public celebrations take place in cities and towns across Spain; in Barcelona, three costumed Magi arrive by boat at the port to dispense candy to children. **Carnaval** (just prior to Lent) in Barcelona is low-key, with dressing up only by groups of children or stall owners in the local markets. Not so in Sitges, the seaside town south of Barcelona, where locals, especially the gay community, go all out with hedonistic costumes, parades, and other forms of revelry.

The Weather

Barcelona is blessed with a Mediterranean climate, and spring and fall are unfailingly pleasant, with sunny skies and moderate temperatures. Even in the winter, days are crisp but not exceedingly cold and often sunny. Snow is rare and never lasts more than a day or two. Most rainfall occurs in April. July and August are hot and humid, even at night, as the temperature often only drops minimally. The surrounding sea is warm enough to swim in from the end of June to early October. Inland, the temperatures drop slightly, as does the humidity. North on the Costa Brava, a strong wind known as the *tramontana* often blows.

Cellphones (Móviles)

World phones—or GSM (Global System for Mobiles)—work in Spain (and most of the world). If your cellphone is on a GSM system, and you have a world-capable multiband phone, you can make and receive calls from Spain. Just call your wireless operator and ask for "international roaming" to be activated. You can also rent a GSM phone. The French-owned store **FNAC** (main branch at Pl. Catalunya, 4; Metro: Catalunya; ☎ 93-344-18-00; www.fnac.es) provides a pay-as-you-go mobile phone package, which actually works out to be cheaper than renting if you're staying just a few weeks or less. North Americans can rent a GSM phone before leaving home from **InTouch USA** (☎ 800/872-7626; www.intouchglobal.com) or **RoadPost** (☎ 888/290-1606 or 905/272-5665; www.roadpost.com).

Car Rentals

Driving in Barcelona isn't advised, especially with the preponderance of inexpensive taxis and metro services. A car is pretty much indispensable, however, for exploring L'Empordà and Costa Brava. North America's biggest car-rental companies, including Avis, Budget, and Hertz, maintain offices in Barcelona and Catalunya, including at El Prat airport and the Girona rail station. **Avis, Hertz,** and **Budget** have offices at Sants railway station and other spots in Barcelona. Two other agencies of note include **Kemwel Holiday Auto** and **Auto Europe.**

Getting **There**

By Plane

From Barcelona's newly expanded **El Prat de Llobregat** airport (www.barcelona-airport.com)—its new

Terminal 1, completed in 2009, is absolutely stunning—12km (7 miles) from the city center, there are several ways to get into town. The most convenient and inexpensive means is the **Aerobús** (☎ 93-384-17-58; 5€ one-way, 8.65€ round-trip), which leaves from just outside terminals A1 and A2 every 15 minutes from 6am to 1am and stops at Plaça Espanya, Gran Vía de les Corts Catalanes, Plaça Universitat, and Plaça de Catalunya (taking about 40 min. to reach the last stop). Another is by half-hourly **rail service** (☎ 902-32-03-20; www.renfe.es; 3€)—temporarily and confusingly rerouted as the **Renfe C2** line ("Norte Aeropuerto–Sant Celoni/Maçanet") due to construction of the Barcelona-Madrid AVE high-speed train. The service departs between 6:15am and 11:40pm from El Prat to Estació Sants (25 min.), which has connections with the Metro. There is also a **TMB bus** (1.40€ one-way; www.tmb.cat) that travels from the airport to Plaça de Espanya from 5:30am to 12:45am. The last but most convenient method of getting to the city from the airport is by **taxi** (about 25€) from ranks outside all terminals.

Travelers arriving from within the European Union on budget airlines such as Ryanair may land at **Girona** airport (103km/64 miles northeast of Barcelona) or **Reus** (110 km/68 miles west of the city). **Barcelona Bus** (☎ 93-232-04-59) travels to Barcelona from the airport in Girona (12€ one-way, 21€ round-trip; 70 min.) and Reus (11€; 90 min.). The train from either city is cheaper, but you'd have to catch a bus to either town's rail station. A taxi to Barcelona from Girona or Reus will cost as much as 120€ or more.

By Car

Highway **A-7** leads to Barcelona from France and northern Catalunya (Costa Brava and Girona). The **A-2** leads to Barcelona from Madrid, Zaragoza, and Bilbao. From Valencia or the Costa del Sol, take the **E-15** north. Close to the city, look for one of two signs into downtown Barcelona: CENTRE CIUTAT takes you downtown into the Eixample district, while RONDA LITORAL is a beltway that takes you quickly to the port area.

By Train

Most national (Renfe; ☎ 902-32-03-20; www.renfe.es) and international trains arrive at **Estació Sants,** Plaça dels Països Catalans, s/n (☎ 93-495-62-15; Metro: Sants). New high-speed AVE rail service from Madrid to Barcelona makes the journey in about 3 hours.

Getting **Around**

By Metro

The **Metro** (☎ 010 or 93-318-70-74; www.tmb.net) is Barcelona's excellent, modern, and clean subway. Its five lines are by far the fastest and easiest way to navigate the city. Red diamond symbols mark stations. Single-ticket fares (*senzill,* or *sencillo*) are 1.40€, although you can get a T1 pass (good for 10 trips) for 7.85€. You can also get free rides on all public transport with purchase of the Barcelona Card discount pass (www.barcelonacard.com). The Metro runs Monday to Thursday 5am to 11pm, Friday and Saturday 5am to 2am, and Sunday 6am to midnight.

The Metro shares some terminals with **FGC Trains** (☎ 93-205-15-15; www.fgc.net), run by the provincial government (they cost the same as the Metro, and you can use the same Metro multitrip tickets) and connecting the city center to upper neighborhoods, including Sarrià, Vallvidrera, Tibidabo, and Gràcia. The only problem you may encounter is when you need to switch between an FGC train and a regular Metro train: You have to exit the first and reenter the second, paying separately for each line.

Transportation Tip

TMB (Transports Metropolitans de Barcelona) has a nice online feature that allows you to plug in your destination and address and mode of transport to get from one point to another (both within and beyond the city): www.tmb.cat/vullanar/en_US/vullanar.jsp.

By Taxi

Black-and-yellow taxis are plentiful and reasonably priced; few journeys cost more than 8€ to 10€. You can either hail a cab in the street (the green light on the roof means it's available) or grab one where they're lined up (usually outside hotels). There's no negotiating over fares; you pay what the meter reads (it starts at 2€). Most locals round up the fare to the next half- or full euro, if they tip at all. Fares will include special supplements for airport trips, as well as luggage. Night fares are also higher. Reliable taxi companies include **Servi Taxi** (☎ 93-330-03-00) and **ZBarna Taxi** (☎ 93-358-11-11). For more information, visit www.taxibarcelona.cat.

By Bus

Buses (☎ **010** or **93-223-51-51;** www.emt-amb.com; same tickets and price as Metro) are plentiful, but much less convenient than the Metro. Most bus routes stop at the Plaça de Catalunya. Routes are clearly marked on each stop, as are timetables—but most buses stop running well before the Metro closes. The **Nitbus** (☎ **010** or 93-223-51-51), which runs from 11pm to 4am and is often the only alternative to the dearth of taxis in the wee hours, is bright yellow and clearly marked with an N; most leave from Plaça Catalunya. Travel Cards and other TMB passes are not valid on Nitbuses. Tickets (1.40€) are bought directly from the driver.

By Car

Trying to negotiate Barcelona's unfamiliar, traffic-clogged streets can be nerve-racking, and parking is an expensive nightmare. However, a car is useful if you plan to head out on day trips to Sitges, Montserrat, or the Penedès wine country, or to travel to the Costa Brava or L'Empordà. See p 162 for a list of rental-car companies.

On Foot

Strolling in Barcelona is a pastime and art, and the compact city is ideal for walking, especially along La Rambla, Passeig de Gràcia, Rambla de Catalunya, and in the labyrinthine quarters Barri Gòtic and La Ribera (Ciutat Vella).

Fast **Facts**

AMERICAN EXPRESS Passeig de Gràcia, 101 (☎ 93-255-00-29) and c/ Llull, 321 (☎ 93-217-10-04).

APARTMENT RENTALS The city's tourism bureau, **Barcelona Turisme** (www.barcelonaturisme.com), maintains a long list of tourist apartments rented either by the day or week, and various online brokers, including **www.visit-bcn.com**, which offers everything from Barri Gòtic town houses to loft-style apartments; **www.friendlyrentals.com**, offering stylish properties at a surprisingly good value; and **www.oh-barcelona.com**, which lists more than 300 apartments for rent. Two buildings with 13 chic, modern apartments for rent in the old city (both Born and waterfront) can be found at **La Casa de les Lletres** (☎ 93-226-37-30; www.cru2001.com), while **Chic & Basic** (www.chicandbasic.com), with hip, minimalist hotels in Barcelona and several other European cities, also offers a nice selection of a half-dozen apartments with a modern aesthetic similar to their hotels in the old part of town.

ATMs/CASHPOINTS Maestro, Cirrus, and Visa cards are readily accepted at all ATMs, which are plentiful throughout the city. Exchange currency either at banks or *casas de cambio* (exchange houses). You can also find currency-exchange offices at the Sants rail station and El Prat airport. Spanish banks include La Caixa, Caixa de Catalunya, BBV, and Central Hispano. Branches of these are located near Plaça Catalunya. Most banks offer 24-hour ATMs. Currency-exchange houses include BCN World and BCN Change & Transfer. Spain uses four-digit PINs; if you have a six-digit number, change it at your bank before you leave.

BUSINESS HOURS Banks are open Monday through Friday from 8:30am to 2pm. Most offices are open Monday through Friday from 9am to 6 or 7pm (in July, 8am–3pm). In August, businesses are on skeleton staff if not closed altogether. At restaurants, lunch is usually from 1:30 or 2 to 4pm and dinner from 9 to 11:30pm or midnight. Major stores are open Monday through Saturday from 9:30 or 10am to 8pm; staff at smaller establishments, however, often still close for siesta in the midafternoon, doing business from 9:30am to 2pm and 4:30pm to 8 or 8:30pm.

CONSULATES & EMBASSIES **U.S. Consulate,** Pg. Reina Elisenda de Montcada, 23 (☎ 93-280-22-27; barcelona.usconsulate.gov); **Canadian Consulate,** Plaça de Catalunya, 9, 1st floor, 2nd office (☎ 93-412-72-36; www.canadainternational.gc.ca); **U.K. Consulate,** Av. Diagonal, 477, 13a planta (☎ 93-366-62-00; ukinspain.fco.gov.uk/en); **Australian Consulate,** Plaza Gala Placidia, 1–3, 1st Floor (☎ 93-490-90-13; www.dfat.gov.au/missions/countries/esba.html); **New Zealand Consulate,** Travessera de Gràcia, 64, 2a planta (☎ 93-209-03-99; www.nzembassy.com/spain).

DOCTORS, DENTISTS & HOSPITALS Dial ☎ 061 to find a doctor. For hospitals, the **Centre d'Urgències Perecamps** (☎ 93-441-06-00), located near Les Ramblas at Avinguda de las Drassanes, 13–15, is a good, centrally located choice. For a dentist, try **Dental Clinic Center,** Passeig de Gràcia, 8, 2º, 2ª (☎ 93-412-16-95).

ELECTRICITY Most hotels operate on 220 volts AC (50 cycles). Some older places have 110 or 125 volts AC.

EMERGENCIES For an ambulance or medical emergencies, dial ☎ 061; for fire ☎ 080. For other emergencies, call ☎ 112.

GAY & LESBIAN TRAVELERS In 1978, Spain legalized homosexuality among consenting adults, and in 1995, Spain banned discrimination based on sexual orientation. Marriage between same-sex couples became legal in 2005. Catalunya has helped pave the way in rights for gay couples, preempting national laws by granting same-sex couples the same official status and conjugal rights as heterosexual ones. Barcelona is one of the major centers of gay life in Spain, and Sitges, one of Europe's most popular resorts for gay travelers (see www.gaysitgesguide.com), is just south of Barcelona. The website www.gayinspain.com has very complete and destination-specific listings for gay travelers.

HOLIDAYS Holidays observed include January 1 (New Year's Day), January 6 (Feast of the Epiphany), March/April (Good Friday and Easter Monday), May 1 (May Day), May/June (Whit Monday), June 24 (Feast of St. John), August 15 (Feast of the Assumption), September 11 (National Day of Catalunya), September 24 (Feast of Our Lady of Mercy), October 12 (Spain's National Day), November 1 (All Saints' Day), December 8 (Feast of the Immaculate Conception), December 25 (Christmas), and December 26 (Feast of St. Stephen).

INSURANCE Check your existing insurance policies before you buy travel insurance to cover trip cancellation, lost luggage, medical expenses, or car-rental insurance. For more information, contact one of the following recommended insurers: **Access America** (☎ 866/807-3982; www.accessamerica.com); **Travel Guard International** (☎ 800/826-4919; www.travelguard.com); **Travel Insured International** (☎ 800/243-3174; www.travelinsured.com); and **Travelex Insurance Services** (☎ 888/457-4602; www.travelex-insurance.com). For travel overseas, most U.S. health plans (including Medicare and Medicaid) do not provide coverage, and the ones that do often require payment for services

upfront. If you require additional medical insurance, try **MEDEX Assistance** (☎ 410/453-6300; www.medexassist.com) or **Travel Assistance International** (☎ 800/821-2828; www.travelassistance.com; for general information on services, call the company's Worldwide Assistance Services, Inc., at ☎ 800/777-8710).

INTERNET Internet access is plentiful, both in cybercafes *(cafés Internet)* and frequently in hotels, several of which now offer Wi-Fi. The **Internet Gallery Cafe** is down the street from the Picasso Museum, Barra de Ferro, 3 (☎ 93-268-15-07). To find cybercafes in Barcelona, check **www.cybercaptive.com** and **www.cybercafe.com**.

LOST PROPERTY Call credit card companies the minute you discover your wallet has been lost or stolen and file a report at the nearest police precinct. Your credit card company or insurer may require a police report number or record. **Visa's** U.S. emergency number is ☎ 800/847-2911, or 90-099-11-24 in Spain. **American Express** cardholders and traveler's check holders should call ☎ 800/221-7282 in the U.S., or 90-237-56-37 in Spain. **MasterCard** holders should call ☎ 800/307-7309 in the U.S., or 90-097-12-31 in Spain.

MAIL & POSTAGE Spanish post offices are called *correos* (koh-ray-os), identified by yellow-and-white signs with a crown and the words *Correos y Telégrafos.* Main offices are generally open from 9am to 8pm Monday through Friday and Saturday 9am to 7pm. The Central Post Office is at Plaça de Antoni López, s/n, at the end of Vía Laietana (☎ 902-19-71-97). Other branches are at Aragó, 282; and Ronda Universitat, 23.

MONEY The single European currency in Spain is the **euro.** At press time, the exchange rate was approximately 1€ = $1.37. For up-to-the-minute exchange rates between the euro and the dollar, check the currency converter website **www. xe.com/ucc.**

PASSPORTS No visas are required for U.S., U.K., New Zealand, and Canadian visitors to Spain, provided your stay does not exceed 90 days. Australian visitors do need a visa. If your passport is lost or stolen, contact your country's embassy or consulate immediately. See "Consulates & Embassies," above. Make a copy of your passport's critical pages and keep it separate from your passport.

PHARMACIES Pharmacies (farmàcies) operate during normal business hours, and one in every district remains open all night and on holidays. The location and phone number of this farmàcia de guàrdia are posted on the door of all the other pharmacies. A very central pharmacy open 24/7 is **Farmàcia Álvarez,** Pg. de Gràcia, 26 (☎ 93-302-11-24). You can also call ☎ 010 or 93-481-00-60 to contact all-night pharmacies.

POLICE The national police emergency number is ☎ 091. For local police, call ☎ 092.

SAFETY Violent crime in Barcelona is a rarity, but criminals frequent tourist areas and major attractions such as museums, restaurants, hotels, beach resorts, trains, train stations, airports, subways, and ATMs. Exercise care around major tourist sights, especially La Rambla (in particular, the section closest to the waterfront); Barri Gòtic; Raval neighborhood; and La Sagrada Família. You shouldn't walk alone at night in either the Gothic Quarter or the Raval district. **Turisme Atenció (Tourist Attention Service),** La Rambla, 43 (☎ 93-256-24-30), has English-speaking attendants who can aid crime victims in reporting losses and obtaining new documents. The office is open 24/7.

SMOKING A law banning smoking in public places, including on public transportation and in offices, hospitals, and some bars and restaurants, was enacted in 2006. Nonsmoking sections in restaurants remain relatively rare, but expect this to change as Spaniards adapt to the new reality. If you feel strongly about avoiding secondhand smoke, ask establishments if they have a *no fumadores* (nonsmoking) section.

TAXES The value-added (VAT) tax (known in Spain as *IVA*) ranges from 7% to 33%, depending on the commodity being sold. Food, wine, and basic necessities are taxed at 7%; most goods and services (including car rentals) at 13%; luxury items (jewelry, all tobacco, imported liquors) at 33%; and hotels at 7%. Non-E.U. residents are entitled to a reimbursement of the 16% IVA tax on most purchases worth more than 90€ made at shops offering "Tax Free" or "Global Refund" shopping. Forms, obtained from the store where you made your purchase, must be stamped at Customs upon departure. For more information see **www.globalrefund.com**.

TELEPHONES For national telephone information, dial ☎ 1003. For international telephone information, call ☎ 025. You can make international calls from booths identified with the word *Internacional.* To make an international call, dial ☎ 00, wait for the tone, and dial the country code, area code, and number. If you're making a local call, dial the two-digit city code first (**93** in Barcelona) and then the seven-digit number. To make a long-distance call within Spain, the procedure is exactly the same because you must dial the city prefix no matter where you're calling.

TIPPING   More expensive restaurants add a 7% tax to the bill and cheaper ones incorporate it into their prices. This is *not* a service charge, and a tip of 5% to 10% is expected in these establishments. For coffees and snacks most people just leave a few coins or round up to the nearest euro. Taxis do not expect tips. Tip hotel porters and doormen 1€ and maids about the same amount per day.

TOILETS   In Catalunya they're called *aseos, servicios,* or *lavabos,* and are labeled *caballeros* for men and *damas* or *señoras* for women.

TOURIST INFORMATION   **Turisme de Barcelona,** Plaça de Catalunya, 17 (underground; ☎ 93-285-38-34), is open daily 9am to 9pm; it offers a hotel-booking service, sells tickets for tours and performances, and has a well-stocked gift shop. **Informació Turística de Catalunya** has information on Barcelona and the entire region; it's located in Palau Robert, Pg. de Gràcia, 107 (☎ 93-238-40-03). City tourism information offices are also at **Plaça Sant Jaume** (c/ Ciutat, 2; Mon–Fri 9am–10pm, Sat 10am–8pm, and Sun 10am–2pm), **Estació de Sants** (Pl. dels Països

Catalans, s/n), **Mirador de Colom** (Pl. Portal de la Pau s/n), and **El Prat** airport (terminals 1 and 2). There are also smaller tourism information kiosks *(cabines)* in several places, including La Sagrada Família, Plaça de Espanya, and aboveground on Plaça de Catalunya. Call ☎ 010 for general visitor information.

TRAVELERS WITH DISABILITIES   Many buildings in Barcelona have stairs, making it difficult for visitors with disabilities to get around, though conditions are slowly improving. Newer hotels are more sensitive to the needs of persons with disabilities, and more expensive restaurants are generally wheelchair-accessible. However, because most places have very limited, if any, facilities for people with disabilities, you might consider taking an organized tour specifically designed to accommodate such travelers. **Flying Wheels Travel** (☎ 507/451-5005; www.flying wheelstravel.com) offers escorted tours to Spain ("Spanish Symphony"), and **Access-Able Travel Source** (☎ 303/232-2979; www.access-able. com) has access information for people traveling to Barcelona. TMB (the public transportation system for both bus and Metro) has a help line for travelers with disabilities (☎ 93-486-07-52), and ECOM is a federation of private disabled organizations (☎ 93-451-55-50).

Barcelona: **A Brief History**

550 B.C. Greeks settle at Empúries in northern Catalunya.

212 B.C. The Romans, using Empúries as an entry point, subjugate Spain.

206 B.C. Romans defeat Carthaginians.

1ST C. A.D. Christians spread throughout Catalunya.

15 Barcino founded by Romans.

70 First Jewish settlements in Barcino.

415 Barcelona occupied by the Visigoths; capital until 554.

719 Moorish invasion of Iberian Peninsula reaches Barcelona.

878 Guifré el Pilós (Wilfred the Hairy) defeats Moors and founds dynasty of Counts of Barcelona (5-century-long autonomous rule).

1064 The *Usatges,* the first Catalan Bill of Rights, is drafted.

1137 A royal marriage unites Catalunya and neighboring region of Aragón.

1213–35 Jaume I consolidates empire; conquers Mallorca, Ibiza, and Valencia.

1249 Barcelona forms the *Consell de Cent* (Council of 100) municipal government.

1283 Corts (Parliament) to govern Catalunya created.

1347–59 The Black Plague halves the city's population. The *Generalitat* (autonomous government) is founded.

1469 Fernando II, monarch of Catalunya-Aragón, marries Isabel, queen of Castile, uniting all of Spain.

1492 Columbus discovers America. The "Catholic Monarchs" expel all remaining Jews and Muslims.

1494 Catalunya falls under Castilian rule.

1522 Under the rule of Charles V, Catalans refused permission to trade in the New World.

1640–50 Catalan revolt known as the *Guerra dels Segadors* (Harvesters' War); Catalunya declares itself a republic, allied with France.

1701–13 Spanish War of Succession.

1759 Barcelona falls to Franco-Spanish army; the Catalan language is banned.

1808–14 French occupy Catalunya in Peninsular War with England.

1832 The Industrial Revolution begins in Barcelona with the first steam-driven factory.

1854–1865 Old City walls torn down; work begins on the "new city"; expansion called *L'Eixample.*

1873 First Spanish Republic established.

1888 First Universal Exposition in Barcelona held at *Parc de la Ciutadella.*

1892–93 Collectives demand Catalan autonomy. Anarchist throws bombs in the Gran Teatre Liceu Opera House.

1909 *Setmana Tràgica* (Tragic Week); anarchists go on anticlerical rampage in Barcelona.

1924 Dictatorship established by General Primo de Rivera; Catalan language banned.

1929 Second International Exhibition held, on Montjuïc.

1931 Francesc Macià negotiates autonomy for Catalunya during the Second Republic and declares himself president.

1936–1939 Spanish Civil War; ends with anarchist-occupied Barcelona taken by Franco's army.

1960s Package tourism boom takes off on Catalunya's Costa Brava.

1975 Franco dies; Juan Carlos becomes king.

1978 King Juan Carlos grants Catalunya autonomous rule; Catalan language restored.

1981 Coup attempt by right-wing officers fails; democracy prevails.

1982 Socialists gain power after 43 years of right-wing rule.

1986 Spain joins the European Community (now the European Union).

1992 Barcelona hosts 25th Summer Olympic Games.

1994 Gran Teatre del Liceu opera house destroyed by fire for second time.

2004 Spanish Prime Minister José Luis Zapatero officially requests that Catalan, along with Basque and Galician, be recognized as a working language of the E.U.

2006 A statute granting Catalunya additional autonomous powers is passed by the Spanish Socialist government.

2009 Barcelona wins the European Champions League football championship.

2010 Spain's financial and debt crisis continues, official unemployment rate hovers at 20%, double the European average, and Spain's credit rating is downgraded. Though Zapatero's presidential term lasts until 2012, there are calls, amid widespread strikes and protests, for early elections. In July, Spain wins the FIFA World Cup (football/soccer) in South Africa to claim the first championship in the nation's history; seven key members of the team represent the local club FC Barcelona.

Barcelona's **Architecture**

Roman (2nd c. b.c.–4th c. a.d.)
The early conquerors of Spain were extraordinary engineers. Relics of the Roman colony of Barcino can be seen in the surviving columns of the **Temple d'Augustus,** originally part of the Roman forum, and gates and sections of the 3rd- and 4th-century walls that encircled the city. The finest Roman ruins are beneath **Plaça del Rei,** in the **Museu d'Història de Barcelona** (see p 33).

Medieval (Romanesque, 9th–12th c.; & Gothic, 12th–16th c.)
Beautiful in its simplicity and austerity, Romanesque architecture featured wide aisles, round

arches, and heavy walls (mostly in churches). Examples abound in the La Ribera and Barri Gòtic districts of the Ciutat Vella. The finest example in Barcelona is **Sant Pau del Camp** (9th–12th c.).

Catalan Gothic emerged in Catalunya in the 12th century, with harsher lines and more austere ornamentation than traditional Gothic architecture. Employed in both civic and religious buildings, it featured pointed arches, soaring buttresses and spires, airy naves, and massive columns. The purest example anywhere is **Santa Maria del Mar,** the basilica in La

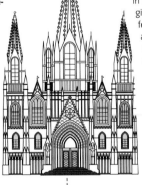

Catedral de Barcelona.

Ribera. Other fine examples include **Església de Santa Maria del Pi** and the **Saló del Tinell** (on the stunning Plaça del Rei). Though the entire Barri Gòtic is named for the style, the neighborhood reflects an evolution and mix of styles, of which the **Catedral** is the best example. See the special-interest tour (p 31) and walking tour (p 61) focusing on the Ciutat Vella's ancient architecture.

Modernisme (late 19th to early 20th c.)

The distinctive *modernisme* style of architecture that dominates much of modern Barcelona is not "modernism," or what is usually defined as 20th-century functionality, but Catalan Art Nouveau, a derivative of the European movement in the arts of the late 19th century. In Barcelona, *modernista* architecture—marked by curved rather than straight lines, ample ornamentation, organic forms, and wrought iron and stained glass, among other elements—was spearheaded by **Antoni Gaudí (La Sagrada Família, La Pedrera),** but many other celebrated *modernista* architects, including **Lluís Domènech i Montaner** and **Josep Puig i Cadafalch**, transformed the city with elegant mansions, concert halls, and churches perfectly suited to the enlightened prosperity of the Catalan bourgeoisie. Perhaps the greatest examples are Gaudí's La Pedrera (Casa Milà), Domènech i Montaner's Palau de la Música Catalana and Hospital de Sant Pau, and Puig i Cadafalch's Casa Amatller. While there are excellent examples outside of Barcelona—in Girona, Valencia, Sitges, Reus, and even the Basque Country—the Catalan capital boasts the highest concentration

La Pedrera.

of *modernista* architecture in the world. The mid-19th-century L'Eixample district, the new city expansion grid by **Ildefons Cerdà,** is the style's finest showcase (it's not called the *Quadrat d'Or,* or Golden Square, for nothing). See the special-interest tour (p 24) and walking tour (p 68) focusing on L'Eixample and *modernisme.*

Modern & Contemporary (1929–present)

The stark pavilion built by **Mies Van der Rohe** for the 1929 International Exposition in Barcelona is a landmark of modern architecture. Barcelona took advantage of the 1992 Olympic Games to reorient the city to the sea and create urban beaches, residential neighborhoods, a port and marina, and ring roads, and to introduce daring public sculptures, promenades, and squares weaving through the Old City. In 1999 the Royal Institute of British Architects presented Barcelona's City Council with its Gold Medal, the first time a city (rather than an architect) had received the accolade. Spanish (**Rafael Moneo** and **Santiago Calatrava**) and international (**Arata Isozaki** and **Norman Foster**) architects have also made their mark on the city, as have

Mies Van der Rohe pavilion.

a number of young, daring Catalans. The French architect **Jean Nouvel**'s audacious Torre Agbar is the newest symbol—at night it's illuminated with the colors of none other than Barça, the beloved local *fútbol* team—along with the stunning new El Prat airport terminal, by native son **Ricardo Bofill,** of a city embracing the future with bravado.

Useful Phrases

Useful Words & Phrases

ENGLISH	SPANISH/CATALAN	PRONUNCIATION
Good day	Buenos dias/ Bon dia	*bweh*-nohs *dee*-ahs/ bohn *dee*-ah
How are you?	¿Cómo está?/ Com està?	*koh*-moh es-*tah*/ com ehs-*tah*
Very well	Muy bien/Molt bé	mwee byehn/mohl beh
Thank you	Gracias/ Graçies	*grah*-thee-ahs/ *grah*-see-uhs
You're welcome	De nada/De res	*deh nah*-dah/duh ress
Goodbye	Adiós/Adéu	ah-*dyos*/ah-*deh*-yoo
Please	Por favor/ Si us plau	por fah-*vohr*/ see yoos plow
Yes	Sí/Sí	see
No	No/No	noh
Excuse me	Perdóneme/ Perdoni'm	pehr-*doh*-neh-meh/ per-*don*-eem
Where is . . . ?	¿Dónde está . . . ?/ On és . . . ?	*dohn*-deh es-*tah*/ ohn ehs
To the right	A la derecha/ A la dreta	ah lah deh-*reh*-chah/ ah lah *dreh*-tah

ENGLISH	SPANISH/CATALAN	PRONUNCIATION
To the left	A la izquierda/ A l'esquerra	ah lah ees-*kyehr*-dah/ ahl ehs-keh-*ra*
I would like . . .	Quisiera/ Voldría	kee-*syeh*-rah/ vohl-*dree*-ah
I want . . .	Quiero/Vull	*kyeh*-roh/*boo*-wee
Do you have . . . ?	¿Tiene usted?/Té?	tyeh-neh oo-*sted*/teh
How much is it?	¿Cuánto cuesta?/ Quant és?	*kwahn*-toh *kwehs*-tah/ kwahnt ehs?
When?	¿Cuándo?/Quan?	*kwahn*-doh/kwahn
What?	¿Qué?/Com?	Keh/Cohm
There is (Is there . . . ?)	(¿)Hay (. . . ?)/Hi ha? or Hi han?	aye/ee ah/ ee ahn
What is there?	¿Qué hay?/Que hi ha?	keh aye/keh ee ah
Yesterday	Ayer/Ahir	ah-*yehr*/ah-*yeer*
Today	Hoy/Avui	oy/ah-*wee*
Tomorrow	Mañana/ Demá	mah-*nyah*-nah/ deh-*mah*
Good	Bueno/Bon	*bweh*-noh/bohn
Bad	Malo/Mal	*mah*-loh/mahl
Better (Best)	(Lo) Mejor/ Millor	(loh) meh-*hohr*/ mee-*yohr*
More	Más/Mes	mahs/mehss
Less	Menos/Menys	*meh*-nohs/*meh*-nyus
Do you speak English?	¿Habla inglés?/ Parla anglès?	ah-blah een-*glehs*/ *pahr*-lah ahn-*glehs*
I speak a little Spanish/Catalan	Hablo un poco de español/ Parlo una mica de Catalá	ah-*bloh* oon *poh*-koh deh es-pah-*nyol*/ *pahr*-loh *oo*-nah *mee*-kah *deh* kah-tah-*lah*
I don't understand	No entiendo/ No comprenc	noh ehn-*tyehn*-doh/ noh cohm-*prehnk*
What time is it?	¿Qué hora es?/ Quina hora és?	keh *oh*-rah ehss/ *kee*-nah *oh*-rah ehss
The check, please	La cuenta, por favor/ El compte, si us plau	lah *kwehn*-tah pohr fah-*vohr*/ehl *cohmp*-tah see yoos plow
the station	la estación/ la estació	lah es-tah-*syohn*/ la esta-*cyo*
a hotel	un hotel/l'hotel	oon oh-*tehl*/ehl ho-*tehl*
the market	el mercado/ el mercat	ehl mehr-*kah*-doh/ ehl mehr-*kaht*
a restaurant	un restaurante/ un restaurant	oon rehs-tow-*rahn*-teh/ oon rehs-tow-*rahn*
the toilet	el baño/ el lavabo	ehl *bah*-nyoh/ ehl lah-*vah*-boh
a doctor	un médico/ un metge	oon *meh*-dee-koh/ oon meht-*jah*
the road to . . .	el camino a/ al cami per	ehl kah-*mee*-noh ah/ ahl kah-*mee* pehr
to eat	comer/menjar	ko-*mehr*/mehn-*jahr*

ENGLISH	SPANISH/CATALAN	PRONUNCIATION
a room	una habitación/ un habitació	oo-nah ah-bee-tah-*syohn*/oon ah-bee-tah-*syohn*
a book	un libro/ un llibre	oon *lee*-broh/ oon *yee*-breh
a dictionary	un diccionario/ un diccionari	oon deek-syoh-*nah*-ryoh/oon deek-syoh-*nah* ree

Numbers

NUMBER	SPANISH	CATALAN
1	uno (*oo*-noh)	un (oon)
2	dos (dohs)	dos (dohs)
3	tres (trehs)	tres (trehs)
4	cuatro (*kwah*-troh)	quatre (*kwah*-trah)
5	cinco (*theen*-koh)	cinc (sink)
6	seis (says)	sis (sees)
7	siete (*syeh*-teh)	set (seht)
8	ocho (*oh*-choh)	vuit (vweet)
9	nueve (*nweh*-beh)	nou (noo)
10	diez (dyehth)	deu (*deh*-yoo)
11	once (*ohn*-theh)	onze (*ohn*-zah)
12	doce (*doh*-theh)	dotze (*doh*-tzah)
13	trece (*treh*-theh)	tretze (*treh*-tzah)
14	catorce (kah-*tohr*-theh)	catorza (kah-*tohr*-zah)
15	quince (*keen*-seh)	quinza (*keen*-zah)
16	dieciséis (dyeh-thee-*says*)	setze (*seh*-tzah)
17	diecisiete (dyeh-thee-*syeh*-teh)	disset (dee-*seht*)
18	dieciocho (dyeh-thee-*oh*-choh)	divuit (dee-*vweet*)
19	diecinueve (dyeh-thee-*nweh*-beh)	dinou (dee-*noo*)
20	veinte (*bayn*-teh)	vint (vehnt)
30	treinta (*trayn*-tah)	trenta (*trehn*-tah)
40	cuarenta (kwah-*rehn*-tah)	quaranta (kwah-*rahn*-tah)
50	cincuenta (theen-*kwehn*-tah)	cinquanta (theen-*kwahn*-tah)
60	sesenta (seh-*sehn*-tah)	seixanta (see-*shahn*-tah)
70	setenta (seh-*tehn*-tah)	setanta (seh-*tahn*-tah)
80	ochenta (oh-*chehn*-tah)	vuitanta (vwee-*tahn*-tah)
90	noventa (noh-*behn*-tah)	noranta (noh-*rahn*-tah)
100	cien (*thyehn*)	cent (sent)

Recommended **Spanish Wines**

Spain has taken the wine world by storm in the last decade. I recommend seeking out the following wines while touring Spain. Catalunya produces some outstanding wines: If you want to drink local, stick to wines from Penedès, Priorat, and Montsant.

Reds (Tintos)

Rioja   Artadi, Bodegas Lan, Castillo de Ygay, Contador, CVNE, El Puntido, Finca Allende, Imperial, La Rioja Alta, López de Heredia, Marqués de Riscal, Muga, Remírez Ganuza, Roda, San Vicente, Sierra Cantabria, Viña Ardanza, Viña Izadi

Ribera del Duero Reds   Aalto, Alión, Atauta, Condado de Haza, Emilio Moro, Flor de Pingus, Hacienda Monasterio, Leda, Mauro, Pago de los Capellanes, Pesquera, Vega Sicilia

Toro   Dos Victorias (Gran Elias Mora), Numanthia, Pintia, Quinta Quietud, San Román

Priorat   Àlvaro Palacios Les Terrasses Cims de Porrera, Clos Martinet, Clos Mogador, L'Ermita, Mas Alta, Mas Doix, Mas d'En Compte, Vall Llach

Jumilla   Casa Castillo, Clio/El Nido, Finca Sandoval

Monsant   Acústic, Can Blau, Capçanes, Joan d'Anguera, La Universal Venus

Others   Gran Claustro/Castillo de Perelada (Penedès), Artazu, Chivite and Faustino (Navarra), Dominio de Tares, Dominio de Valdepusa/Marqués de Griñón (Toledo), Paixar (Bierzo), Torres (Penedès)

Whites (Blancos)

Albariño (from Galicia)   Lagar de Cervera, Laxas, Martín Codax, Pazo de Señorans, Terras Gaudia

Penedès   Castillo de Perelada, René Barbier

Rioja   Allende, López de Heredia, Marqués de Riscal, Muga

Rueda   Belondrade y Lurton, Dos Victorias José Pariente, Martinsancho, Viñedo de Nieva Pie Franco

Other

Cava (sparkling wine from Catalunya)   Agustí Torelló, Avinyó, Gramona, Juvé y Camps, Raventós i Blanc, Segura Viudas

Sherry   San León, La Guita (manzanilla), Tío Pepe (fino), Alvear (Pedro Ximénez)

Recommended Vintages for Rioja, Ribera del Duero & Priorat

YEAR	RIOJA	RIBERA DEL DUERO	PRIORAT
1994	Outstanding	Excellent	Very good
1995	Outstanding	Outstanding	Very good
1996	Excellent	Outstanding	Very good
1997	Good	Good	Good
1998	Excellent	Excellent	Very good
1999	Excellent	Excellent	Excellent
2000	Excellent	Excellent	Good
2001	Outstanding	Outstanding	Outstanding
2002	Average	Average	Good
2003	Good	Good	Very good
2004	Outstanding	Outstanding	Outstanding
2005	Excellent	Very good	Excellent
2006	Good	Very good	Very good
2007	Very good	Excellent	Very good

Index

See also Accommodations and Restaurant indexes, below.

Photo **Credits**

Notes